The Franchising Bible

The Franchising Bible

How to plan, fund and run a successful franchise

Second edition

Kim Benjamin
Brian Smart, Director General, bfa

Published in association with the British Franchising Association

crimson

The Franchising Bible: How to plan, fund and run a successful franchise

This second edition published in 2012 by
Crimson Publishing Ltd, Westminster House,
Kew Road, Richmond, Surrey TW9 2ND

First edition published in 2010

© Crimson Publishing 2012, 2010

Authors: Kim Benjamin and Brian Smart
Additional material supplied by John Bensahlia

British Library Cataloguing in Publication Data
A catalogue record for this book is available from the British Library

ISBN 978 1 78059 047 9

Typeset by IDSUK (DataConnection) Ltd
Printed and bound in the UK by Ashford Colour Press, Gosport, Hants

CONTENTS

FOREWORD

The British Franchise Association (bfa) has been representing British franchising since 1977 and during that time we have seen the industry go from strength to strength. With the development and maturity of the industry came the development of stronger ethics and best practice. Today Britain, along with its European colleagues, is considered one of the most important hubs for world franchising.

The industry has grown into a community of possibilities, enabling people to own their own businesses across a multitude of business disciplines and markets. From the fast food industry to modern business services, and from home-based businesses to international high street brands – franchising has more to offer than you may expect.

This book will give you the starting point in your journey to see if franchising is right for you; looking at the market, the ethics and many of the key areas to consider when choosing the right business. Time and again, franchising has greatly outperformed other start-up businesses. Its formula of a locally owned and run enterprise, driven by a small-business owner, with branding, economies of scale and support from the wider network, gives the consumer the best of both worlds and the business a far better chance of success – but only if done correctly.

It is an industry worth £13.4 billion and which employs 594,000 people, so it is not a cottage industry. It is a serious and professional business format and one that you need to approach with serious consideration.

Franchisors will be very careful about whom they take on as new franchisees in their network, as they will want to ensure that only those that can contribute positively and add value to the network are part of the brand. As a franchisee, you should take just as much care over the businesses you consider. A great deal of commitment is required for successful franchising, so you'll need to plan your options and proceed carefully; don't cut corners; and make the most of the information in this publication.

We have put together some core advice, real-life examples and insight from those in the industry. However, although the book is comprehensive, this is not where your research ends. With a growing interest in franchising, the resources now available to take advantage of the industry are extensive.

Franchising could well be your next step into a new life as a business owner, but don't rush into it. Understand what you want, understand what you can commit to and understand what the business can deliver.

I wish you the all the best in finding out if franchising is your route to a new life, knowing that you have taken the right steps and asked the right questions of both yourself and the franchise along the way.

Brian Smart,
Director General,
British Franchise Association

INTRODUCTION

Everywhere we look in today's society, running your own business is THE thing to do. Turn on the TV and shows such as *Dragons' Den* or *The Apprentice* demonstrate that with the right approach and sense of business nous, running your own business can be a highly profitable venture. Read the papers, and in the finance pages you will find stories of how people have gone from rags to riches – just by launching their own business. Even take a walk down the high street, and you will be passing by big brand names that started out as a self-made business.

So with that in mind – and especially bearing in mind the fragile economy (which is still leading to redundancies), starting your own business is the way to go for many people. However, starting a brand new business is a highly daunting experience, especially for those who have no real idea about how or where to begin. What sort of business would you want to run? Would running a business in a field that you have knowledge of be better than going into a brand new sector for a new challenge? And don't forget the great big, black void of the unknown.

> **If you are sure you want to go out on your own, but don't have all the confidence or knowledge, then a franchise is the answer. It is a 'security blanket' which you can use when you run out of the answers yourself.**
>
> *Maeve Larkin, Leaps and Bounds*

That's where franchising comes in. Basically, a franchise is the term granted by a business owner (the franchisor) licensing another person (the franchisee) to use their business idea (often within a defined geographic area). The great benefit of becoming a franchisee is that the franchisor provides help and support, not to mention the reassurance of a proven brand name and business model.

A franchise allows you the autonomy of running your own business, but with the benefit of having that all-important support from the franchisor. You will receive training in all quarters: advice on aspects of starting and running a business such as raising finance, creating a business plan and marketing your business. On that score, marketing will also be a key benefit, since the franchisor will help to promote and market your new business in stylish, eye-catching ways. The level of support will vary, according to the franchise and sectors that you want – but the fact that you will be working from a proven business idea will stand you in good stead.

> **I love being the decision maker and I get excited about the potential the business has to grow. The staff are loyal and we have a great team. The customers are happy and we get lots of positive feedback, so I'm very motivated.**
>
> *Juliet O'Connell, The ZipYard*

It's worth bearing in mind that the franchising sector continues to grow in popularity. According to the 2011/2012 NatWest/bfa Franchise Survey, it's an expanding field with more than 594,000 working in franchising. It is estimated that there are 929 active franchise systems in the UK, with more than 40,100 units. Bearing in mind that in the previous year that there were 897 active franchise systems, that's a significant increase, indicating that franchising is a hugely popular notion. And with a healthy 91% of franchisees trading profitably, that's further cause for encouragement.

However, it's also worth noting that starting out in franchising is by no means a picnic. A lot of hard work, determination, patience and dedication are required on your part to enable your business to become a success. *The Franchising Bible* will help you to assess whether franchising is the right path for you and also to select the right franchise for you, and show you how to get started. The book features a mix of advice, guidance and information, as well as contributions from franchise entrepreneurs, who will impart their knowledge and expertise to you.

The book includes features on whether franchising is right for you and, if so, which franchise sector is right for you, as well as the different types of franchise available to you, to give you an idea of which one to choose.

> **Joining a franchise was a big leap of faith, but looking back on it, it has worked out for me beautifully. I was bored in my last job. I am now much happier – I am selling a service people want and are very happy with in general.**
>
> *Steven Hook, Greensleeves*

The Franchising Bible also includes information on buying an existing franchise, and how this differs from investing in a new one; financial aspects, and how to go about getting the money for investment; the legal issues, clauses and contracts, and how to source the right legal advisor; business planning; the initial start-up phase and, of course, developing and growing your franchise.

This is the second edition of the title and is fully updated with an entirely new chapter dedicated to the popular topic of buying an existing franchise, whereby a franchisee sells an existing franchise. With franchising already having the reputation of being a lower risk than starting an entirely new business, resales are particularly pertinent, as the incoming franchisee is often able to take on a money-making franchise. But it may not be quite as simple as that, so this book has plenty of useful advice to help you make the right decisions.

Franchising may seem like a daunting prospect at the beginning, but with the right amount of hard work and commitment, and a positive, dedicated attitude, the financial and personal rewards will be great. *The Franchising Bible* is your complete guide to approaching a franchise, with a wealth of information and advice from industry experts and franchisees to help steer you in the right direction. And by taking on board some of the ideas and facts in this book, you too could become one of the success stories that people will be reading about in the future.

1.0

INTRODUCING FRANCHISING

IN THIS CHAPTER

Having established the meaning of franchising and how it works, there are now several questions to ask yourself. Do you have enough motivation for a franchise, with the long hours and hard work involved? Will you be able to afford a franchise, and, if not, will you be able to obtain funding, such as a business loan? Are you happy with the relationship that exists between franchisors and franchisees?

This introductory chapter will explore these themes in more detail, so as to determine whether a franchise is the right business system for you. The chapter features a section on the origins and history of franchising, recent statistics from both UK and global franchise industries, and an analysis of growth levels and what the future holds for the franchise sector. By the end of this introductory chapter, you should be able to gauge whether franchising is the path you want to take, and whether you have the commitment and drive to fulfil the full potential of a franchise.

In this chapter, we'll cover:

- what franchising is
- how it started
- how the UK franchising industry is faring
- international prospects
- future growth of the market.

What is franchising?

According to the website of The British Franchise Association (bfa), the voluntary, self-regulating governing body for franchising in the UK:

'The term "franchising" has been used to describe many different forms of business relationships, including licensing, distributor and agency arrangements. The more popular use of the term has arisen from the development of what is called "business format franchising".'

Business format franchising is the granting of a licence by one person (the franchisor) to another (the franchisee). This allows the franchisee to trade under the trademark/trade name of the franchisor. A franchise comes as a complete business package deal in that you pay the franchisor for the following:

- the right to use the brand name, products, technology and business model over a set time period on a renewable contract (the initial run is often for five years)
- support: from the initial training period, support will always be available from the franchisor, including ongoing training, help with marketing and promotion, assistance with finding and buying any necessary equipment, and financial matters such as accounting and tax. Help in this area will vary between business type and size of franchise
- premises/transport: in some cases, where you will be operating from the high street, you will be paying for the premises which you will work from. Other franchises may provide a vehicle such as a van or car – for example, franchises that involve gardening, pet care or home repairs. In other cases, overhead costs will be lower, especially if the franchise can be run from home.

Although as a franchisee you do retain some degree of autonomy, you must remember that the franchisor has control over the way in which the business is run, and how products and services are sold. You will also be running the business in accordance with the franchisor's standards and guidelines. The franchisor–franchisee relationship can be a crucial element in how well the business does. However, the 2011/2012 NatWest/bfa Franchise Survey shows promise in this regard: 80% of franchisees say that they are satisfied with their franchisor relationship, which is a higher percentage then in any previous survey.

To be honest I didn't really relish this prospect as I perceived a franchise to be too restrictive. [But the earnings potential] was the carrot for me. I love wheeling and dealing – nothing appeals to me more – selling is what gives me the buzz! What amazed me is that I became accustomed to working within Snap-on's constraints and programmes, and I'd even go so far as to say I fell in love with the whole business. 🙿

Tim Adkin, Snap-On Tools

How it started

The elements of franchising – providing a service in a specified area in return for a fee – date back several centuries and are said to have originated as far back as the Middle Ages. More recently, the Singer Sewing Machine Company is credited with being the very first example of a franchised business, introducing the first franchise in the mid-1800s in the USA. It operated a mass manufacturing service that enabled the company to price its products competitively. However, for repairs and maintenance, it was unable to replicate such a service and, instead, it set up a distributed franchise rather than a central operation. Those whom it employed as franchisees also made sales for the company.

Automotive company General Motors was another business that helped to shape the franchise model at the turn of the 20th century, developing car dealerships that were granted exclusive territories in which to sell cars, a business model that still exists today. Other sectors followed suit and adopted the franchise model as a cost-effective way of expanding their brand and increasing sales, including the likes of soft drinks giants Coca-Cola and Pepsi.

A franchise boom in the 1950s increased the popularity of franchising as a business model, but a decade later, growth had slowed on both sides of the pond, for various reasons. In the UK, franchising began to be confused with pyramid selling, a marketing scheme that attracted bad publicity. Consequently, its reputation began to suffer.

In 1977, the major franchising companies in the UK decided to set up their own association, the bfa, to establish standards for the UK franchise industry and to ensure that the sector continued to build a solid reputation. Founder members included Dyno-Rod and Wimpy, and the standards these established names represented brought credibility back into the industry in the UK. This backing for recognised industry standards was crucial, as the franchisors' ability to attract potential franchisees to invest in their systems depended very much on their reputation. Today, the bfa acts in the interests of the industry as a whole – its franchisees and franchisors, and their funders and advisors – by assessing and accrediting franchising companies against practical standards.

A growth industry

In recent years, franchising has outperformed other start-up businesses, largely because, in franchising, much of the groundwork needed to set up and run a business exists already. Franchising offers the format of a locally owned and run company, with branding, a business system, economies of scale and support from a wider network that can offer a business a good chance of success. And there are plenty of facts and figures on the industry to support this view. Each year, the bfa and NatWest commission a survey of the franchise industry, which is carried out by independent researchers, so there is a wealth of up-to-date information available. The latest statistics, released in June 2012 based on fieldwork carried out between December 2011 and February 2012, examine the performance of the industry in 2010, in relation to both franchisors and franchisees. They make for very encouraging reading, particularly in light of the tough economic conditions in the UK.

Franchise businesses continue to grow. In 2011, the industry contributed £13.4 billion to the UK's economy, a growth of 8% on the previous year. The average turnover figures for a franchised business was £349,000, an increase of 4% on the previous year. With an increase of 2% on the previous year, 27% of turnovers were more than £500,000 and there remained 44% of turnovers of more than £250,000. The survey also revealed that, as compared to the 1990s recession, fewer franchise businesses today are trading at a loss. In 1990 only 70% of all franchise businesses were profitable, compared to 91% in 2011. One notable increase was the number of businesses franchising. Having risen only from 835 to 842 in 2009, the growth was far more significant in 2011, showing an increase to 929.

If you are looking to become a franchisee, you'll certainly be in good company. There are an estimated 40,100 franchise units in the UK. And it's never too late to consider starting a franchise – the average age of a franchisee is 49, while for those just starting out it's 41. The stability and maturity of the sector is also highlighted in the average length of time franchisees have been running their businesses. In 1992, the figure was 3.9 years, and in the most recent survey it was 8.4 years – however, again, with the economic climate in mind, more franchisees regard their franchised business as a stable place to be.

❝❝ **I wanted to be my own boss, but I just wasn't sure that I would have the experience or all the business acumen that would be necessary. Therefore having a source of information and a team of experts to speak to when I needed to seemed to be the right solution for me. 🙿🙿**

Maeve Larkin, Leaps and Bounds

The sectors covered

When it comes to choosing a sector, you'll be spoilt for choice. Mention the word 'franchise' and, for most people, the words 'burger bar' automatically come to mind. This is hardly surprising, as McDonald's, Burger King and Wimpy are all franchised businesses. However, many different types of businesses are run as franchises today, and besides fast food they include cleaning and maintenance, automotive, health and fitness and financial services, to name but a few. And you'll have a difficult decision to make if you are looking to set up a franchise in the UK, as there are just under 930 businesses to choose from in the UK alone.

FRANCHISING AT A GLANCE

- You don't have to come up with a unique selling point: a franchise uses an existing business model that has already been tried and tested.

- You'll get access to training in areas that could prove challenging, such as sales and marketing, although the level you get varies from franchise to franchise.

- If you choose to join one of the larger, more recognised franchises, you'll often have the backing of a national advertising campaign, offering you invaluable marketing support.

Costs and raising finance

What will it cost you to start a franchise? You'll pay the franchisor an initial fee at the start, together with an ongoing management service fee, so if you are looking to start a business on a shoestring, starting a franchise is probably not a viable option. The bfa tells us that the management services fee is usually based on a percentage of either annual turnover or mark-ups on supplies. (See Chapter 8 for an in-depth look at raising finance.) In return, the franchisor has an obligation to support the franchisees in their network in areas such as training, product development, advertising and promotional activities, and with a specialist range of management services.

According to the NatWest/bfa Franchise Survey, initial outlay varies in accordance with two different types of franchise package – the turnkey and the non-turnkey. A turnkey solution (in which the franchisee gets everything required to start up a franchise) can cost from £2,000 up to £280,000.

Banks are the most important overall source of finance and there are three main lenders in the UK: Royal Bank of Scotland/NatWest, Lloyds TSB/Bank of Scotland and HSBC. Less than half franchisees surveyed, 46%, borrowed money to set up. The average amount borrowed in 2010 was £66,500, with one in five needing to borrow more than £100,000.

The average annual management service fee amounts to 9.7% of sales. However, don't concern yourself too much with these average costs, as they won't necessarily offer an accurate reflection of the fees for your chosen sector within the franchise industry.

In Chapter 8, we'll outline in detail everything you need to know about buying and setting up a franchise, including how much you can borrow and how quickly the business can become profitable.

> In today's economic climate, quick-service restaurants are a booming industry. Our family has already tapped into some leading franchises, such as Subway and Papa Johns, and we are confident that SFC will follow in the same footsteps as these established and successful brands.
>
> *Romina La Bella, Southern Fried Chicken*

Future prospects

The franchising market-place as a whole is generally optimistic about the future prospects for the industry, although less so about the economy generally. When asked about their expectations in 2010 over the next 12 months, 42% of those surveyed expected to stay with their franchise for the long term, with 19% expecting to stay for the medium term. The former figure is an encouraging increase from the 32% expecting to be in their franchise for the long haul when asked in 2009.

SEVEN FACTS ABOUT FRANCHISING

1. There are approximately 40,100 franchisees in the UK.

2. There are 594,000 people employed in the industry.

3. There are 929 franchise systems operating in the UK.

4. Compared with the 1990s recession, fewer franchise businesses today are trading at a loss.

5. In 2010, the industry contributed £13.4 billion to the UK's economy.

6. The average age of a franchisee is 49; for those just starting out it is 41.

7. On average, it takes a franchisee two to five months from first contact to sign for a new franchise.

TaxAssist Accountants
The franchise where taking the plunge couldn't be safer.

With a TaxAssist Accountants franchise you enjoy all the benefits of running your own business, but without that feeling of being alone in unchartered waters.

As an award winning franchise with the largest network of small business accountants across the UK and Ireland, we provide you with all the technical, marketing and field support you need.

We even give you your own protected area and supply you with new business leads within it.

So come on in, the water's fine. To find out more call

0800 0188 297

Email info@taxassist.co.uk
or visit www.taxassist.net

Gold Winner
bfa HSBC
Franchisor
of the year 2010

TaxAssist Accountants
The Accountancy and Tax Service for Small Business

The franchise deal that adds up.

2.0

ABOUT THE bfa

IN THIS CHAPTER

If you find that you have invested your hard-earned cash in an opportunity that turns out to be much less than you expected, it will not be easy to get your money back. This is why it's vitally important to research as much as possible before committing.

One of your first ports of call for research should be the British Franchise Association (bfa), the only self-regulatory body for the UK franchise sector. Its website, www.thebfa.org, has a wealth of information about franchising, including case studies of existing franchises and a directory of experts you can turn to for advice.

In this chapter, we'll look at:

- the bfa and its role
- the different types of membership available
- membership benefits
- the future of the bfa
- what the bfa can do for you.

All about the bfa

The British Franchise Association (bfa) was established in 1977 and is the only voluntary self-regulatory body for the UK franchise sector. Its aim is to promote ethical franchising practice in the UK and help the industry develop credibility, influence and favourable circumstances for growth. It does this with a standards-based approach to membership of the association. In addition, the bfa works to increase awareness of ethical franchising by communicating with government, academia, the media and the UK public on what constitutes franchising best practice.

As a result, one of the bfa's main roles is to help potential franchisees recognise the good, the bad and the ugly in the franchising industry for what they are. It also helps businesses involved in franchising to secure their own position among the 'good' operators. The ability of franchisors to attract potential franchisees to invest in their systems depends crucially on their own reputation, and on the reputation of franchising in general.

Membership types

Membership of the bfa is divided into three types – Full, Associate and Provisional listing, while professional advisors to the franchise industry can apply for affiliate membership status. As a potential franchisee, these membership types will help to give you some additional insight into the business.

- **Full members:** These are established franchised businesses with a proven trading and franchising record. They are prepared to have their reputation examined by the bfa, and have an established network of franchisees from whom the bfa takes confidential references on their franchises.
  Monthly subscription: £267.60 + VAT
  Annual subscription: £2,890.00 + VAT
- **Associate members:** These are franchisors that have proved their ability to launch and support at least one franchised outlet for 12 months and are now in the business of building their network. They must meet the same operating standards as full members but they will not have established their trading or franchising record over the same length of time.

Monthly subscription: £257.00 + VAT

Annual subscription: £2,772.00 + VAT

- **Provisional listing:** For those at the beginning of their development in franchising. Although the franchise may only be at the pilot stage, there is a real business up and running where end-products and services are being sold successfully to consumers. The franchise agreement is sound and, by joining the bfa, the company has committed itself to developing the business in accordance with bfa industry standards.
  Monthly subscription: £180.00 + VAT
  Annual subscription: £1,943.00 + VAT

- **Affiliates:** These are the banks, solicitors, consultants and other professionals who are able to demonstrate their expertise and specialism in franchising. If you are looking for finance or need legal documentation checked, you would be foolish not to seek out a bfa-accredited lender, lawyer or other professional advisor. You wouldn't go to an interior decorator to have your portrait painted. So don't go to a conveyancing lawyer to get your franchise agreement checked.
  Monthly subscription: £267.60 + VAT
  Annual subscription: £2,890.00 + VAT

More and more franchise businesses are joining the bfa (typically around 20–30 new members a year). For a complete list of members, please visit the bfa website at www.thebfa.org.

> The initial training was vital for me as a non-accountant and I took every last ounce I possibly could from the course, often asking the trainers to stay late to give me extra support . . . which they were happy to do.
>
> *Renee Mackay, TaxAssist*

Membership benefits

For franchisors

Franchisor members have to meet the standards set by the bfa in order to establish that their franchise represents a fair, ethical and disclosed opportunity. The standards are adopted from the European

Franchise Federation (EFF) code of ethics (see Chapter 7). Although the credibility of membership and the associated opportunity to promote an ethical and proper approach to franchising is one of the most obvious benefits for franchisors when joining the bfa, there are also many other aspects to the membership. These include platforms to share best practice and opportunities to raise their profile, make new contacts and influence their business environment.

For the franchisee

In addition to the benefits for franchisors, membership of the bfa also has a number of benefits for franchisees. If a franchisor has the credibility of bfa accreditation, this can help you as a franchisee to access finance, as banks that specialise in franchise financing will look positively on bfa accreditation of the brand. These benefits will then continue through the life of the franchise, even to the point at which you may want to sell the business. For a franchisee who is looking to sell their business, being part of a brand which is bfa-accredited means that potential buyers will have more confidence, and in many cases a better sale can be achieved.

Using the bfa

The bfa provides educational seminars across the UK and works with various media to provide objective information that will help those who are right for franchising – and also to help those who are not suited to it – to recognise this before entering into any costly agreements.

The bfa lists only those companies that it accredits on its website (www.thebfa.org) in non-promotional and unbiased lists, which provides you, a potential franchisee, with a wealth of information in order to help you decide whether franchising is right for you.

The future of the bfa

During the last year, a number of developments have taken place within the bfa. As launched in 2010, the new qualification of Qualified Franchise Professional (QFP) has been awarded to over 20 successful delegates – each of the delegates has proved their commitment to professional development and ethical franchising.

The bfa website has also been completely rebuilt. In order to accommodate the wealth of information available for online users, the website has created new resource zones for each of the groups in an efficient and accessible fashion, and, in addition, the new structure of the website means that there are a greater amount of franchising resources for online users to look at. With the evolving nature of the website, further developments are planned for the future.

The bfa also organised a crucial meeting between leading franchise figures and 30 UK MPs in October 2011. The meeting was to increase the awareness of franchising in Parliament, and the future relationship could help to increase the education available on the subject.

Importantly, the bfa also continued to develop its engagement with franchisees by appointing a third franchisee to its board of directors. This sits alongside the development of direct membership for franchisees, with access to new benefits from the association and with franchisees becoming part of the official industry governance.

WHAT THE BFA CAN DO FOR YOU

- It offers objective information and advice to potential franchisees.

- It accredits franchises, which can make it easier for you to recognise ethical franchise businesses and raise the necessary finance to set up a franchise business.

- You can access educational seminars across the UK.

3.0

IS FRANCHISING RIGHT FOR YOU?

IN THIS CHAPTER

Franchising isn't suited to everyone, so it's important that you are comfortable with the concept and that you do as much research as possible to ensure it's the right decision for you. As outlined in the previous chapter, buying a franchise can be a quick way to set up your own business and get off to a flying start. And as such a vast number of products and services are now franchised businesses, you're bound to find something that appeals to you or in which you have experience and that would make an attractive business opportunity.

But while there are plenty of positives to starting a franchise, there are some potential disadvantages you'll need to consider before deciding whether franchising is the right move. Such a convenient, guided approach to business can be too inflexible for some people. Others may want to have a bigger say in how their business is run and operated, but feel that this is not possible within a franchise business, as the franchisor will always retain a significant level of control over how the company is run.

In this chapter, we'll cover:

- the pros and cons of franchising
- who it's suited to
- the reality of running a franchise
- buying a franchise.

Franchising: the pros and cons

For every action, there is an equal and opposite reaction – as Isaac Newton discovered. This mantra can apply to franchising. There are many benefits to franchising, but at the same time there are some potential issues to be raised, and depending on your point of view, these can be problematic.

This section will look at the two sides of each argument, dividing them into 'pros' and 'cons'. It's worth bearing in mind that starting your own business from scratch will also have its own list of pros and cons, and this chapter will look at this aspect as well.

> Joining a franchise was a big leap of faith, but looking back on it, it has worked out for me beautifully. I was bored in my last job; I am now much happier. I am selling a service people want and are very happy with in general.
>
> *Steven Hook, Greensleeves*

The business system

Pros

A strong brand is a great advantage because there are already customers for those products and services. These customers know what they can get from you when they see your brand. But brands begin somewhere and, when you start searching for the right franchise, you might end up looking at a relatively new business that has yet to establish the reputation of its brand in its market.

The most important advantage you will still be buying into is that the business model has been proven in practice. It's not just an idea on paper: it will exist out there in the real world as a real business doing business with real customers. If there isn't such a business for you to go and look at, it's not a franchise. Don't pay for the business development work that has not been done.

There is a greater risk of failure with a stand-alone business start-up. It's not easy to get the product and service mix, pricing, marketing and sales strategy, equipment and product supply arrangements, and location decisions right first time when starting a new business. A small error on just one of these elements could leave you with a business that puts a 5% net loss on the bottom line rather than a 5% net profit. In a franchise, these issues have been tried, modified and tested for you, usually over a reasonable period of time – which has got to be at least one or two years – in at least one or two locations.

The less testing and time the business system has had to prove itself, the greater the risk that the business might not work in your location. But even with one location and one year of successful trading, you're still streets ahead of a stand-alone start-up.

Cons

While a franchise's business system may be tried and tested, the downside is that this is a rigid format. By buying into a franchise, you are contracted to run your business by adhering to the guidelines laid down by the franchisor.

There is no specific UK legislation for franchising, but it is regulated under European competition law. In terms of legal documents, you'll need to sign what is known as a franchise agreement. This sets out the rights and obligations of the franchisor and the franchisee and what is expected of the relationship between them. The franchise agreement includes restrictions on how you run the business.

The merits of this will depend on your own viewpoint about starting a business from scratch. Yes, it's true that in a franchise you are allowed the autonomy to run a business – the only catch is that it's not on your own terms, but the franchisor's. Your franchise must be run in accordance with a proven business system rather than your own. You may like the franchise but there may be some aspects of the business system that you want to change. In a stand-alone business, this would not be a problem, since you would be devising your own business plan. But with a franchise, you have no choice.

If you have any of your own ideas or changes that you want to contribute, this is only possible if you consult the franchisor and suggest these changes. It's possible that the franchisor may like your idea – suggestions for promotions or products may be welcomed. If the franchisor does not agree, however, and you choose to implement the changes regardless, this will be more damaging than you think, and could result in you losing your business. Not only are you putting the reputation of the brand at risk: you're also jeopardising the careers of other franchisees who are perfectly happy to adhere to the business system.

Right from the outset, you need to determine whether you are happy to work this way. If you are not, and you wish to have complete autonomy, then starting your own business from scratch is a better bet. At the end of the day, you have to weigh up whether independent thinking is a good substitute for the benefit of having a proven and supported business system in place.

A defined trading territory

Pros

Some franchised businesses offer exclusive trading territories and some don't. Some set prime marketing areas and some don't. Retail shops, particularly at the lower customer-spend end of the spectrum, will rarely have an exclusive territory. Shops have their own natural territory. People just don't travel 20 miles for the benefit of buying their preferred burger from you rather than the outlet near their house. Territories come into their own with van-based mobile franchises, on the other hand – where it's easier to travel to a customer just that bit further away – and with higher value business-to-business sales where one customer might spend £50 and another £5,000.

In these circumstances you don't want your high-value customers being picked off by just a handful of the early, high-flying franchisees in the network, leaving the later franchisees with the low-value customers to trade among. Set territories for each franchisee prevent this from happening.

Cons

At first glance, a defined territory in which you have the exclusive right to trade looks attractive, but don't forget that all the other territories will have the same protection, so you will not be able to trade outside your territory even if it has fewer customers in it than you expected.

When you're researching franchising, find out what the different approaches are to exclusive and other kinds of territory and what the franchisor's reasons are for their particular approach.

Raising finance

Pros

One of the big advantages of franchising is its track record of being a much lower-risk option. This, combined with the fact that you can see the success of other franchisees in the same network, means that banks look upon franchising very favourably. There are a handful of the high street banks that have dedicated franchise departments and these can lend up to 70% of the value of the business – much more than for a non-franchise start-up.

This process can also be aided by the franchisor, who may be able to help with the introduction to the bank or provide guidance on the business plan.

Cons

The main disadvantage with regard to finance in franchising is that you need to be sure not only that you can make a living from the business, but that you can also make all the necessary repayments in the time required. In some business start-ups a start-up loan may have various options for the repayment term. With a franchise the bank will not want to make the repayment term any longer than the franchise term. As most initial franchise agreements run for five years, this will probably be the time period that you will also need to make the full repayment of any bank loan.

Costs

Pros

Looking at the upside of the additional costs required with a franchise, it's worth considering the bigger picture. Yes, there may be extra costs charged on top of the initial franchise fee, and in some cases you will be charged for overheads that you would need to pay for in a regular business – but then a good number of franchises offer the turnkey package. Which is to say that you will have everything you could possibly need in making your business a big success and allowing you to afford the required costs, as well as enough money to earn you a decent living. You will get some or all of the following: territory; office; vehicle; equipment; stationery; marketing campaigns; training; support. All of these combine to give you the best opportunity available to make enough money.

However, these will vary between businesses – and another point to make is that any established franchise network will benefit from a better buying power for a number of core supplies. In some cases, there will be deals struck by the franchisor that the franchisee can choose to take advantage of.

Cons

Invariably, taking on a franchise doesn't suddenly stop with the initial franchise fee. There will be ongoing fees included in the mix, such as management service fees (which pay for the ongoing support and services that you get from the franchisor). You also may be contracted to buy products from the franchisor.

In the case of a tight profit margin, you will also need to be aware that the management fee will be taken off your turnover rather than the surplus that you make (see Chapter 9 for more information on fees). And when the initial contract term ends, you may also have to pay to extend your time with the franchisor.

Factor in the overheads needed to run a business – electricity, phone bills, even food costs – and again, you do need to make sure that running a franchise is financially viable for you. You need to ensure that you have enough funds to afford all these extra costs – so devise a detailed breakdown of costs prior to making a decision as to whether or not to proceed with your franchise.

Network of support

Pros

One of the great things about being part of a franchise is the support that you can get. Support can be provided in a number of ways. Some networks offer a mentor scheme in which well-established franchisees offer the benefit of their experience to newcomers through the initial start-up phase. Advice can be given through the internet, on the phone or in person. The other important aspect of this is that it's a great way to make new friends; a large number of franchises pride themselves on the camaraderie that they create through their franchisee networks, and in some cases, they can organise special events and parties to bring the network closer together.

> **The support continues long after you've set up and there's always someone available to offer advice and help if you need it. It's also very helpful having a whole network of franchise owners to talk to and share ideas with.**

Juliet O'Connell, The ZipYard

Cons

Although support among fellow franchisees is quite common in franchising, you also need to make sure this advice is still in line with the objectives and standards of the franchisor. The last thing you want is biased or subjective direction from one disgruntled or unsuccessful franchisee in the network. While it's worth getting feedback from other franchisees, your first port of call should always be the franchisor.

You should also note that while the franchisor, mentor or support team can offer advice and help, at the end of the day, only you as a franchisee can take action. Make sure that you have the right willpower and determination to see any difficulties through rather than rely on hand-holding, because it's your job to make the business a success.

Marketing and PR

Pros

Some franchises offer a marketing and PR campaign in order to groom you for your big launch. Maximum publicity will be the order of the day here – the problem with starting your business from scratch is that marketing the business is a very costly deal indeed. Advertising in magazines, radio and TV – they all cost a lot of money. Even the comparatively simpler methods of online advertising, search engine websites and printed flyers all cost more than you realise.

So a franchise can make good use of this promotion, because it's part of the package that you buy into. And, provided the campaigns and methods are effective enough, these will see you well on the way to your franchise generating a lot of feedback and interest.

> " I try to attend all training days and I have always received a lot of support from office staff. I keep in close contact with the staff and ask for their help whenever I need it. In the recent past, they have accompanied me to open days, school assemblies, carnivals and student award ceremonies, as well as helping out with leafleting. "
>
> *Vicky West, Kumon*

Cons

However, not all franchises provide marketing and PR – in some cases, the onus will be on the franchisee to generate publicity. If you feel that you have the necessary expertise to create a cost-effective but memorable way of promoting the business (for example, if you have previously had experience of marketing and PR), then this shouldn't be such a big obstacle.

With respect to the franchises that do offer marketing and PR campaigns, a potential problem is that you won't have as much freedom as to how you promote your business. With a franchise, publicity is usually done in a 'uniform' fashion – that's to say that every franchisee in that network will get the same sort of promotional campaign. However, if you want a bit more creative input into the advertising idea and you want to make your own mark on the marketing ideas, there's less opportunity to do so, because the franchisor will want to do it a certain way. Again, you have to consider whether you're the sort of person who wants to have a considerable amount of creative freedom in your business. If you're unsure about the 'uniform' style of marketing, and you have sufficient funds to start your own business and promote it in your own way, this may be the better option for you.

Training

Pros

Franchisors will want to make sure that their new franchisees know every last fact about how to run their business, and so training courses are provided. The courses will teach the franchisee about the product or service that they are providing, in addition to selling techniques, finance, book-keeping and customer service.

This initiation can take different forms, whether it's hands-on, practical training – either on the job with another franchisee or in an imaginary scenario – or whether it's more formal classroom teaching. The outcome is that the franchisee will be very well versed in all aspects of his or her franchise. Ongoing training will also take place in most franchises after the franchisee has gone through initiation.

> The course covers all the aspects that you need to know before you can begin work. It is structured in a certain way so that you get dedicated periods of time on a particular aspect.
>
> *Steven Hook, Greensleeves*

Cons

What if a potential franchisee wants to join a franchise because he or she has some prior experience of the field? It may be that they have been in a similar franchise that had to fold for whatever reason, financial or otherwise. In theory, training may not be as necessary – in practice, however, each franchise has a set of specific systems and working practices, so training will need to be given – even if the incoming franchisee has had prior experience. A good number of franchisors tailor the training sessions – so that franchisees work to the specifics of an individual system – choosing to concentrate more on the working practices and systems that they require of the franchisee. This aspect of training is not a con as such, but generally, you will still have to pay for training, no matter how much you choose to do.

Sharing profits

Pros

Part of the deal with franchising is that you will need to pay the franchisor ongoing fees, which at times you will undoubtedly resent. However, the reason that franchising is so successful is mainly on account of the many benefits you get in return for these fees. It is these fees that provide the ongoing support, protection, development and guidance that give you such a stable platform to work from. At times you will forget this point and not see the value, but you will need to remind yourself about how much all of these benefits have helped you and what an advantage they are.

Cons

It's also important to consider the worst that could happen. For example, the franchisor might go out of business or other franchisees could give the brand – and your business – a bad name. This could drag your profits down, as well as your reputation. You should also bear in mind that all profits you make are shared with the franchisor, and seeing your hard-earned profits going elsewhere could be painful to bear for some.

Worst of all, if you breach the contract with your franchisor this could result in an abrupt end to your business. Other people's decisions could sink your franchise – your lack of complete control over your franchise means that even if you run a profitable outlet, you can still lose everything if your franchisor makes bad business decisions and the firm fails. As well as seeming vastly unfair, such catastrophes can come out of the blue if your franchisor doesn't keep you up to date with developments. When franchisors fail, and sometimes they do, their franchisees can often go on trading, either under their own name or as part of another network that can profit from bringing more good businesses under their brand. But don't underestimate the difficulties you would face in such circumstances.

Growth prospects

Pros

The great thing about being a franchisee is that there is potential for expanding the business. The latest NatWest/bfa Franchise Survey says that while 73% run just one franchise unit, the remaining, multiple-unit franchisees have an average of under three. This indicates that while most franchisees are perfectly happy with just one franchise unit, the potential for expansion is there if desired. And if the next franchise unit proves to be just as successful as the first one, and meets increased consumer demand, the financial rewards will be big.

Cons

When you are with a franchisor, you do not have the freedom simply to open up another outlet yourself, as you would do with your own business. The decision would have to be made with the franchisor – if both you and the franchisor feel that you are doing well, then proceedings can begin for a second territory.

However, if you do proceed, there is still that same element of risk as with the initial franchise. Just because that went well, it does not guarantee that the second one will too. Not only does the outcome depend on the still shaky economic climate: there's also the added risk of the franchisee taking on too much work too soon. Be sure that you are in a financially stable position to proceed before committing yourself to a second shot that may entail the risk of missing the target.

FRANCHISING PROS AND CONS AT A GLANCE

- You won't have to come up with a business idea.

- You can make use of your franchisor's advertising and marketing material.

- You'll get access to support and training.

- It can be easier to raise finance.

- Depending on the type of franchise, you could get access to prime trading areas.

But . . .

- The costs of buying or starting a franchise can be high.

- As a franchisee, you'll have to run your own business according to someone else's rules.

- The future of your business could be jeopardised if a bad franchise ruins the brand's reputation.

- As a franchisee, a percentage of all your turnover goes to your franchisor.

Franchising: to whom is it suited?

Franchising has proved to be the safest way of starting your own business, and nine in 10 franchises say they are making a profit. But this doesn't necessarily mean it's the right opportunity for you. You'll need to assess your strengths and weaknesses before you start to evaluate potential franchises.

The success of a franchise and its location depends very much on you – the franchisee – following a set of rules and ensuring that customers have a similar experience, no matter where they visit the franchise. This means that your product, branding, design, packaging and operations have to be the same as the next franchisee's. Implementing the standard working practices of your franchisor and then improving on them is a massive task, and one that takes dedication and a lot of support from family and friends.

If you don't feel that this is an environment you can thrive in, then a franchise probably isn't suited to you – ultimately, it could lead to clashes with your franchisor, which would make the ongoing relationship extremely difficult. If, however, you prefer to have a business whose future prospects can be clearly mapped out and where you follow a set of rules, then it may be the right choice.

It's a delicate balance though. As mentioned above, one of the advantages of starting a franchise is receiving support and advice from the franchisor and a network of franchisees, but you shouldn't expect to receive help with everything. The basis of franchising is this: although your franchisor will tell you the best method of doing whatever needs to be done in your business, they won't do it for you. That's your job as a franchisee. If you think you might benefit from more rather than less support, it may be worthwhile seeking out a franchise that is well established, with solid operating systems in place, and that can offer you this extra level of support.

Don't break the rules

As mentioned above, before you enter into a franchising deal, you need to work out whether a franchise is suited to your personality, particularly if you prefer to be running the show. Because a franchise contract binds you to working by the franchisor's set of rules and established business system, this will not suit those who want a little bit more freedom in their business. If you're more of a maverick who likes to march to the beat of his or her own drum, then a franchise will not be suitable. As also mentioned above, the franchisor will determine not only how your business is run, but also how it is promoted and marketed. You may not agree with the franchisor's methods – and so running your own show is the safer option here.

Turn on the charm

The franchisor will look for someone who is hard-working, dedicated – and also easy to get on with. That's one of the most crucial aspects of becoming a franchisee. You have to be pleasant, good humoured and willing to get on with the job without kicking up any fuss or hassle.

A lot of franchises require customer interaction, so you will need the above qualities in abundance. It's the same as working in a shop – if the customer comes in to be confronted by a surly, miserable face, they'll walk out again. It's the same trick with a franchisee – he or she needs to smile and genuinely engage with his or her customer. That way, the customer will always return, leading to repeat business and good prospects for your franchise.

The right personality

The other aspect of dealing with the public is that some people – although pleasant and good humoured – may be exceedingly shy. Therefore, if this applies to you, then a franchise in which you have daily dealings with the public is not a good option. It's no reflection on you or your capability to do the work, but being a franchisee in the public eye requires someone who is outgoing, with bags of confidence. So make sure that you choose the right franchise for you and one that you're fully comfortable with.

Support from all quarters

Support does not just apply to your work environment. Before making your final decision about starting a franchise, remember to involve your friends and family. Being a business owner – whether you are starting from scratch or running a franchise – will take up more of your time and energy than you could possibly imagine and it's essential that you prepare your family and friends for what lies ahead. If your family (spouse, children, parents) aren't on board with you 100%, at some point you, your business and/or your family will bear the consequences and will be most affected by your workload.

You'll also need to seek out support from industry experts before taking the plunge. It's vital that you speak to a legal expert who specialises in franchising to help you understand the ins and outs of the franchise agreement.

Ask yourself the following question before committing to any franchise: is the franchisor happy for you to talk to existing franchisees for advice and further information? If not, then it could be a sure sign of one franchise to avoid – there is nothing more invaluable than the thoughts and tips of someone who has been there before.

Working hard to reap the rewards

Many of the personal qualities that determine whether a franchise is right for you also apply to anyone thinking of starting a business. Above all, you must be willing to work hard to reap the rewards – buying into an existing business concept does not mean you are buying into a get-rich-quick scheme. Working weeks of 60 hours or more are not unheard of among franchisees attempting to get their business off the ground. You have to be fully committed – if you get behind with the running of the business, or let standards slip, your business will be failing and neither you nor your franchisor will be best pleased.

> **Of course it's hard work, but then so is working for someone else – the difference is that you get to create wealth for yourself and your family rather than someone else.**
>
> *Andy Rees, Ableworld*

Managing the workload

As a franchisee, you are a business owner, and businesses need to be managed. You have to manage the accounts, credit control, local advertising, public relations, VAT returns and everything else that's part of running your own business. Your franchisor will have processes and training methods that relate to all these management tasks, but you'll still have to do it. Depending on the type of franchise you opt for, in the early days you may have to take on many of the day-to-day tasks yourself, but as your profit margin increases, you'll want to consider employing staff. In these circumstances, management experience will be beneficial and franchisors will be on the look-out for people who can manage and motivate staff.

As with any other business, it's important to choose a franchise that you'll enjoy running, in a sector which you can be passionate about. Most companies succeed if their owners are behind them and their products and services 100%. If you choose a sector that you are really interested in, you are likely to learn faster and to improve your skills in a shorter space of time.

However, don't think you *need* to have previous experience in the sector. Many franchisors prefer candidates who don't bring other people's methods with them. Aptitude and passion count more than existing skills.

FRANCHISING QUIZ

Can you answer 'yes' to the following?

- Do you have the financial resources to buy a franchise, or if not, can you see yourself getting the money elsewhere?

- Do you enjoy working with others?

- Are you prepared to give up a degree of independence and run the business according to someone else's rules?

■ Are you comfortable giving your franchisor a share of your profits?

■ Do you have any management experience, or are you willing to learn?

Running a franchise: the reality

Once you've decided whether or not you have the necessary aptitude and mind-set to become involved in franchising, the next step is to research what it's like to run a franchise and to consider whether this is something you can do successfully.

One of the keys to a successfully run franchise is choosing the right franchisor in the first place. It's important to look for an established company with a proven track record and a good reputation, and you should make sure that it belongs to the bfa and runs its business in accordance with the association's best-practice guidelines. All of the bfa's members have chosen to be vetted against a strict code of business practice. If a company is not a member of the bfa, that does not mean it is disreputable, but you would be wise to seek additional expert advice to ensure that you are protected as much as possible, and ask why it is not a bfa member.

You'll also need to be able to sell, and to attract customers – while you'll get a ready-made business with a franchise, you won't get customers. And what can you expect on a day-to-day basis? It's essential to maintain a good working relationship with your franchisor and to keep in touch on a regular basis. A problem shared is a problem halved – and whatever challenges you encounter, it's likely that someone, somewhere, has already faced a similar situation and your franchisor will be able to assist you. Use your franchisor's experience rather than learn the hard way! That is why you have joined a franchise and not set up on your own.

Keeping on top of your finances and monitoring cash flow is also key. It's important to refer back to your business plan (see Chapter 8 for more on this topic) and to ensure that your figures are in line with your expectations. It's perfectly normal to keep reviewing and changing your business plan in line with what the actual figures are telling you. This will also allow you to keep a close eye on your cash flow and prepare for any unforeseen difficulties that may arise.

You can call on the support of your franchisor for marketing, but the truth of the matter is that no one is better placed than you to market your business. This is why it is so important to choose a franchise in an industry that you are interested in or have a passion for. Enthusiasm is contagious – if you can convey enthusiasm for your service or product, then you are likely to be more successful at converting and retaining customers.

Buying a franchise

Investigate the different types of franchise on offer. It's all too easy to feel overwhelmed by the number of options open to you, but there are three main areas you need to consider when buying a franchise:

1. the level of capital investment needed (what you are prepared to put into the business)
2. how much, if necessary, you can afford to borrow
3. whether you want your franchise to primarily serve consumers or other businesses.

If you need to borrow money from the bank, you'll need to find out whether it will consider a loan. Consider whether you would be capable of starting your own business in the same market as some franchises (for example, car repair or plumbing), as some require you to have previous experience. You'll also need to assess the market, and it's important to look at the overall picture rather than just relying on past performance. If you're serious about buying a franchise, you'll need to know just as much about the industry and market as if you were starting your own business from scratch, which will involve writing a detailed business plan. While your franchisor will be able to give you a certain amount of support, you can't expect them to do the research for you or to answer all the questions you may have.

If the franchise you are considering buying has a single, defined product or service, you must ensure that there is sufficient demand now and in the future. Franchises, like any other start-up business, will face competition and it's important to identify who you'll be competing with and how their products and services differ. You may even find that the stiffest competition comes from other franchised businesses.

> **The most important advice I can give on buying any franchise is to ensure that you choose a franchisor that you can trust to offer you the ongoing knowledge and support you will need to allow your business to thrive.**
>
> *Nigel Toplis, ComputerXplorers*

Background check

Be sure to obtain a detailed history of the franchised operation. Consider how many franchises were in operation a year ago, as compared to today, and how many are planned over the next five years. Ask yourself the following questions.

■ Have any franchises ceased operations, and if so, when, where and for what reason?
■ What support will be available and what training will be provided? Will it be given to you before you start the franchise or can you expect to have a level of ongoing support?
■ Does the marketing and promotional material meet your expectations and is it up to date?

It goes without saying that getting as much financial information as possible up front will be crucial. A franchise is a partnership that thrives on communication between the franchisor and the franchisee – and that includes all things financial. If you find that the franchisor is unwilling to disclose the information you require, then you should tread carefully. Every good franchisor will give you access to their franchisees. Indeed, they will insist that you spend time with existing franchisees to get a first-hand view of what it's like to be in the business. You might get a mix of opinions, but overall, you should be able to build up a good picture of how the franchise is performing.

BUYING A FRANCHISE: QUESTIONS TO ASK

■ Is the business viable: is it as good as it sounds?

■ Who else has made a success of the business, and is the franchisor giving you realistic targets and projections?

■ Does the business appear capable of supporting the marketing, advertising and training that it has promised you?

■ Is the business legal and ethical and is the company a member of the bfa?

We're not like the rest

BCR Associates is a cost reduction company helping businesses boost profitability by cutting overspend on essential running costs.

We stand out from the crowd because, unlike others in the marketplace, 100% of the savings we realise are passed on to our clients without any commission or fees - instead we get an introducer's fee from our supply chain. This unique business model provides our franchise owners with a residual income and no barriers to sale.

We have built a team of successful franchise owners who have the passion to build their business with our proven business model and we are seeking other like-minded people to expand our brand across the UK. Be part of it.

BCR Associates Franchise Opportunity
www.bcrassociatesfranchise.co.uk
Call 0844 880 9838
Email franchise@bcrassociates.co.uk

4.0

WHICH FRANCHISE IS RIGHT FOR YOU?

IN THIS CHAPTER

There are hundreds of franchises to choose from, covering all manner of sectors, so how do you go about choosing the right franchise? You can narrow down your search for franchisors by the industry sector you're interested in, the type of franchising opportunity you're seeking and your minimum personal and total investment.

Franchising is not just about the business opportunity, however. Once you've decided that it is the right business for you with regard to investment and type of industry, it's important to ask yourself exactly what you want from the business in terms of support, day-to-day responsibilities, work–life balance, skills required and opportunities for ongoing learning.

In this chapter, we'll cover:

- different types of franchise
- what each franchise needs and offers
- how to work out what you want from a franchise
- buying an existing franchise.

Different types of franchise

There are different types of business-format franchising model, and within these models many different types of business, so knowing where to start can be daunting. Business-format franchising models can be roughly broken down into the following categories.

- **Job franchise:** these are also referred to as 'single operator' franchises and are so called because you are, in effect, buying a job for yourself, with no responsibility for other employees. They start from £5,000, usually rising to £20,000. Examples include car-dent repair franchises.
- **Executive franchise:** these are in fact job franchises but provide a professional service; hence they are often referred to as 'white collar' franchises. They involve providing consultancy in areas such as financial services. Most people operating in this type of franchise work from home and travel to clients' premises.
- **Management franchise:** as a franchisee of a management franchise, you'll be marketing and managing a business while trained staff carry out actual business activities. The majority of your turnover will be generated from business-to-business activities rather than retail. Examples include parcel delivery franchises.
- **Master franchise:** as a master franchisee, you would secure exclusive rights to develop an international franchisor's brand, trading style and system in the UK, or in a major area of the UK. These are franchises that have a proven system in another country but which do not yet have a presence in the UK. As the franchisee, you would be responsible for introducing the franchise into the UK and then running it. You would be taking on the role of franchisor.
- **Investment franchise:** these franchises require you to put in a substantial amount of investment – at least £100,000 – and cover bigger businesses such as hotels and restaurants. The money is required to purchase the property and necessary equipment.

There are also other kinds of business-format franchises, some of which are used by very successful companies. For example, exclusive distribution is the format adopted by motor vehicle manufacturers for their dealerships. Some of the great brands in perfumery use selective distribution to get their products to market.

At the bottom end of the 'business opportunity' market there are many product distribution schemes, some of which use multi-level marketing formats – the new name for pyramid selling – where great care is needed. You must ensure that you don't buy into obligations to purchase products for resale without any real prospect of, or help in, making those sales. Operators of these schemes often call their opportunity a franchise to make unwarranted up-front fees look legitimate. These examples are all the more reason to find an industry-approved franchisor.

Fortunately, with bfa accreditation, and your own common sense to go by, it's not difficult to recognise a good business-format franchise, provided you do your research. The best option is to research the different types of franchise as much as possible and think about your strengths and weaknesses so that you can choose a franchise that makes the best use of your aptitude and interests.

We've listed below some of the more popular types of business-format franchise you'll come across, and the skills they require.

Retail

These tend to be popular high street chains, occupying retail premises and selling products or services to walk-in customers. The business will be very dependent on its premises, so it's vital that they are in the right location, making it easy for customers – who will be your main source of turnover (the volume of business over time) – to visit.

You'll need to be prepared to work long hours and at weekends too, and will most likely need to hire additional staff, so management and recruitment experience would be a plus. Above all, you'll need to feel comfortable dealing with the public and providing customer service.

Retail franchises cover a wide variety of sub-sectors, including food and takeaway, hairdressing and carpets. Examples include fast-food chain McDonald's, shoe store Clarks, sandwich makers Subway and window blinds retailer Marla Custom Blinds. The costs vary widely. A McDonald's franchise, for example, costs between £125,000 and £325,000 and you'll need to provide at least 25% of the value of the business, whereas the minimum total investment for Marla Custom Blinds is about £18,000.

> **We wanted to run a business that is ethical and fulfils a need in the community in which we live. We have seen plenty of poor service in the retail sector and we hope to bring our experience in the hospitality trade into a new sector.**
>
> *Mark Hennis, Ableworld*

Care services

Care provider franchises place care workers – and in some cases nurses – with both private and public clients, from individuals to hospitals. Contracts might run for just a few days, to fill in for someone off sick, or for several months – perhaps to cover for maternity leave.

Carers are generally recruited through local advertising or the Jobcentre. Some franchisees send out flyers or even put cards in the windows of newsagents. But the main point is that the advertising is as cheap as possible. Franchisees should aim to have upwards of 100 carers to run a viable business and they need to recruit constantly. You would also need to employ staff to help run an office.

In the care services industry, it's vital that you, as the franchisee, keep up to date with the relevant legislation and that you know as much as possible about the social services provided in your territory. It's also worthwhile gaining accreditation with the social services and relevant local authorities, as these can be good sources of referrals. Staff and training are likely to be your biggest expenditure.

Estate agencies

You don't need any formal qualifications to become an estate agent franchisee, but many come from a financial background. The two industries complement each other, as many people buying houses are also seeking mortgages. The property industry has been very hard in recent years, however, so you'll need considerable people skills in order to inspire trust and confidence in your potential customers.

Financial services

Franchises in this sector are generally based around business advisory services, operations designed to help businesses reduce their costs or to assist with their tax and accounting needs. As well as making initial audits, you can generate work by monitoring and making recommendations.

As this is a professional franchise, existing contacts in a white-collar industry can be beneficial. It goes without saying that you'll need to have a head for figures and an analytical mind. Thanks to the nature of this type of business, all franchisors vet potential franchisees carefully before taking them on. You must be prepared to travel and to spend much of your day out and about, visiting clients.

In most cases, financial experience is not a pre-requisite. Obviously, you must be able to handle money issues, but relevant contacts and management-level experience are more important. The overheads are low because you start from home.

Cleaning services

A host of domestic cleaning franchises have sprung up in recent years, but a cleaning franchise can also cover furniture, upholstery and carpet cleaning as well as domestic services. Most cleaning franchises are run from the franchisee's home, as you hire a pool of external cleaners – moving into premises generally comes as a matter of course later on. This means that the franchise has more flexibility in terms of working hours. Cleaning franchises attract a large number of women, who work from home and fit the work around childcare, for example.

Good people skills are essential – you'll need to visit people's homes in order to assess their cleaning needs and you'll also be managing a number of employees. While you can initially keep your overheads down by working from home, you'll incur other expenses such as staff wages and, in some cases, you may have to provide vehicles for your cleaners (which you would lease or hire, rather than buy outright). Expect to do a lot of leafleting as part of your marketing activity and to spend money advertising in local directories such as *Yellow Pages*. There are also commercial cleaning franchises, some of which guarantee contracts to a specified level of turnover. But be aware that a guarantee of turnover is no guarantee of profit.

Working with children

If you choose a franchise that involves working with children, the work can be very rewarding, as well as fun. To work with children, you have to be flexible and patient – many of the franchises involve work during term time only or in the mornings or afternoons. While this can work for franchisees who are looking for a job that fits around their own children, you'll be expected to do preparation outside of this period. Work is based around movement, music and reading. Some of the franchises operating in this area include Monkey Music, Tumble Tots and Jo Jingles. Classes normally last around 45 minutes.

You can work from home, although the classes will be held in hired halls. You'll need to hire space over a set period of time and not per individual class, so you'll need to ensure that classes are pre-booked for that period and that you can collect money up front. As these tend to be part-time franchises the returns are not typically that high.

> Kumon is ideal when you have a young family. Most of the work is done at home, when I can pick it up and put it down when my own children dictate! It enables me to keep my children at home with me rather than having to put them into full-time childcare. I carry out my enrolments in

the evenings when my husband is home to look after the children and put them to bed. Apart from my Saturday-morning class, we have the luxury of spending all our weekends together. 🙶🙶

Vicky West, Kumon

Internet

An interest in computers, technology and the internet is helpful if you want to make a living in this field. You'll need to be the type of person who enjoys learning, as new products are being launched every week that could reshape your business. However, you don't necessarily need a high level of IT skills to compete in this sector. For many internet franchises – and there is a huge amount of diversity – just basic IT skills will be fine. Former sales people are often well suited to internet franchises that involve a particular emphasis for the franchisee on selling.

Internet franchises may involve selling online advertising, or may be concerned with IT consulting or support, web design, online publishing, administration and search marketing services, to name a few popular models. Franchisees purchase the right to trade under the franchisor's name and are given support and training to increase their chances of success. They mostly work from home, so overheads are kept relatively low. There are a wide range of internet franchises and the costs to run them vary greatly.

Print shops

Location is one of the most important factors for success, and printing franchises also cost quite a bit of money to set up. The business, however, can be quite lucrative, although you'll need to work at it for several years. As it can cost upwards of £100,000 to set up a franchise, print shops appeal to older franchisees, and it comes as little surprise that franchisors will be looking for people who can demonstrate some work experience – particularly in sales or management.

As the cost is quite high, one of the most important factors in your success as a print shop franchisee will be your relationship with your bank.

Recruitment

If you choose the recruitment business, you'll be joining an industry that ranges from finance to catering, engineering to sales. As far as franchising goes, there are broadly two kinds of recruitment.

At the commercial recruitment end of the scale, you should recognise the high street names. They cover a familiar market that handles work placement in a low- to mid-range pay bracket for both temporary and permanent contracts, such as Select Appointments. At the other end of the scale is executive search, or headhunting.

Your role is to liaise between employers and employees, with a view to finding a perfect fit. In the beginning, your job will be to sell yourself. For commercial recruitment, this will probably mean cold calling, hopefully leading to face-to-face meetings and establishing contacts. And even when you have clients, you'll have to work at keeping them while looking for more. Inevitably, at the start you'll have to do whatever is needed to get the business going and keep it running. You should expect to have to juggle looking for premises, talking to the bank, managing your team, hiring and training staff, all on top of acting as a recruitment consultant. Ideally, you should come from a senior management or sales background, as this will give you the right mind-set to make the business work.

Automotive/car-repair franchises

Car-repair franchises fall broadly into two categories. First, there is mobile repair work, fixing worn-out parts or more superficial damage. Revive!, for example, specialises in repair to paintwork, plastic bumpers, windscreens, alloy wheels and interiors.

It's vital to have excellent customer service skills in the car-repair business and to build up a loyal client base. Being part of a franchise with a big name can be your best advert, but much of your work is likely to be generated by word-of-mouth referrals, from one satisfied customer to another. It helps to have some interest and experience in mechanics and, unsurprisingly, this franchise tends to be dominated by men.

The franchise fee and set-up costs vary. There is obviously a big difference between a mobile business and a workshop-based one, although the cost can also depend on which package you go for. The initial fee for a Revive! franchise costs £28,500, but total investment, including legal fees, plant and equipment, premises renovation and start-up promotional funds will amount to £145,000.

Parcel courier

Parcel-delivery franchises fall broadly into two categories. There is a depot-based franchise where you are responsible for vans, drivers and liaising with the network; and a courier franchise where you operate with a van and your own territory – usually working from home, until there is the opportunity to expand. Franchisees generally make their own work within an area strictly designated by postcode.

You'll also have to be prepared for long and often unsocial hours. Working in a depot is a 24-hour, seven-day week business and you'll probably find yourself working 12-hour days initially. The same applies for couriers, though the hours are more likely to be irregular and long, since you'll take on jobs as and when they come.

Costs range from £20,000 to £50,000 for a regional, depot-based franchise and from £6,000 to £20,000 for a courier franchise. The main factor in the price variation is the size of the territory you are given.

Plumbing

Demand for plumbers in recent years has been high and continues to grow, and the industry employs people from a wide range of backgrounds. Franchise opportunities in this area include formal training and qualification in areas such as water regulation and domestic gas safety, so you don't need to have existing plumbing skills.

Franchisees buy the license for a business where they will be the exclusive operator for a territory and where they will have the right to trade under the franchisor's name, use their logo and benefit from the company's training and support. However, the work can take a toll on you both mentally and physically, as you can be on call at all hours of the day. It can involve heavy lifting too, and working in cramped, uncomfortable conditions. On the other hand, the rewards can be well worth it.

Remember that by becoming a plumbing franchisee you are not just a plumber, but also a business owner. You'll have to be able to manage your employees, and this can be a daunting task for those unfamiliar with staff management.

Gift cards

Starting out as a greeting cards franchisee can be a scary prospect. You won't be required to create a range of cute birthday cards or write a witty rhyme for the inside, but you'll have to cold call independent businesses and persuade them to sell your particular range. On the plus side, though, you'll operate on a sale or return basis – so all the retailer has to do is give you some of his or her shelf space on trust. And accepting something almost for nothing is something most small businesses find hard to resist. As a business, it is quick to set up and can be run from home with low overheads.

Working out what you want from a franchise

You've narrowed your search down to several franchises. All of them promise great support and have a solid track record, with good training opportunities. But how can you get a better idea of what you'll really get from each of them and ensure you are making the right choice?

One of the main benefits of running a franchise is that you don't have to figure everything out on your own. There is a wealth of information out there to help you pick the franchise system that's right for you.

Think about the word 'support' and what that looks and feels like to you. Does it mean someone holding your hand in the run-up to opening your franchise and being available thereafter, or does it mean someone handing you a manual and checklist and letting you get on with it? Do you feel reassured by knowing that there is support in your area close by, or would you prefer to have less frequent visits from your franchisor?

> **Running a business is always going to be a rollercoaster affair, with challenges along the way, but the support and dedication provided by the Driver Hire team and network has meant that I know I'm not alone and can push forward with a positive outlook. Being recognised for the hard work is an added bonus and certainly helps to motivate me and the team.**
>
> *Manjit Singh, Driver Hire*

You'll need to look into how each franchise model fits in with your lifestyle or how you want it to shape your lifestyle. Are you looking for something you can run from home, for example? Do you want to deal with people face to face or would virtual interactions be preferable? And what are your ultimate aims? For example, would you like a franchise that will supplement the household income or something that can expand, and provide you with a retirement fund? The more you understand what's important to you, the more likely you are to find it.

Do your research

You can find out about franchise opportunities and do more research from a range of sources. The bfa website is a good starting point as it provides contact information on all bfa members' franchise opportunities, whether they are offering new franchises or existing ones for resale.

Franchise opportunities are also widely advertised in the national press, such as the *Daily Express* and the *Daily Mail*, and in specialised business publications such as *Business Franchise* magazine, and there are plenty of events, ranging from seminars to exhibitions, held throughout the year.

Make a list of the elements of franchising that are most important to you. Once you've reviewed the list, start talking with the prospective franchisors and their existing franchisees. The more people you can talk to, the better. Also, look for support information in writing. Does the franchisor have manuals for training you and for training your employees? Find out how often they are updated and whether the franchisees use them. If not, why not? Talking to existing franchisees in a business you are interested in is probably the most important part of your research, once all your initial investigations have been done. Franchisors won't invite you to start visiting their franchisees straight away. First, they will want to make sure you are a serious candidate, not a time waster, or worse, a competitor!

But once your prospective and cautious franchisor is sure that you are a serious candidate for their business, they should be encouraging you to visit some of their franchisees.

You must take up these opportunities. They are your best assurance that what you are being told about the business is what you really get in practice. There's another benefit to talking with existing franchisees. You'll find out what they do during a working day and their range of activity in a working week. There's no point buying into a franchise to build yourself a better life if you're going to hate what you do every day.

Remember that no franchise system is going to have everything. A smaller franchisor will often have fewer of the things that may be important to you, and that's why it may cost less to get into their system. A more mature franchisor will often have more of these, and that's why it may cost more to become part of their network.

For more on how to conduct effective market research, see Chapter 5.

> Prior to joining Expense Reduction Analysts I had been in corporate life for the last 20 years across a range of different roles. I enjoyed a number of them, but this franchise opportunity definitely works well for me, and it gives me the lifestyle that I always wanted.
>
> *St John Rowntree, Expense Reduction Analysts*

Buying an existing franchise

Rather than starting up a franchise from scratch, you may want to buy an existing one. Such an opportunity may occur if an existing franchisee wishes to retire, for example. An existing franchise business can be bought or sold much like any other business, the only difference being that the franchisor will need to be involved in any negotiations and the sale cannot be completed without their approval. You'll also need to meet the franchisor's criteria, the same as if you were taking on a franchise from scratch.

You'll be able to assess the business's current and past performance, giving you an idea of whether you can realise its potential. Even if the business has not been profitable in the past, you may relish the challenge of turning it around. There are other advantages, too, of buying an existing franchise: the business is already up and running and will therefore have an existing client base, and you can benefit from support from the outgoing franchisee.

Buying an existing franchise is not necessarily more expensive than starting one from scratch (this depends very much on the sector chosen), but you'll need to make a substantial investment to take on a going concern and you'll also have to factor in additional solicitors' and accountants' fees, which will be required to complete business transfer documents.

For more information on what you'll need to consider to buy an existing franchise, see Chapter 6.

CHOOSING THE RIGHT FRANCHISE: TOP TIPS

- Take as much time as possible to do your research, and make use of the resources available: publications, seminars and exhibitions held nationwide.

- Buying an existing franchise could give you a head start, but will require considerable investment.

- Get as detailed a background as possible of the business you have targeted, but also look at future growth projections.

- Check out the financial status of the franchisor. Can they also provide you with the right level of support on an emotional and practical level?

- No franchise system is going to have everything, so be realistic in your expectations.

5.0

HOW TO FIND THE RIGHT FRANCHISE

IN THIS CHAPTER

One of the questions you'll ask yourself when considering becoming a franchisee is, quite simply, how to get started. It's worth remembering that a franchise is a hybrid between working for an established corporation and starting a business from scratch. Therefore, aspects of both will be evident in the running of your franchise company. You'll need to assess your own skills, strengths and weaknesses and match these to a suitable franchise opportunity.

Likewise, the franchisor will need to assess your abilities and financial status and decide whether you are the right person to join the group of franchises, known as a network.

In this chapter, we'll discuss:

- starting up
- methods of finding the right franchise
- researching the market
- start-up costs
- investment levels
- meeting the franchisor
- the 10 questions you should ask a franchisor
- deposits
- what type of business can be franchised
- the 10 attributes of a good franchisor
- evaluating a franchise.

There are a numbers of factors you must bear in mind when evaluating a franchise opportunity.

- Get as detailed a background as possible of the business, as well as information on its future growth plans.
- Assess how and why the business has expanded and over what length of time.
- Check how many franchises were up and running a year ago, compared to the present time, and find out what the business's plans are over the next few years.
- Find out whether all the franchises that were launched a year ago are still running – if not, establish whether the franchisees terminated their contracts and why, or whether others have failed or stopped trading for other reasons.
- Assess what you'll get in terms of support and ongoing professional development.
- For every franchise you are interested in, examine its marketing strategy in detail. How much has been spent over the last 12 months, for example, and which elements were successful?
- When it comes to buying a franchise, it's not just your skills that are under scrutiny – check out the financial status of the franchisor.

Starting up

Franchisees come from all walks of life. You may be looking to start a franchise following a period of unemployment or redundancy, you may have always wanted to run your own business or you may have already been self-employed but wish to take on a new challenge.

Just as different factors motivate franchisees, so too do franchisors vary in how they recruit and select potential franchisees. If you want to start a franchise, you'll need to make the first move and deal with the franchisor direct, although the franchisor will ultimately select those people who they feel best fit within their network. The best-known brands, for example, receive many speculative applications and enquiries from individuals keen to learn more. Check out a franchise's website to see if you can make an initial enquiry or download a form. Many franchises advertise information days on their website where you can find out more about the business and have the opportunity to meet franchisors and existing franchisees.

Given my background, I knew how to sell and market products and services – the issue was that although I had lots of ideas for starting

a business of my own, I had less idea of how to get them off the ground. The good thing about a franchise is that all this is done for you. 🎵

Steven Hook, Greensleeves

Methods of finding the right franchise

Other recruitment methods include newspaper and magazine advertising. There are several publications dedicated to franchising, as well as a host of general business magazines that have sections focusing on franchising. These include the *Daily Express, Franchise World, Business Franchise* magazine*, The Franchise Magazine* and *What Franchise Magazine*. You can also visit online franchise directories such as the bfa's (www.thebfa.org) or Whichfranchise.com – both of these carry listings only from those companies that are accredited against the bfa's standards.

Exhibitions and conferences will also give you a great opportunity to learn more about the industry and to meet franchisors in person. Franchisors use exhibitions to distribute promotional material, meet potential franchisees and arrange additional meetings for those keen to take things further. You won't be expected to sign up to anything on the spot – and if you are asked to, it's a sign of a franchise that is best avoided. The bfa website has a list of educational seminars running at various locations in the UK, for both franchisees and franchisors.

All franchisors will have a brochure or information pack that you can pick up at an exhibition, request via the post or download from the internet – but be prepared for the quality of information and the way it is presented to vary enormously between franchisors. One of the key elements of your research is to get a feel for what different kinds of franchises cost and what kind of returns can be made. Looking at several franchise offers is the only way to get an idea of what represents value for money and to be able to pick out a good deal from one that is overpriced.

The aim is to reach a position where you can be reasonably sure that you are going to make a specific application to join a franchise that you can afford; that suits you and your expectations; and that is good value for money. You'll then be expected to fill in an application form for the franchise that you have selected. This will give the franchisor an idea of whether you are suitable, as you'll be expected to include a history of your career and skills to date, as well as an in-depth report of your financial situation and how you plan to raise finance, if you need to. Every good franchisor will want to know a great deal about you and your family before agreeing that you can join their network. If the franchise is properly constructed, the franchisor will get a return on his or her investment only if you succeed. If you find yourself talking to a so-called franchisor that is only keen to take your money, walk away.

Researching the market

You do need to do your homework prior to signing on the dotted line. Conducting your own market research, in particular, is a great way of assessing not only whether the franchise is right for you, but whether it's a commercially viable proposition. You can do this by visiting websites, looking at online forums and reviews, looking around your local area and finding out if there is any competition, or speaking to the franchisor.

First up, you need to look at the product or service that the franchise is selling. Is there a demand for this product or service? In these uncertain times, when austerity still seems to be the watchword, more and more people are buying products that they need, rather than want. If that product will make a fundamental difference to the buyer, or if it's something that's an irresistible purchase or service, then there's a good chance that the franchise will do well – as long as the service and the delivery provided are up to a high standard.

> **Check it fits your skill set and is the kind of role you would enjoy. Also, ensure you have sufficient funds in reserve to see you through those initial times – things might take longer than your plan indicates. Be realistic but not pessimistic. The more effort you put in, the better the results.**
>
> *Trevor Grinsted, The Christmas Decorators*

Another problem with the product, though, is assessing how unique it is. It may well be that there are several other types of product or service in existence, so what does the particular franchise you're interested in do to make its offering stand out from the crowd? What's the unique selling point? Does it have potential to stand head and shoulders above the competition?

Research the target audience, and also how well your chosen area of operation relates to that target audience (eg: gender, class, age). If you want to go for a business that provides a service for children (eg: play/dance/drama schools or suppliers of toys), then you want to make sure that your area will include enough young couples with children.

And of course, identify any threats that may put a dampener on the franchise. Are there any similar sorts of business in the area already? It may well be that there are, but they're not doing quite so well, which would make your franchise a breath of fresh air. Is the product or service still relevant today, or is it outdated – could there be some brand new innovation threatening to steal the thunder? Assess the state of the economy, and whether the franchise could be threatened by the omnipresent financial gloom.

Start-up costs

There are several issues to be aware of when starting a franchise, as compared to starting a conventional business, and finance is probably one of the most important. Starting a business from scratch and starting a franchise both require initial investment on your part. Although a franchisor will relieve you of much of the financial risk compared to a conventional start-up, there are still significant initial costs to running a franchise.

The initial fees and costs in a franchise vary from a few thousand pounds to hundreds of thousands. In all cases, the bulk of the fees should relate to the real costs the franchisor has to meet, such as recruiting, selecting and training you, site searches and launch costs. If the proportion of initial fees that are attributed to the intangible right to join their network is too high – that is, if there is a significant profit for the franchisor in merely selling you the franchise – then be cautious.

Investment levels

The investment levels will vary according to franchise sector. When it comes down to it, the investment level of a franchise will reflect what you get in the package. The more expensive franchises tend to be those where you are buying into a high street retail brand or a restaurant or fast-food outlet. Food franchises tend to cost around £85,000 to £100,000, and sometimes more. This is because you are taking on a high street premises, and in addition, all of the equipment, bills, staff, food and drink stocks.

The middle-tier costs, typically between £25,000 and £50,000, tend to be those where you are not buying a high street franchise, but one that still needs a lot of equipment, in addition to an office and/or transport. For that reason, gardening franchises (typically around £25,000 to £35,000) and print/photography/signage (around the £30,000 mark) require investments that reflect the costs.

Lower costs tend to be for franchises that can be worked from home – in some cases, all you need is your own home office set-up (in other words, a telephone, computer and fax machine, for example) as well as your own transport. In addition, pet care/pet food-delivery franchises are lower in cost; for example, because, in the case of pet food, you are delivering a smaller number of food products – around the £10,000 to £20,000 mark.

Don't forget though that the quoted figures are general averages and, in some cases, the price will differ in accordance with each franchise package. Some franchise packages may contain more or less elements (such as equipment, training, support systems, stock, marketing, etc.) than what's expected, and so the amount you pay will reflect this.

In addition to the investment level, the franchisor will charge a fee for services, known as a management service fee. Sometimes this can take the form of a set monthly fee, but normally it is in the form of a percentage of the franchisee's monthly turnover. Although the flat fee structure can work well with some businesses, there is a preference for the percentage structure, as this provides an incentive for the franchisor to help you prosper.

Meeting the franchisor

Once you've sent in your application and the franchisor has received it, the next stage is arranging to meet the franchisor, and in most cases this will be at the company's headquarters. This will be the first stage in your assessment by the franchisor as a potential franchisee. But bear in mind that franchising is all about the relationship between the franchisor and franchisee, so this meeting will give you a chance to get to know the franchisor too.

Take this opportunity to clarify all the areas you will need more information on, and to get answers to the outstanding questions you will have. Have any other franchisees failed, and if so, why? Can the franchisor give you a clear overview of the business/industry and its future prospects? When will it be possible to meet other franchisees?

At this stage, you should be able to get a good feel for whether you and the franchisor will be able to work together over the long term. A good working relationship is fundamental to the success of your franchise, so it pays to get this right from the beginning. Your visit to the franchisor's headquarters should have given you, and your prospective franchisor, a good insight into whether to take the relationship further. Different franchisors will have different recruitment and selection programmes. There may be several forms to fill in, there may be more than one interview stage, and the franchisor may insist on visiting you at home. You will not be given all the information on day one, as your franchisor needs to be sure you are a serious candidate. Before you are given, or shown, some of the details about the business, you may be asked to sign a confidentiality agreement.

Next, you should contact existing franchisees to find out more about their experiences. It's a good idea to ask your chosen franchisor for a list of franchisees whom you can contact in your own time. Again, take the opportunity to have a frank, honest discussion with them about trading prospects and the future for the business. Did they reach their targets and achieve the financial forecasts originally discussed with the franchisor? What challenges have they come up against? Are they optimistic about future prospects for the business?

The 10 questions you should ask a franchisor

1. Can you give me a clear overview of the business, its background in franchising and its vision?
2. What support and training are provided at the start and later?
3. How well is the business doing financially? (Ask for past performance figures.)
4. How many franchisees have failed in the last 12 months, and why?
5. What makes your product or service stand out from your competitors?
6. What are the costs involved, both initially and in the future?
7. Can you provide me with a list of franchisees for me to speak to?
8. What obstacles do you see for the business in the near future?
9. What makes up the franchise package and how are the costs attributed?
10. How many franchisees are you looking to recruit in the next 12 months and how will you support them?

For an extended list of 50 questions to ask a franchisor, visit the bfa website: www.thebfa.org.

Deposits

In a fair number of franchises you will be asked to pay a deposit once the franchisor has decided that you a serious candidate, but prior to your committing yourself by signing the franchise agreement.

This is often the case in franchises that offer exclusive territories and when the franchisor is reserving a territory for you, turning away other applicants while you build a business plan and arrange your financing.

Deposits are also sometimes involved in a franchise where the franchisor will incur considerable expenses from site searches and negotiation with landlords before you sign up. In all cases, under rules for bfa members, deposits must be refundable against the real costs incurred by your franchisor. Get an idea of what those costs are likely to be before you sign a deposit agreement.

What type of business can be franchised?

As you'll come to find, the franchising pool is deep and varied, with countless sectors to choose from. Where else can you find pets, stage schools, fitness clubs and plumbing all in the same place?

The main answer to the initial question is that any business can be franchised if it so desires, as long as it can prove a number of requirements. The first is that the business must be a credible, proven proposition. It must have a sound business formula that can be replicated by potential franchisees in order for that business to successfully expand. With that in mind, the business must be successful and be profitable – in order for it to provide a good return.

In order to be a good franchise, the business must be one that can be taught in a matter of months rather than through years of convoluted teachings. It should be simple and also easy to replicate in order to establish a uniform pattern among its potential franchise network.

The business should offer a product or service that can be classed as competitive, offering the best possible customer service, together with value-for-money products. It should also be a business that's transferable, with the ability to operate in more than one location.

The 10 attributes of a good franchisor

1. A proven business in the way in which it is being franchised.
2. A competitive product or service that has the capacity to attract interest.
3. Profitability and evidence that the business is financially successful.

4. A clear idea of the business goals and objectives.

5. A well-organised and structured franchise system built upon the bfa's ethics of franchising.

6. Good support and solid training, both in the initial stages and on an ongoing basis.

7. A collaborative approach to making sure that the franchisee's business is a success.

8. Good potential for return on investment.

9. Openness towards feedback and communication from the franchisee.

10. An honest, transparent and fair approach to the business and the franchisee.

EVALUATING A FRANCHISE

■ Meet your prospective franchisors face to face, as this will give you a good idea of what your future working relationship may be like.

■ Be sure to interview other franchisees working for your chosen brand and ask them about their experiences and their thoughts on the future of the company.

■ Don't sign up to anything until you are completely sure it is the right opportunity for you.

■ Ensure that any information you are given is checked over by a legal expert.

6.0

BUYING AN EXISTING FRANCHISE

IN THIS CHAPTER

Sometimes, when looking at buying a franchised business, a potential franchisee may look into the possibility of an existing franchise. There are a number of substantial differences between starting a new franchise and taking on a franchise that is already in operation. The latest NatWest/bfa Franchise Survey statistics demonstrate the growing trend towards buying an existing franchise. Because of the maturing franchise industry, it's a fact that more and more resale opportunities are coming up. In addition, some franchise networks have reached full capacity, so they can no longer offer opportunities for green-field sites.

In this chapter, we'll discuss:

- the reasons for resales
- the advantages and disadvantages of buying an existing franchise, or a new one
- the differences between buying an existing franchise and a new franchise
- the process and costs involved in buying an existing franchise
- the availability of resales, and sourcing them.

Introduction: what is a resale?

A resale is an existing and operating franchise which is now up for sale. Thus, instead of starting a brand new franchise business in a new area, you would be taking over an existing operation. This brings with it a number of new considerations, advantages and disadvantages.

There is also a need to understand why the resale has become available, which may be for a number of reasons, both positive and negative. So let's look at the causes in greater detail.

Why do resales occur?

In many cases a resale is just a natural part of franchising, where existing franchisees retire and the business becomes available as a resale. This is something that has become more common as a growing number of networks in the industry become established. This maturity causes the balance to tip towards the availability of existing franchises over the opportunity for new areas.

Derrick Simpson, director of Franchise Resales Ltd, says:

> Some franchise networks of course are 'full' and have no further territories or locations available for new franchisees. In these mature networks exit planning is a vital part of their support processes to encourage franchisees to prepare for a structured exit, as this will enable the franchisors to bring new franchisees into the network to drive future business growth.

> The UK franchise industry is now reaching a state of maturity and many of its franchisees are seeking retirement. Some long-established franchisors have been successfully selling on franchises for many years as their owners seek an exit.

Each franchisee enters into the franchise for a defined period of time, the most common of which is a five-year term with the option of renewal. Many franchisees choose to run their business longer than five years, whether it's 10 years or considerably more. It's not unheard of for some people to run a franchise for 30 or even 40 years. However, all good things come to an end, and inevitably, there will come a point when the franchisee will choose to leave and therefore sell his or her business. The average time span for a franchisee to work will be between 10 and 15 years, during which time he or she will aim to increase the value of the business and therefore make a profit when the time comes to sell.

Chris Gillam, who heads franchisee recruitment at Mail Boxes Etc., comments:

> **Many franchise resale opportunities arise like this when franchisees want to retire. The benefits associated with financial stability should provide a solid foundation from which to develop and grow the franchise.**

> **Buying an established franchise, particularly as an existing franchisee, may provide a faster return on investment than starting a new venture from scratch because all the systems and procedures are already in place, enabling a new franchisee to integrate quickly into the local market-place.**

This is why, in many cases, the upfront fee for a resale will be higher than that of a new franchise.

However, not all resales are a result of pre-planning by the franchisee. In some cases, unforeseen circumstances will mean the franchisee needs to sell earlier than expected. This can be due to a number of reasons. The franchisee may be suffering from ill-health or the consequences of an accident. They may be affected by personal issues such as bereavement, divorce or depression. They may be moving away to another town, county or even country.

In these cases where the franchisee chooses to sell the business – whether it's due to planned retirement, the prospect of moving on to new things, benefiting from added value, illness or bereavement – this is recorded in franchise statistics as 'voluntary'. The latest NatWest/bfa Franchise Survey shows that currently, the annual percentage of franchisees leaving franchising each year through voluntary channels is 5.1%. Most of these cases will result in the business being up for resale.

Unfortunately, not all resales are for voluntary reasons. While 5.1% of franchisees leave franchising for voluntary reasons, 3.2% leave for forced reasons. If market changes force a business to fail commercially, then this will be unlikely to result in a resale because the concept of that business in that location has failed.

However, there will be cases in which the business concept has worked, but the franchisee has not stuck to it. This may be a result of the franchisee failing to put in enough work. Alternatively, they may have broken the terms of the initial contract, to the point where the franchisor has had to take the business back from them. In some of these cases, the business may be sold at a lower than expected cost because it has struggled or failed to live up to its potential under the ownership of the old franchisee. The franchisor will therefore look to find the right person to get the business back on form.

However, it's a two-way street – the franchisee may become disillusioned with the franchise. They may think that they don't have as much autonomy as they might have hoped. They may think that they are not getting enough support from the franchisor. They may not be happy with the territory that they are working in. In some cases, a planned and amicable exit can be agreed by both franchisee and franchisor if the franchisee is either underperforming or is no longer enthused by the concept. For whatever reason, the franchisee can bring their time with the franchisor to an end, leaving a gap for someone new.

THE REASONS FOR RESALES AT A GLANCE

Planned or voluntary:

- the franchisee has reached the end of his or her contract

- retirement through success

- sale to gain more capital

- sale to go on to do new things

- personal issues (ill health, bereavement, illness, financial problems, forced relocation).

Forced:

- the franchisor is not happy with the current franchisee's performance

- the franchisee is not happy with the franchise.

Advantages and disadvantages of buying an existing franchise

Advantages

As Derrick Simpson explains, demand for franchise resales is growing:

> **More and more purchasers are actively seeking existing businesses to buy rather than starting from scratch with a new operation. There is less perceived risk to the purchaser in acquiring a franchise resale and prospective franchisees are naturally seeking to minimise their financial risk as they start in business.**

The main difference between buying a new franchise and buying an existing business is that a new franchisee taking on an existing franchise will find this prospect less daunting because many of the elements required are already in place. New franchisees do not have to worry about finding their first customers, because a ready-made customer base is already waiting for them. Although they will need to manage the ongoing stock, there will be no worries about setting this up and gauging initial levels (in some cases, the franchisor may be the main supplier of stock, so this will not make a difference). If they are applying for a franchise that involves hiring staff, then the staff will already be in place – a further plus point is that the staff will already be trained and should have good existing customer relationships. If the previous franchisee has done well with the business, there will be a strong sense of recognition and goodwill in the area.

The franchisee will know about the projected revenue from the previous franchisee's figures. So long as the new franchisee sticks to the same business plan and the same method of generating business, then he or she will do well – the existing business will give the franchisee realistic expectations and the results to match.

Whereas someone starting a franchise business from scratch may take longer to generate income, with a resale, the process is shorter because the new franchisee will have practically everything in place. Of course, one of the conditions of a franchisee taking on a business, whether green-field or existing, is that they complete the training satisfactorily. As soon as they have done this, they will be ready to start operating the business.

Another benefit of taking on an existing business is that it may be possible to get it for a very reasonable price if that business has not been performing as well as it could have done. This is an opportunity for those who feel that they are up to the challenge of turning the struggling business around and making it into a profitable enterprise. The key here is to understand why the business was underperforming.

The prospect of buying an existing franchise can be very appealing. Here are some examples of franchisees who bought an existing business for one of the reasons we have been considering.

Patrick Villinger and David Baker, Driver Hire

Having grown up in South Africa, Patrick Villinger moved to the UK 13 years ago, when the faster pace of life in this country appealed. Having happily settled in the UK with his family, Patrick wanted to leave his consulting job and build up his own business. Faced with two options – either buying a franchise or starting up a stand-alone business, Patrick began to explore franchising avenues in late 2010. 'I decided that I should look for something that I could operate from within the M25 zone, and preferably it should be an existing business,' says Patrick. 'I knew there would be a higher entry cost but I would be able to improve the existing turnover rather than start from scratch.

'I had a few franchises on my shortlist – I went to a couple of talks at a franchise show, and as I was browsing through the exhibitors I saw the Driver Hire stand; they had sent me some information a few weeks before so I decided to stop for a chat.'

Driver Hire is a recruitment franchise that specialises in the logistics sector. Franchisees manage their client portfolio while maintaining an extensive pool of staff with a wide variety of skills to match with their clients' needs.

After the show, John Warren from Driver Hire got in contact with Patrick, and after a meeting at the company's head office, plus contact with new and longer-term franchisees, Patrick decided to buy a resale franchise.

'It wasn't just one thing that cemented Driver Hire as my franchise of choice. I had 25 items on my list and they had ticked off most of my personal requirements. I knew that this was something I wanted to be a part of and on 1 June 2011, I took over Driver Hire Slough.'

And for Patrick, there were many benefits in buying an existing franchise.

> **Buying a resale franchise meant that from day one, I could concentrate on getting to know my clients and provide a continuity of service. It also means that you can spend time getting to know the drivers who are representing you in front of those clients, and take time to become familiar with the business, how it works and the regulations that must be adhered to.**

Just like Patrick, David Baker realised that by buying a resale there would be less risk and a more certain income in the short term. Having wound down his own motor vehicle electronic diagnostics business, David looked at the option of buying a resale franchise. 'Whoever chooses a new start-up needs to be a keen marketer, and while I had built one business on my own before, I preferred the idea of a current business with existing customer goodwill.'

David regards the company as a 'rock steady brand and a well-established big business'. 'I hadn't looked at recruitment before and talking to people afterwards I thought I could get to grips with the concept easily. I also liked the idea of buying a business that was already up and running and part of a network of around 100 offices.'

David took over Driver Hire Kingston on 23 May 2011 and he says that he picked up the nuts and bolts of the industry fairly easily. 'There is the basic job of matching the client's need with our most suitable driver, but there is an awful lot of industry compliance procedure and the Driver Hire bespoke computer system is a great help with that. The full-time experienced member of staff who stayed with the business as I took over also helped massively.'

Osman Ahmed and Faraz Ahmad, Mail Boxes Etc.

Despite being in their 20s and having been franchisees for less than two years, Osman Ahmed and Faraz Ahmad already own five central London Mail Boxes Etc. stores – two of which are resales.

Osman and Faraz opened their first store in Belgravia, having bought it from a franchisee who felt he did not have sufficient resources to manage multiple stores and decided to sell so he could focus on just one. Osman and Faraz say: 'We saw immediately how well the Mail Boxes Etc. model works, its strength in a niche market and the benefit of having a well-known name.'

Osman continues:

> It was a great opportunity for us starting out, as buying an existing store offers a number of benefits and advantages. It is likely to be much faster than starting a franchise business from scratch, with all that's involved in the process, particularly in retail: finding suitable premises, negotiating a lease, fitting out the store, and ordering stock and equipment as well as recruiting and training staff.

After their initial success in Belgravia, Osman and Faraz wanted to expand, and were beginning to think about buying another Mail Boxes Etc. franchise when they were approached by the owners of the Victoria store, a couple in their early 60s who wanted to retire after eight years as franchisees.

The store had much to offer, as the business was already well established, with a loyal customer base, good regular turnover and growing overall profit. Once again, Osman and Faraz appreciated all the advantages of buying an existing business with a good local reputation and a team of trained and competent people, headed by a dedicated manager. They took over Victoria in June 2010 and closed it for a week to begin a store refit and make some other small improvements. This investment has had a direct effect on sales and increased turnover by around 10%. 'In Victoria the customers are very loyal and we see the same people almost every day,' Osman explains. 'The location couldn't be better, as it is directly next door to the biggest supermarket in the area and there is huge potential for some proactive marketing of our wide range of services to all the local businesses and hotels.'

Laura Macrae, Cafe2U

When Laura Macrae's husband gave her a cup of coffee provided by mobile coffee franchise Cafe2U, little did she know that a resales opportunity would be just around the corner. Having worked for a survival training company, Laura wanted to start her own business and, if possible, through a resale franchise.

'I knew I didn't want to start a business from scratch – it was too big a risk,' says Laura. 'I already knew about franchising from the big players like McDonald's and Subway and so I searched on the internet for more information. It was the Cafe2U concept that caught my eye and the excellent reviews I had received from my husband about their quality products and service that drove me to find out more.

'After discussions with the Cafe2U team, I was really keen on this established and thriving concept and it was clear that there was a good support mechanism in place. I also loved the van, which was fitted out with everything you could need.'

After four weeks of research, Laura decided to go ahead with the purchase.

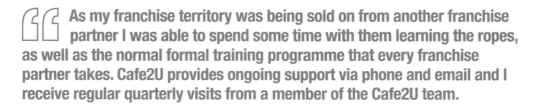

As my franchise territory was being sold on from another franchise partner I was able to spend some time with them learning the ropes, as well as the normal formal training programme that every franchise partner takes. Cafe2U provides ongoing support via phone and email and I receive regular quarterly visits from a member of the Cafe2U team.

My advice to anyone looking at buying a franchise is to research ALL the details, and especially the small print. Make sure you will always

get ongoing support and backup from your franchise brand's head office, not just when things go wrong. 🎝🎝

Shaun and Dawn Brigden, OSCAR Pet Foods

When Shaun and Dawn Brigden heard that their OSCAR Pet Foods franchisee was due to retire, they didn't hesitate to make contact. They felt that buying an existing franchise was an ideal opportunity because all the elements were in place and it was just what they were looking for.

Shaun explains the origins of their interest. 'We knew the product and our three dogs, Vegas, Max and Freddie, were enjoying the benefits of a complete pet care service and nothing but quality food. We were tempted, and applied for an information pack. The purchasing experience was thorough and all at a pace to suit our needs.

'Having been self-employed, without the support of a much larger enterprise, I was capable of handling the ups and downs of business, while Dawn's work at pre-school for the last 10 years still gave us the chance to enjoy family life. A change of career could not disrupt our lifestyle and OSCAR, as we see it, will allow us the chance to run a successful business with even more time together.'

Disadvantages

Although there are many benefits in buying an existing franchise, you still need to be aware that there are potential challenges and drawbacks. Because you are taking on an existing business, there will be an element of the unknown when you start. In order to maintain a profitable business, you will need to have the best resources and staff available. Although key equipment will be to a standard stipulated by the franchisor, it is possible that some element may need servicing from day one, or may need replacing in a shorter time period than expected.

With staff, this is an even greater challenge in a number of ways. Personnel issues can be a problem, whether it's high levels of absenteeism or disagreements between some of the staff members. While the staff may have been what the previous franchisee wanted, they may not be up to the standards that you have in mind. Another potential problem is that some of the staff members may be used to the old way of working with the previous franchisee, and may be wary of the new arrival. Most of the time, this is not a problem, but in some cases, some of the staff may find it difficult to get used to the new regime.

Another potential problem is that of the existing customer base. If the previous franchisee was successful, especially with customers, there is always a chance that the existing customer base may be wary of a stranger taking over the business. It's rare, but it has been known for existing customers to leave simply because they don't have the same kind of relationship with the new franchisee.

The state of the existing franchise can be seen as a drawback, whether it's in positive or negative health. If it's positive, then this will command a higher upfront fee because it is a golden opportunity to invest in a business that's doing very well. On the other hand, if the business isn't doing so well and is going for a cheaper fee, it is still up to you to put in more work to turn it around. In particular, repairing relationships with customers or suppliers will be a difficult task. You will have to earn their trust, and that may take some time. If there are many spiralling cost problems, this will also need to be dealt with as swiftly as possible.

So, when you buy a resale franchise, you will need to hit the ground running – more so than if you were to take on a new one from scratch. With a new business, there is ample opportunity to build up the customer base and earn money, but you need to be on the ball from the word go if you are taking on an existing business.

ADVANTAGES AND DISADVANTAGES AT A GLANCE

Advantages:

- existing customer base
- existing goodwill and recognition in the area
- business from the moment you start
- faster set-up time
- if the business has staff, then they will already be trained and knowledgeable about the business
- faster return on business.

Disadvantages:

- staff issues
- bad feeling with customers and suppliers, or debts left by the previous franchisee
- the existing customer base may find it hard to adjust to a new arrival
- possibility of higher upfront fees if the business is a success
- the need to hit the ground running is greater than ever with a resale.

The differences between taking on an existing franchise and starting a new one

One key area that all incoming franchisees need to be aware of is the TUPE Regulations. TUPE is an acronym of Transfer of Undertakings (Protection of Employment) and these rules apply when a business unit is being transferred, so as to protect the employees of that business unit.

Basically, the rules state that all employees transfer along with the franchise unit. If any one of these employees is dismissed prior to or at the point of transfer, this will automatically be counted as unfair – even in the case of redundancy. Dismissal can take place only if there is a valid economic, technical or organisational reason. The rules also state that the employees must be employed on the same terms as with the previous franchisee.

So the incoming franchisee will need to make sure that they have the right indemnities and warranties for all TUPE issues as well as the indemnities and warranties to protect themselves from matters occurring prior to the transfer.

Let's assume you've covered the TUPE issues and bought the business with staff. Then it will be your job to make sure that you run a well-oiled machine and keep your staff in check. Be approachable and down to earth, but at the same time make sure that they do the job to the best of their ability. You will need solid management skills in order to deal efficiently with any staffing problems that may arise. In any case, at the recruitment stages of your resale business, potential problems should be raised in order for you to proceed smoothly.

With respect to dealing with an existing customer base, taking on a resale business needs a different approach as compared to starting one from scratch. You must deliver fantastic customer service from the word go. Now obviously, this is a vital aspect of starting a new franchise, but because you are building up customers from scratch, there is a more measured approach. You are getting to know the customers, but at the same time, the customers are getting to know the business. With an existing customer base, the ability to hit the ground running is more crucial than ever, in order to win over the existing customers (who may have been used to the old franchisee and the old way). Customers in an established franchise will already know the business, so you will need to adapt very quickly.

Be friendly. Be courteous. Be professional. Win the sceptics over with your charm. Provided that you have the right professional attitude, you should be able to retain your customers – who may even recommend plenty of new ones for you!

You must also build on your existing customer base. A franchisor will have taken you on for a reason. They believe you have what it takes to build your business, increasing your customer base and increasing your revenue. So while buying an existing franchise may seem easier than taking on a new one, it needs to be emphasised that you still need to put in a lot of hard work not only to maintain existing customers, but also to take that customer base to the next level. Work as hard as you can to attract new customers.

Taking on an underperforming business has some more crucial differences. This is not a job for the faint-hearted. You will need to have the ability, business sense and also confidence to turn the business around. First of all, you will need to work out where things have gone wrong, exactly. What did the previous franchisee do that made the business dwindle? What mistakes were made? Can these problems be overcome? It is also important to look at the bigger picture when figuring out what went wrong – look at other franchisees in the network, at the whole market (for further advice on research, see both the section below and Chapter 5 for more details). Take all of this information into consideration when drawing up your business plan.

There are some notable challenges to taking on an existing business. But these can be overcome if you are prepared to put in the hard work and dedication that any good franchise needs. You will, as mentioned before, need to hit the ground running in order to maintain the strength and profitability of the business – but provided you meet the challenges with thought, care and practicality, they can be overcome.

The process and costs of a resale

Because an existing business provides a strong foundation for a new franchisee, this means that a good number of resales can command higher investment levels. Derrick Simpson says:

The value and therefore price of a franchise resale is determined by the level of profitability it generates. It is likely this will be higher than purchasing a new green-field franchise from the franchisor, but once the level of additional capital required has been factored in for a new business, it is quite likely, especially in a premises-based franchise which requires equipment and fitting out, that the additional set-up costs of a new location and working capital required to launch it can equal the costs of purchasing an existing franchise.

The good news, though, is that banks will be positive in this regard when potential franchisees apply for a business loan. With a brand new franchise, the bank can go on projected revenue streams, turnover and profit when deciding whether to lend the money. An existing franchise business, on the other hand, has all these figures in black and white as a record of actual experience, and provided that the business is doing well, securing a bank loan should be straightforward.

For those franchises that have previously struggled and are now up for sale, the initial investment is likely to be less. However, you will need to show the bank why you are different from the previous franchisee; that you have identified where the problems were; and, most importantly, that you know what needs to be done to make it a success. Prior to the resale, a sale and purchase agreement will be drafted to sit alongside the franchise agreement for the process of selling the business to someone new. The agreements will include input from the franchisor, including their consent to sell and the approval of the new franchisee. Therein lies a fundamental difference from buying an existing franchise – for a resale, you will be buying from the franchisee and franchisor, rather than just the franchisor.

There will also be fees included at this stage. A fee will need to be paid to the franchisor for their approval of the new franchisee. A percentage of the initial fee you pay will be paid back to the franchisor for the administration and training costs involved in the resale. If the franchisor has found the replacement franchisee, then they may also have the right to charge a percentage of the sale price as a finder's fee.

The outgoing franchisee will have much to do – they will need to collate as much data as possible relating to their franchise. Every aspect should be covered, including financial figures, performance history, customers and, if these are involved, staff and premises. Derrick Simpson comments: 'The selling franchisee, either in conjunction with their franchisor or through a specialist broker, should prepare a full information document (prospectus) describing their business in detail. This is to include the background to the business and the market-place, how it has grown, the historic and current trading performance; details of any staff and premises, plus owned and leased or hired equipment. If this is not freely available, the purchaser would be wise to be cautious and seek clarification before proceeding. Without this level of detail a purchaser and their advisors will find it difficult to accurately assess the business and make an informed decision to purchase.'

Nothing should be left out – even if there are or have been problems with the franchise, these should be included. It is up to the outgoing franchisee to be as honest as possible in order to allow for a fair exchange.

Both parties should use solicitors with experience of both franchising and franchise resales. Derrick Simpson says: 'Purchasers will require the same advice about the franchise agreement as with any new franchise, but additionally they require advice on the contractual elements of the sale and purchase agreement, so it is important to use a specialist firm for this.' Details of these can be found on the websites of the bfa (www.thebfa.org) and Franchise Resales Ltd (www.franchiseresales.co.uk).

If the incoming franchisee has thoroughly investigated the franchise and is happy to proceed, then the final stages can begin. Just as in the final process of buying a property, contracts will be exchanged between the incoming and outgoing franchisee. The incoming franchisee must pay a proportion of the asking price and must complete the training to a satisfactory level. As soon as this has been done, and all outstanding conditions are met, then completion goes ahead – and the business belongs to the new franchisee.

Availability and sourcing of resales

The latest NatWest/bfa Franchise Survey throws up some interesting findings with regard to resales. In 2011, the projected number of resales was 1,830; although, looking at the longer-term trend, there are a growing number of resale opportunities, owing to the maturity of the franchise industry.

The report goes on to claim that 36% of all franchisees are running units which they bought as resales. Because some franchise systems have expanded as much as they can, franchisors can sell only existing businesses as they become available.

There are many places where you can find out about resales. Most of the franchise magazines, including *Business Franchise*, have resales columns or adverts. In addition, these magazines offer background information and advice on buying an existing franchise.

It's worth pointing out that in some cases the franchisor will not be advertising specifically for a resale opportunity. If you are particularly interested in a franchise, then it is worth making the first contact. Call or email the franchisor to see if there are any resale opportunities available. If there are not at that point, then find out when one is likely to become available.

Information will also be available at the franchise exhibitions held across the UK. These take place throughout the year, including two National Franchise Exhibitions at the Birmingham NEC; the British & International Franchise Exhibition at London's Olympia, and the British Franchise Exhibition at Manchester Central. For more details about the dates and opening hours of these exhibitions, please visit the bfa website at www.thebfa.org. An advantage of these exhibitions is that there will be other franchisees on the stands. They can advise you on the realities of running a franchise. It's worth speaking to other franchisees to get the full low-down on what's required and to make sure that this is still the right career avenue for you.

Also, research the franchise in as broad a capacity as you can. Find out how well the franchise was performing, and what the franchisee did to make the franchise such a success. And in some cases, find out what the franchisee did wrong if the business was not performing so well. In the latter case, do as much research as you can to find out what other, external factors may have caused problems, such as competitors, the market or the economy.

RESALES AT A GLANCE

■ Conduct detailed research into the franchise up for sale.

■ Meet with the franchisor and get the full picture of the available franchise.

■ Make sure that you have the right funds for buying an existing franchise.

■ Engage an experienced franchise solicitor to deal with all agreements.

■ Be prepared for any possible challenges, such as taking on existing staff.

■ Read up on TUPE regulations.

■ Work as hard as you can to build the customer base and take the franchise to the next level.

7.0

ETHICS OF FRANCHISING

IN THIS CHAPTER

Time and again, franchising has greatly outperformed other start-up businesses. Its formula of a locally owned and run enterprise, driven by a small-business owner, with a business format, branding, economies of scale and support provided by a wider network, gives the consumer the best of both worlds and the business a far better chance of success.

Franchising encompasses a range of business types and consumer markets and opens up countless opportunities for people looking for a new start. However, all of this is based on one core requirement – that it is done correctly and that all the parties involved adhere to a code of practice.

In this chapter, we'll look at:

- an introduction to ethics in franchising
- how they have developed over time
- why ethics are important for the franchising industry
- the different obligations for franchisors and franchisees
- issues to be aware of.

Ethics: an introduction

Franchises can and do fail, but their success rate is still significantly higher than for those businesses that choose to go it alone. As a potential franchisee you are tied to a franchisor, and it is the latter's responsibility to set acceptable standards and ethics. Put simply, unethical behaviour will lead to long-term problems with the business model and, ultimately, could result in failure. As a franchisee, you'll have enough challenges to overcome without having to deal with a franchisor who is not behaving ethically.

What might be best practice for most franchises, however, might not fit the exact circumstances of others. It is important, therefore, that you do your homework thoroughly before committing to one and understand why a code of ethics is important for the industry.

While you are conducting your research you may come across a franchise that is badly structured. You may spot this before you enter into a binding contract, but in some cases your task is made harder if the franchisor is deliberately setting out to mislead you. As the bfa outlines, often those who embark on deceptive practices will use the term 'franchise' wrongly to describe what they are offering, in order to attract interest in a less-than-viable business opportunity. This is why you, as a potential franchisee, must understand thoroughly what franchising is, what it involves and whether it is right for you.

A history of ethics in franchising

Following the creation of the bfa in the late 1970s, a core set of standards and ethics were outlined by those in the industry, with the aim of differentiating good franchising from bad and from those misusing the term. This code of ethics was specific to the bfa. The European Franchise Federation (EFF), to which the bfa now belongs, created the first European code of ethics in 1972. The EFF is an international non-profit association whose members are national franchise associations or federations established in Europe. At this time most franchise associations across Europe tended to have their own codes of ethics, although they are broadly similar to the European code of ethics.

In 1990, the bfa formally adopted the common European code of ethics, along with some extensions and interpretations specific to the UK franchise industry. These set out the principles of best practice across all key areas of the franchise operation, from promotion to support, and from disclosure to legal agreements.

The full details of this code of ethics, which all of its members agree to adopt, and how to interpret it can be found in the bfa's publication *The Ethics of Franchising*. This is a fairly comprehensive publication and will enable you, as a potential franchisee, to gain a deeper understanding of what good franchisors sign up to and how it will affect you.

Why ethics are important

The code of ethics was first written to provide a best-practice guide for good franchising. It aims to protect the image of the franchising business model as well as the people who work in the industry. For the franchisor, it acts as an ideal checklist against which to gauge their own business, ensuring they are taking the right steps to building a proper franchise business.

As a potential franchisee, understanding the code of ethics and knowing if the franchise you are looking at complies with this code can give you a lot of confidence. This can be invaluable when you are thinking of starting a business. Much of what the code of ethics contains is there to protect franchisees. For example, it aims to ensure that you are able to invest in a real business, that you are given a fair opportunity to succeed and that you are able to realise your investment and hard work by selling the business, including the added value you have created.

Selling your franchise may be the last thing on your mind if you are thinking of starting one, but if and when the time comes to sell your franchise, being part of a brand that is in line with the code of ethics will also help with the sale of the business. Potential buyers are more likely to have confidence in the franchise and the model, increasing their ability to make a success of the business.

> I also wanted to build something for the future, an asset I could sell when I'm ready. And it was with this clearly thought through exit strategy I joined TaxAssist Accountants.
>
> *Renee Mackay, TaxAssist*

The easiest way to know whether someone is adhering to the code of ethics is to check whether they are a member of the bfa. However, there are also some key areas that you can investigate yourself, as you will see.

THE CODE OF ETHICS EXPLAINED

There are some guiding principles behind the ethics that affect both the franchisor and the franchisee. The bfa says that these provide the basics of any good franchise relationship.

The obligations of the franchisor

- The franchisor shall have operated a business concept with success, for a reasonable time and in at least one pilot unit before starting its franchise network.

- The franchisor shall be the owner, or have legal rights to the use, of its network's trade name, trademark or other distinguishing identification.

- The franchisor shall provide the individual franchisee with initial training and continuing commercial and/or technical assistance during the entire life of the agreement.

The obligations of the individual franchisee

- The individual franchisee shall devote its best endeavours to the growth of the franchise business and to the maintenance of the common identity and reputation of the franchise network.

- The individual franchisee shall supply the franchisor with verifiable operating data to facilitate the determination of performance and the financial statements necessary for effective management guidance, and allow the franchisor, and/or its agents, to have access to the individual franchisee's premises and records at the franchisor's request and at reasonable times.

- The individual franchisee shall not disclose to third parties the know-how provided by the franchisor, neither during nor after termination of the agreement.

The ongoing obligations of both parties

- Parties shall exercise fairness in their dealings with each other. The franchisor shall give written notice to its individual franchisees of any contractual breach and, where appropriate, grant reasonable time to remedy default.

- Parties should resolve complaints, grievances and disputes with good faith and goodwill through fair and reasonable direct communication and negotiation.

What to be aware of

There are some key areas relating to ethics that will help you evaluate further franchise opportunities. This will help you to spot the ones to avoid, or give you an idea of further questions that you may want to have answered before you commit. They cover areas such as advertising for the recruitment of franchisees, what to look out for if you are asked to sign a pre-contract, and details contained in the franchise agreement (the legally binding contract between a franchisor and a franchisee – see Chapter 9 for more details on this).

Promotion and advertising for recruitment

The code states that 'Advertising for the recruitment of individual franchisees shall be free of ambiguity and misleading statements.' An example here would be an advert promising a guaranteed turnover without any note to explain that a guarantee of turnover is not a guarantee of net profit.

The code states that 'Any publicly available recruitment, advertising and publicity material containing direct or indirect references to future possible results, figure or earnings to be expected by individual franchisees, shall be objective.' This means that any statistics and figures relating to the franchise should be presented in an unbiased fashion – the source of figures should be given as well. Both the statistics and source should allow the potential franchisee to make his or her mind up without prejudice. In an established franchise, projections of turnover and costs will often be based on the average results for all, or for the middle range, of existing franchisees. In a new franchise they may be based on the results of a pilot store. Wherever the numbers come from, you should be told what that source is so that you can decide how reliable they are.

The code states that 'In order to allow prospective franchisees to make a binding agreement with full knowledge, they shall be given full and accurate written disclosure of all information material to the franchise relationship, within a reasonable time prior to the execution of these binding documents.' This means that the franchisor must present all information relevant to the potential franchisee in good time – even if this means any issues or problems that have occurred within the franchise at any time. In other words, if you are being offered, for example, a territory where a previous franchisee has tried to build a business but failed, you must be told.

The code also covers incidences of a franchisor's requiring a prospective individual franchisee to enter into a pre-contractual obligation. In these cases, the following principles should be respected.

- Prior to the signing of any pre-contract, the prospective individual franchisee should be given written information on its purpose and on any consideration he may be required to pay to the franchisor to cover the latter's actual expenses, incurred during and with respect to the pre-contract phase; if the franchise agreement is executed, the said consideration should be reimbursed by the franchisor or set off against a possible entry fee to be paid by the individual franchisee.
- The pre-contract shall define its term and include a termination clause.

■ The franchisor can impose non-competition and/or secrecy clauses to protect its know-how and identity.

Selection of individual franchisees

The code says that 'A franchisor should select and accept as individual franchisees only those who, upon reasonable investigation, appear to possess the basic skills, education and personal qualities and financial resources sufficient to carry on the franchised business.' This means that the franchisor must carefully choose the right candidate for the franchise, based on their qualifications, personality, experience, skills and financial status. This requirement is more important and further reaching than you might think. In a properly structured franchise, the franchisor will not make any serious profit from the initial fees they charge for recruiting you and setting you up in business. The franchisor's opportunity to make a return on their investment in the business model, and in you, comes from their continuing fees – ordinarily taken as a percentage of your turnover, or as a mark-up on the goods that you are buying from them and selling on to your customers.

In this structure, the franchisor starts making a serious return only when you start doing real business, and if you're controlling your costs, that means making a real profit. The franchisor succeeds only if you succeed, and that makes it vitally important for the franchisor to recruit someone who can do well.

The franchise agreement

The franchise agreement (see Chapter 9 for more on this) should comply with the national law, European community law and the code of ethics.

The agreement shall reflect the interests of the members of the franchised network in protecting the franchisor's industrial and intellectual property rights and in maintaining the common identity and reputation of the franchised network. All agreements and all contractual arrangements in connection with the franchise relationship should be written in, or translated by a sworn translator, into the official language of the country the individual franchisee is established in, and signed agreements shall be given immediately to the individual franchisee.

The franchise agreement shall set forth, without ambiguity, the respective obligations and responsibilities of the parties and all other material terms of the relationship.

For more details on what your franchise agreement should cover, see Chapter 9.

FRANCHISING ETHICS AT A GLANCE

- ■ The code of ethics is a core set of standards that all good franchisors should stand by.

- ■ It aims to protect the image of the franchising business model, as well as the individuals who work in the industry.

- ■ Understanding the code of ethics and knowing whether the franchise you are interested in complies with this code can give you extra confidence.

- ■ The easiest way to know whether someone is adhering to the ethics is to check whether they are a member of the bfa.

- ■ Understanding the code of ethics will help you to better evaluate franchise opportunities.

dennis & turnbull
chartered accountants
& strategic advisors

Specialist franchise accountants

If you would like to speak with one of the team please call 01793 741600

www.franchiseaccountancy.com

8.0

RAISING FINANCE FOR A FRANCHISE

IN THIS CHAPTER

If you are looking to raise finance for a franchise, then in the majority of cases you should not have too much difficulty, provided that you have a sound credit history and a robust business plan. You'll rarely need to look further than your bank.

In this chapter, we'll look at:

■ where to go for franchise finance

■ how much it costs to set up a franchise

■ the role of the business plan

■ the financing options that are available.

Where to go for finance

There are a number of different options when it comes to raising the money for a franchise. You may be able to fund the franchise yourself – maybe you have savings in the bank, or you may have received a substantial redundancy payment.

You do not have to use your usual bank to obtain a loan, but you should approach a bank that has a dedicated franchise department, as there are some clear advantages in doing so. In the UK, banks that provide dedicated franchise finance and advice include NatWest, RBS, Lloyds TSB and HSBC.

The banks' franchise departments will have a good knowledge of franchises and how they have performed over the years, including who the reputable and successful franchisors are and what level of risk they are taking. They will also know what the business plan should include and how the franchise will perform in the early days, and will aim to structure any offer of finance accordingly.

If you want to join an established, successful franchise, you'll be able to raise a greater level of finance for your start-up costs and working capital requirements. For example, this could be up to 70% of the total finance required. For new franchises, the figure will be around 50% or 60%. This compares well against raising finance for an independent start-up business that does not have a brand and a proven model behind it. Thus, you will typically have to find one-third of the total start-up funds yourself (many people use savings or redundancy payments) and the bank will advance you the other two-thirds as a business loan.

Many franchisors have ongoing relationships with several banks that will look favourably on franchisees approved by the franchisor. Therefore, your franchisor may well suggest that you talk to a particular bank or banks – although do bear in mind there is never a guarantee that you'll get a loan. There may also be other related banking products that are offered on special terms to franchisees.

Despite the recent period of economic recession, finance has been made available throughout to people looking to start up a franchise. Business failure in the franchise sector is lower than in the start-up market as a whole, making franchise finance more attractive to a bank. The 2011/2012 NatWest/bfa Franchise Survey reported that 91% of franchisees were trading at a profit. This figure does vary from one area to another, however, so it pays to do your research thoroughly.

How much will it cost to set up a franchise?

Graeme Jones, head of the franchise team at banking provider NatWest, says that costs depend upon what type of franchise you opt for. Some franchises can cost less than £10,000 and, at this level, can typically fit in with your other financial commitments. Those that require premises and are very much a full-time occupation can require significantly higher levels of finance, the average cost being in the order of £65,000. Included in the cost are items such as the franchise fee, equipment, stock and working capital.

Without a doubt, says Jones, the most capital-intensive franchises are those in catering and store retailing. Some franchisors in this sector will insist that a potential franchisee has available capital of over £100,000, and any bank finance will be in addition to that. On the other hand, franchises in the areas of personal services, for example hair and beauty, fitness and weight, care and education services, mobile and home distributions, and computer and telephone services, while having a similar level of cost in terms of the franchise fee, will have a much smaller spend requirement for equipment and stock, and so the level of finance required will be lower.

As franchising matures, a greater number of franchises are being sold as established trading businesses. Purchasing such an existing franchise has its advantages, as the business will already have customers and be known in the district where it trades, and it will already have the existing staff and the necessary equipment. In some instances this may be the only way you can get into the franchise of your choice, as there may not be a 'vacant' franchise territory in the area where you want one. Some franchise systems have grown to full capacity in the UK and if they were to open more franchises they would simply cannibalise the existing business rather than generating new business. Of course, the cost of purchasing an established franchise varies, in the same way that the cost of setting up a new franchise depends on the sector that it operates in, how much equipment is required and the need for premises, for example.

> Carl and the team at Dennis and Turnbull do accountancy stuff really well! That should be no surprise; they have all the right qualifications. What sets them apart for me is that they care about the really important stuff – like me, their client. They care about understanding and helping my business, the franchise world that I operate in, and they care about me and what I'm trying to achieve.
>
> *David Tovey, Dennis and Turnbull client*

The business plan

As a prospective franchisee you should produce a business plan, regardless of whether you intend to borrow money from a bank – but if you going to apply for a business loan, it is a 'must-have'. The bank will require one as part of the process of deciding whether or not to lend you the money. In the plan you'll need to cover all aspects of running the franchise. For more details on making your business plan and setting targets see Chapter 10. There are certain financial details that you must have in your business plan before you can be considered for a bank loan. In particular, you need to set out clearly the following.

- Where and how you are going to establish the franchise – remember, it can take up to six months to get the franchise up and running.
- Evidence that you know who your competitors are (local and national) and how you are going to deal with them.
- Where you are going to get your customers from.
- What resources you need to use in the business.
- The financial implications of all of the above and how you are going to meet your ongoing expenses (these could include the cost of premises, franchise fee, ongoing fees due to the franchisor, stock purchases, wages, personal drawings). You'll need to factor in your financial forecasts too and work out how to repay any money borrowed from the bank.
- A personal assets and liabilities statement. The bank will need to know what security may be available if required, and also what your typical monthly outgoings are and how these relate to any drawings (money taken out of the business for your own personal use) you intend to take from the franchise.
- If you are going to be purchasing the franchise through an existing business, then details of the historic financial performance of that business will also be required (typically three years' accounts).
- If you are purchasing a franchise that is being resold, then its past financial performance is very important in assessing the business plan – again, three years' accounts will be required.

The business plan should demonstrate that any money that you borrow will be repaid – it is not in either your or the bank's interest to proceed with a franchise opportunity if the chances of success are slim.

The different types of finance

There are a variety of ways to structure the finances of your franchise.

- **Loans/leasing:** As a general rule, those costs which are part of the fabric of the franchise, such as the franchise fee, equipment and fitting-out costs, will be financed by way of a loan or through leasing over a period of years.
- **Overdraft:** The other costs, such as stock purchases, wages and monthly bills (known as the working capital), will be financed by way of an overdraft facility – over time, this should swing from overdraft into credit.
- **Asset finance:** A form of finance enabling you to purchase the equipment you need for your business (such as cars, vans and technology).
- **Invoice discounting:** For some franchises, such as those involved in recruitment, where you are not taking money on a day-to-day basis, a type of finance called invoice discounting is a more appropriate method of providing the working-capital element of finance.

Your bank, particularly if it has a dedicated franchise unit, will be able to advise you on the most appropriate method and mix of bank finance.

Loans

Loan repayments will be spread over a period that is linked to the length of your franchise agreement or of the lease of any premises you'll operate from, whichever is the shorter. Loan features will include:

- Fixed interest rates, so that you can budget with certainty what your monthly repayment will be.
- Variable interest rates linked to Bank of England base rate. While repayments may vary as the base rate rises or falls, you will usually be able to repay the loan early without incurring an early repayment charge.
- Capital repayment holidays of up to three years. These can be very useful during the early stages of setting up your franchise, as you'll have to pay only the interest on the loan for the period of the capital repayment holiday. As an example, if you have a seven-year loan with 12 months' capital repayment holiday you will pay interest for the first year and then interest plus capital repayments over the following six years.

- Short-term loans with a lump sum repayment. At NatWest, for example, the bank frequently provides loans for the payment of VAT on the start-up costs of the franchise. These are repayable once the VAT refund has been received.

WHAT BANKS CAN OFFER FRANCHISEES

- Loans
- Knowledge and support from franchise managers and experienced staff
- Strong connections with people in the franchise sector, such as solicitors and accountants
- Realistic repayment schemes
- Capital repayment holidays
- Overdrafts
- Insurance opportunities

Overdrafts

For the working-capital element of your franchise, overdrafts are commonly used, as these are flexible and can be used at any time during the agreed overdraft term. They can be cost-effective, as you pay interest on only the amount you have borrowed. Bear in mind that interest rates are linked to the Bank of England base rate and interest is calculated daily and charged to the account every quarter.

A number of banks, including NatWest, will guarantee to keep overdrafts in place for the duration of the agreement.

Asset finance

Paying cash for an asset can be a significant drain on your working capital. Leasing an asset, however, gives you access to that asset without paying for it all at once. All forms of leasing are basically rental agreements giving you (the lessee) the right to use an asset owned by the leaser (finance company) for a specific period of time in return for regular payments (rental payments).

Asset finance includes hire and lease purchase as well as finance leases, operating leases and contract hire. This is a form of finance that is particularly suitable for financing the cost of vehicles and equipment that you'll use in your franchise.

- **Hire or lease purchase** is a straightforward repayment facility like a loan where you end up owning the asset at the end of the period of finance. Interest rates can be fixed or variable and repayments structured to suit your cash flow.
- **Finance lease** is a flexible method of funding and offers all the practical benefits of ownership of the asset, but without any of the potential burden. Payments are structured to suit your cash flow and the rental payments can normally be offset against taxable profits.
- **Operating lease** is particularly effective for high-value and specialised assets and vehicles. An operating lease guarantees the residual value of the asset to the leaser, meaning that the repayments are lower. Rentals can be matched to cash flow and can normally be offset against taxable profit.
- **Contract hire/purchase** is a form of operating lease (often used with cars and other vehicles) that includes a number of additional services such as maintenance, management or replacement if the asset is in good repair – for example, servicing and taxing the vehicles used in the franchise. At the end of the contract period, in the case of hire you hand the asset back, while in the case of purchase you can keep, sell or return it. There are fixed monthly repayments and the costs can usually be offset against profits.

“ **The van was on hire purchase, and proved to be the better option for me, as I made a nice return when I sold the van.** ”

Melanie Cheung, Riverford

Invoice finance

Invoice finance is particularly relevant to those franchisees where the sales ledger takes time to collect and where the business needs to make payments to suppliers or to staff before the sales revenues are received. It involves releasing cash secured against your business's invoices. Its advantage is that the cash flowing from this form of finance is directly linked to the expansion of the franchise. Sectors where it is used include recruitment agencies and domiciliary care providers.

There are two forms of this type of funding:

1. **Invoice discounting:** One of the advantages of this is that the customers of the franchise need not know that the arrangement is in place, which appeals to some people. You simply issue your invoices and collect the payment as you would do normally, so that you are fully in control of your entire sales ledger. You are able to access up to 90% of the value of the invoices as soon as the invoice discounter has received them. The remaining 10% you receive, less charges and interest, once your customer has paid their invoice in full.

2. **Invoice factoring:** This is very similar to invoice discounting but the administration of the sales ledger is handled by the invoice factor. This can save you time and costs, as well as providing immediate access to working capital. Some franchisors, as well as banks, provide invoice discounting or invoice factoring services to their franchisees.

Security issues

When assessing your business plan and request for finance, the bank will also consider the need for security. In cases where the total borrowing is less than £25,000 and where you'll be trading either in your sole name or in a partnership it may well be that security is not required. If you are proposing to trade as a limited company, then a personal guarantee will be required; whether additional security will be required in support of this will depend on the total amount of finance needed. In addition, the bank will also require a mortgage debenture from your business.

THE ENTERPRISE FINANCE GUARANTEE SCHEME

The Enterprise Finance Guarantee Scheme (EFG) is a government scheme that is designed to provide support to people who have a robust business plan but don't have security to back up their request for bank borrowing.

This scheme was launched in 2009 and supports lending to viable businesses with an annual sales turnover of up to £25 million who are seeking loans of £1,000 through to £1 million. It is available to most business sectors, including most of those covered by the franchise industry.

Finance is repayable over a period of between three months and 10 years. Overdrafts are also guaranteed for up to two years. Invoice finance facilities can be guaranteed as well.

By providing the bank with a guarantee (for 75% of the loan value) the government charges the borrower a premium equivalent to 2% per annum on the outstanding balance of the loan, and this is assessed and collected quarterly throughout the life of the loan. Many banks support this scheme, with NatWest providing more finance under the EFG than any other bank.

A mortgage debenture provides the bank with a fixed and floating charge over the assets of the business (such as stock, money owed relating to products sold) and also the power, if it so wishes, to apply for the appointment of an administrator. In effect, the administrator would take over the running of the business to protect the bank and ensure that any monies collected were used first to repay the bank borrowing.

Other than the above, if security is required, it will usually take the form of a mortgage (typically a second mortgage) over a property. Other assets can also be taken as security, such as stocks and shares in quoted companies. The good news is that raising finance to start up your franchise or to buy an existing one is comparatively straightforward if you approach it in the right way and do your research. Some of the banks, such as those accredited by the bfa, have a dedicated franchise unit with local franchise relationship managers who can help to speed up the process and ensure that you get the appropriate level of finance, structured in the right way. More importantly, banks' dedicated franchise departments will have their own intelligence on the franchisors that are available and any existing experience of how franchisees are performing.

Finally, just because you can raise money by borrowing, this does not mean that you should. The bigger your franchise loan, the more money your business has to make in order to meet the monthly repayments. If you have one or two bad months you could be under pressure. And don't forget that if the franchise is set to become your major source of income it will have to generate enough profit to pay not only its own bills but your household expenses too.

> d&t is knowledgeable about franchise-specific tax legislation, has experience of how franchise networks operate and offers franchisees low, fixed monthly fees. Our franchisees who have already adopted d&t as their accountants also enjoy guaranteed turnaround times, a fixed price menu of fees, a personal relationship manager and, most importantly, a guarantee of 100% satisfaction. We have listed d&t as our recommended accountant for all existing franchisees, whilst all new franchisees who go with d&t get three months' free accounting paid for by EnviroVent as part of the franchise package.
>
> *Phil Harrison, Dennis and Turnbull client*

TIPS ON RAISING FINANCE

■ Ensure that you have sufficient capital – you'll need at least a third of the start-up costs, and half for a less established franchise.

■ Examine costs closely, in particular the franchise fee and monthly management fee, and whether they are reasonable and value for money. Will the margins be sufficient to support the business after payment of regular fees to the franchisor?

■ Seek professional advice from an accountant about income and profit projections and from a solicitor about the legal agreement. Both should have a good understanding of franchising, and preferably be affiliated to the bfa.

■ Talk to your bank's franchise section about the financial aspects of franchising and ask it to put you in touch with your nearest franchise relationship manager.

LINDER MYERS
S O L I C I T O R S

LOCAL • NATIONAL • INTERNATIONAL

Experts in Franchising Agreements

Contact us now to arrange an informal discussion

Paul Willan
Franchising Expert
Corporate and Commercial department

0844 984 6188

paul.willan@lindermyers.co.uk

www.lindermyers.co.uk/franchising

9.0

THE FRANCHISE AGREEMENT
In association with Linder Myers LLP

IN THIS CHAPTER

Being a franchisee means entering into a legally binding franchise agreement. If you don't like what you've signed, you'll have to challenge it in the civil courts, which can be a timely and costly process.

The best way to avoid future legal wrangling is to prepare thoroughly for the deal. You'll need to be aware of the sorts of contract to expect, typical clauses and terms, and how much room for negotiation there is.

It's essential that you have the franchise agreement contract looked over by a solicitor who specialises in franchising, so be prepared to invest time in finding the right legal advisor.

In this chapter, we'll look at:

- what a franchise agreement is and what it typically contains
- your legal obligations as a franchisee
- terminating a contract
- where to find the right legal advisor.

Signing up to a franchise

When you and your prospective franchisor are satisfied that all the questions have been answered, you can then proceed to signing what is known as the franchise agreement. The franchise agreement determines the rights and obligations of the franchisee and the franchisor and specifies the rules under which the franchise must operate. It is essential that you get this document checked over by a legal expert experienced in franchising. The bfa has a list of accredited legal experts.

Signing an agreement involves committing to the franchise for a set period of time, which can normally range from a renewable period of five years for smaller franchises to up to 20 years for some of the biggest, more well-known ones.

Before you sign

The process of signing up to a franchise is relatively simple but you need to be absolutely sure you have made the right choice before you put pen to paper. Be wary of signing up to a franchise before you have thoroughly researched the idea, are comfortable with the prospect and have had all your questions answered. Under no circumstances should you sign up to anything without doing due diligence (assessing the commercial aspects of the franchise, such as history of trading, performance of other franchises, future prospects).

The franchisor will most probably have given you an information pack (a document outlining the franchise opportunity, with all the necessary, key information) at the outset of your research about the business, but do not rely just on this. It's not unheard of for franchisors to pressure you into signing by telling you that you won't get another opportunity like this. Ensure that you read all the information you have several times over.

Initial steps

Signing up to a franchise is the first step on the road to starting your franchise and is normally followed by an intensive training programme with your chosen franchisor. The cost of this training is usually included in the total fees you pay, although you'll need to pay your own travel costs to and from the training venue, and accommodation if necessary. The length of training really comes down to the type of franchise; for example, for a franchise with Domino's Pizza you'll take part in a four-week intensive franchise-development programme covering everything from pizza making and people management to customer service and computer systems. With Burger King, the training lasts 15 weeks and is held at a dedicated training centre.

The essential minimum terms of the franchise agreement are:

- the rights granted to the franchisor
- the rights granted to the individual franchisee
- the goods and/or services to be provided to the individual franchisee
- the obligations of the franchisor
- the obligations of the individual franchisee
- the terms of payment by the individual franchisee
- the duration of the agreement, which should be long enough to allow individual franchisees to write off their initial investments specific to the franchise
- the basis for any renewal of the agreement
- the terms upon which the individual franchisee may sell or transfer the franchised business and the franchisor's possible rights in this respect
- provisions relevant to the use by the individual franchisee of the franchisor's distinctive signs, trade name, trade mark, service mark, store sign, logo or other distinguishing identification
- the franchisor's right to adapt the franchise system to new or changed methods
- provisions for termination of the agreement
- provisions for surrendering promptly upon termination of the franchise agreement any tangible and intangible property belonging to the franchisor or other owner thereof.

Some of these areas will be explored in more detail later in the chapter.

BEFORE SIGNING UP: CHECKLIST

- Thoroughly check out the financial health of the franchisor and the business sector itself.

- Carefully examine exactly what the franchisor has on offer, including the depth of knowledge and operational support you'll have access to.

- Check out your rights as laid out in the franchise agreement.

- Ensure you get your contract checked by a legal advisor experienced in franchising.

Franchising is essentially a licence arrangement whereby the franchisee is permitted by the franchisor (the entity granting the franchise) to operate a business under the franchisor's trade name or trade mark and to use the franchisor's established business system.

Andrew Brown, partner in the corporate commercial department at legal firm Linder Myers, gives the following advice on dealing with legal issues and contracts. As part of purchasing the right to operate a franchise, you, as the franchisee, will be required to enter into a franchise agreement with the franchisor. The franchise agreement contains the franchisor's standard terms and is drafted, as you would expect, with the franchisor's interests very much in mind. In the vast majority of cases the terms of the franchise agreement will be non-negotiable. They will also, obviously, be legally binding on the parties. Therefore it is very important for you, as the franchisee, to be fully aware of the contents of the franchise agreement and to understand the consequences of entering into it.

The franchise agreement will set out in some detail how the relationship between franchisee and franchisor will operate and cover issues such as fees, advertising, training and the sale of the business, among others. But bear in mind that franchise agreements can vary widely. The most important thing to remember is to sign nothing until you have received legal advice. While this may come at an additional cost to you, it could save you from entering into something you do not understand and which, ultimately, could cost you more.

Your obligations

Location and territorial rights

Typically, the franchise agreement allows the franchisee to operate the franchised business for an initial renewable term of five years. If a defined geographical area or territory is offered, the franchise agreement may prohibit the franchisee from actively seeking new business outside their allocated territory, but you will also benefit from the similar restrictions in other franchisees' agreements prohibiting them from operating in your territory. For the purposes of clarity, it is important that the territory is precisely defined by reference to postcodes or a map.

In almost all cases franchise agreements will allow the franchisee to renew the franchise for a further term of five years after the expiry of the initial term. For this to happen though, there are usually certain preconditions that you'll have to meet. These include, for example, that all sums owed to the franchisor are paid and up to date and that there are no outstanding breaches of the franchising agreement.

Operations manual

As a franchisee, you'll be provided with an operations manual that will set out in detail the procedures and policies you need to adopt when running the franchised business.

The franchise agreement will contain an obligation to operate the business strictly in accordance with the franchisor's operations manual. It's a good idea to find out how often this is updated and also how up-to-date the version is that you have been given and how likely it is to change in the future. The manual aims to give you all the skills you need to run the business, so it's vital that you have a thorough understanding of this document so you that can fill in any gaps in information that you may have.

Costs and ongoing fees

On entering into the franchise agreement you'll pay an initial fee that is generally calculated to cover start-up costs, the franchisor's administration fees, the costs of the initial training to be provided by the franchisor and a return for the franchisor on their initial investment in providing the business model. You'll also need to take out and maintain appropriate insurance cover at your expense. This should be detailed in the franchise agreement or in the operations manual.

As a franchisee, you'll also be under an obligation to pay a management fee, and often also an advertising fee (usually as a contribution to the franchisor's costs for national advertising). These are typically paid to the franchisor on a monthly basis.

Usually, the management fee and the advertising levy are calculated at a certain percentage of the turnover generated by the franchisee's business. However, in some franchise arrangements these fees can be a fixed monthly amount. This could have implications for the future prospects of your business – a fixed-fee arrangement may create cash flow problems for you in the first few months of trading and also during periods when you may suffer a downward dip in trade. It is vital that any ongoing payments to the franchisor are factored into your planning at the outset so that you can be sure to have funds to meet this obligation and create a viable business.

If you fail to make payments to the franchisor when they are due, you risk giving the franchisor the right to terminate the franchise agreement, or to charge interest on late payments, or both. Bear in mind, too, that the right to set off, whereby one debt can be set off another, is generally enforceable in most business-to-business relationships, but does not apply to a franchise agreement. As an example, A owes B £1,000, while B owes A £250. A 'sets off' the £250 owed to him by B, and pays B only £750. Franchise agreements typically contain provisions that prevent a franchisee from withholding payment to the franchisor on the basis that the franchisor owes the franchisee a sum of money.

Keeping accurate records

As a franchisee, you'll also be expected to maintain accurate and up-to-date accounting records relating to the business. Many franchise agreements also stipulate an obligation on the franchisee to submit financial information to the franchisor on a weekly or monthly basis.

While this may seem quite onerous, it's a good way of instilling discipline in your accounting practices. Franchise agreements may also state that the franchisor can gain access to your premises during normal business hours to inspect accounts, records, customer lists and other relevant documentation.

Training

A reference to training will usually be included in the contract. The franchisor will provide initial training, the costs of which are typically included in the initial fee. Any additional training that is deemed compulsory under the terms of the franchise agreement will be conducted at your expense.

You'll also be responsible for ensuring that any employees you take on have the necessary training, as prescribed by the franchisor.

Advertising

Arrangements in respect of advertising tend to vary, but commonly, as well as paying the advertising levy referred to above, you'll be responsible for promoting the business in its allocated territory and you'll sometimes be under an obligation to apply a certain stipulated amount towards this end.

It's worth remembering that franchise agreements often state that any advertising conducted by the franchisee must be in accordance with the franchisor's operations manual and that otherwise you'll have to seek the consent of the franchisor.

Selling the business

If you are thinking of starting a franchise, selling the business might be the last thing on your mind, but it's something you should give consideration to. A central feature of ethical franchising is that as well as the franchisee earning an ongoing profit from trading the franchised business, the franchisee will also be able to sell the franchised business as a going concern, thereby benefiting from a capital return on their investment.

> ❝ I also wanted to build something for the future, an asset I could sell when I'm ready. And it was with this clearly thought through exit strategy I joined TaxAssist Accountants. ❞
>
> *Renee Mackay, TaxAssist*

Details regarding the sale of the franchised business by the franchisee are typically set out in the franchise agreement. This process will vary from one franchise business to another, but broadly, if you receive an offer from a third-party purchaser you must submit such information to the franchisor. The franchisor will then have the right to purchase the business on the same terms.

If the franchisor does not take up the option to purchase the business, you can then sell to the third party. Before any sale can take place, however, any third-party purchaser will need to satisfy the franchisor that he or she would be a suitable franchisee.

If you do decide to sell the business, the franchisor will generally charge you a fixed amount or a percentage of the sale value of the business to cover their expenses in dealing with the sale and providing training to the new franchisee. The franchisor may also want to charge you a commission based on a percentage of the sale price, in circumstances where the franchisor has introduced you to a third-party buyer. If such conditions apply, they should form part of the franchise agreement.

Death and illness

While you may not want to think about circumstances such as death and illness, it is important to plan for every eventuality when running your own business. Generally, in the case of the franchisee's death there would usually be an opportunity for the franchisee's relatives or beneficiaries to take over the franchise. Again, the franchisor would need to be satisfied that the potential new owners meet its criteria for franchisees. If no transfer to a relative or beneficiary is available, the franchisor will have the right to purchase the business or terminate the franchise agreement.

In order to preserve the franchisor's interest in the franchise, most franchise agreements contain wording that enables the franchisor to appoint a manager to the business. This would apply where, in the opinion of the franchisor, you are unable to operate the business to the standard required, due to death, illness or otherwise. You would need to bear the cost of employing the manager.

Terminating the agreement

Some franchise agreements contain performance targets that you, as the franchisee, must achieve. If you don't, then the franchisor has the right to intervene, and persistent failure to reach targets will ultimately give the franchisor the right to terminate the agreement. It is therefore vitally important that you understand what is expected of you in terms of performance targets and that you are confident that you can readily achieve those targets, based on your business plan (see Chapter 10). The bfa has rules on the levels of performance requirements that are ethical, which also includes the consequences of a failure to meet the targets. Here again, bfa accreditation can be a worthwhile reassurance that performance targets are reasonable.

There are other circumstances in which the franchisor can terminate the franchise agreement. These include, but are not restricted, to the following:

- if you fail to pay any amounts due to the franchisor when they are due
- if you are in material breach of the franchise agreement
- if you provide false or misleading information to the franchisor
- if you cease to conduct the business or if any insolvency issues apply to you.

On termination of the agreement, you must pay all outstanding amounts to the franchisor, cease to operate the business, change all telephone numbers and return all stationery and other documentation or equipment to the franchisor.

Terminating the agreement is generally the preserve of the franchisor; it is not common for the franchisee to do so, and you would only be able to terminate the agreement with the consent of the franchisor. Be aware that, as the franchise agreement generally contains a fixed monthly management fee, you, as a franchisee, will be taking on a considerable obligation for the duration of the term (usually five years), which you should weigh up carefully before committing to it.

Legal restrictions

As mentioned earlier, the terms of the franchise agreement are drafted with the franchisor's interests very much in mind. A franchisee is generally under an obligation to devote his or her full time and attention to the business and is not permitted to be involved in any other business without the franchisor's consent.

In order to protect the franchisor and other franchises in the network, a common feature of franchise agreements is 'restrictive covenants'. Such clauses prevent the franchisee both during the term of the franchise agreement and within a certain period following termination (the period can vary, but is usually one year) from doing any of the following (sometimes within a specific geographical area):

- setting up a business in competition with the franchised business, the franchisor's business or the business of any other franchisee in the franchisor's network
- approaching, soliciting or attempting to entice away employees, customers or suppliers of the franchised business, the franchisor's business or the business of any other franchisee in the franchisor's network.

Most franchise agreements will contain a clause where the franchisee indemnifies the franchisor against any breach of the franchise agreement and/or in respect of any loss the franchisor may suffer in connection with the franchised business. An indemnity means that the franchisee is under an obligation to reimburse the franchisor on a pound-for-pound basis. Bear in mind that these clauses are widely drafted in terms of the circumstances to which they could apply and therefore are strongly biased towards the interests of the franchisor.

The franchisee will be under an obligation not to disclose confidential information to unauthorised third parties. Confidential information means information disclosed by the franchisor to the franchisee that relates to the business, the operations manual, the services and/or the products (as applicable).

Purchasing an existing franchised business

If you are purchasing an existing and trading franchised business from the incumbent franchisee (as opposed to simply acquiring a fresh franchise from the franchisor), then you'll need to take other factors into consideration. For example, you will need to investigate the existing business to ensure that there are no adverse issues that should be brought to your attention. Ensure you get legal advice; a legal expert will prepare a business sale and purchase agreement, recording in writing the terms of the transaction.

Finding legal advisors

It is essential to have a solicitor review the terms of the proposed franchise agreement, and it would be foolish not to use a solicitor with specialist knowledge of franchising as accredited under the bfa's affiliation scheme. The bfa's list of specialised solicitors who will help you is available on its website at www.thebfa.org. The solicitor should provide you with a report explaining the terms of the agreement, highlighting where they are particularly onerous and where you might need further clarification from the franchisor. Regardless of whether or not you are a legal expert, it is also a good idea to look over the franchise agreement contract thoroughly yourself. You're the one who will be responsible for the business, so it's important that you thoroughly understand all issues covered in the contract.

LEGAL ASPECTS AT A GLANCE

- Ensure that the franchise agreement contract is looked over by a solicitor who specialises in franchising.

- Sign nothing until you have received appropriate legal advice.

- Pay close attention to the operations manual and don't be afraid to ask for additional information if anything is unclear.

- Remember that the franchise agreement is drafted very much with the franchisor's interests in mind.

- Understand what is expected of you in terms of performance targets and be confident that you can readily achieve the targets, based on your business plan.

10.0

BUSINESS PLANNING AND SETTING TARGETS

IN THIS CHAPTER

A proven franchise model is without doubt a less risky way of starting a business – it has, after all, been tried and tested numerous times by others.

But even with this model and the training, guidance and support from your potential franchisor and fellow franchisees, your business is more likely to succeed if you plan it from the outset and monitor it continuously. A franchise may offer you a ready-made business, but this may not help you with all the issues of running operations on a day-to-day basis or dealing with sudden challenges.

Your ability to build a successful franchise will therefore depend on the quality of your business plan. A good business plan will give you something to refer back to when making tough decisions and should be a working document that you update as the business progresses.

Certainly, there's no avoiding writing a business plan; and the more you embrace it, the more likely you'll be to find it a meaningful and useful process rather than merely a way of appeasing the bank.

In this chapter, we'll look at:

■ why you should write a business plan

■ the basics of a business plan

■ budgeting for the year ahead

■ making revenue forecasts.

Why write a business plan?

Don't be put off by the idea of writing a business plan. It's not difficult, and if you do it properly it won't be tedious either. It should be a labour of love and every bit as exciting as the initial idea that generated your enthusiasm for starting a franchise. Writing a business plan should further feed that enthusiasm. Why? Because by the end of the process you should feel that you're able to progress from idea to business, from dream to reality. What's more, you should have a document that will enable others to believe in you.

Having a well-researched and logical business plan will help you not only to get your venture off the ground, but also to keep it on track when it is up and running. In the first instance, unless you have a strong plan, you are unlikely to secure any funds and you could fall at the first hurdle. It will also provide reassurance as well as a means for everyone, yourself included, to measure your business's performance. A business plan is also essential for raising finance. Your business plan plays an important role in allowing you to manage your cash flow. It's vital to establish just how much you intend to spend, and when. Whether it's to buy stock, order uniforms or lease equipment, unless your finances match your requirements at the right moment, your business might stall. How far ahead to plan will again depend on your own aims and the type of business, but a year, broken down month by month, will be a minimum.

Once you've established a time frame for your plan, you need to identify the criteria that will determine your business's success. One of the benefits of starting a franchise is that many of these elements, such as product and branding, and marketing and accounting systems, are already decided for you. Your franchisor will also be able to advise you on the minimum investment needed to get the franchise up and running and how much working capital you are typically expected to have for the first year.

Review your research into potential franchises. Find out how well other franchisees in your chosen sector have done in the last year and what particular milestones they have reached. These could include reaching a certain number of sales by a set date through an aggressive marketing campaign, or expanding in terms of staff or product lines. Are these goals that you want to aim for, or are there other targets that you think you could realistically achieve?

Whatever your goals turn out to be, you need to think hard about them and not make too many assumptions. Because the franchise model is tried and tested, you will have a good idea already of what does and doesn't work, but this doesn't mean your franchise will automatically be a success if you just follow what others have done. Consider that your business might fail in two or three years' time, and try to imagine the reasons why it might do so.

Writing a business plan: the basics

Before you start putting a plan together, ask your bank, or the bank with which the franchisor has an existing relationship, what sort of document they expect to see. There are plenty of business plan templates available that you can study to guide you through the process. Your franchisor may also have examples of past business plans you can draw on for inspiration.

Your franchisor should also provide the basic elements to help you build your business plan, such as what your franchise business will do and key financial and commercial information. However, you'll need to do a fair amount of work yourself. This includes doing detailed market research in your proposed areas to check there will be enough demand for your proposed service or product.

Don't worry too much about the design and layout of your business plan at this stage. As with CVs, people often worry unnecessarily about the best format, structure, length and layout. It's far more important that the document contains all the necessary information and is clear and easy to understand. Most importantly, it's your business plan – however much help and guidance you may have had from your franchisor and other professionals. If it says you're going to need a sales turnover of £10,000 a month by month six, it's you that's making that prediction of what you believe you will achieve in your business.

As a franchisee, you may be working with a particular customer group or in an allocated territory, so it's important to outline the demographic profile of your market and the direct and indirect competition you are likely to face. If you'll be running a retail business, the expected traffic or footfall in your area will be critical. You should also include details of any restrictions placed on the business by the franchisor. This could include territorial limits (the area in which you are allowed to trade) and the length of the time that you are bound to trade under the franchise agreement.

The list might sound fairly exhaustive, but it should be. Your business plan should present a watertight argument of why and how your franchise business will work. If it doesn't, then you should be asking yourself if it's still such a great idea.

Be honest with yourself. Don't exaggerate revenues and underplay overheads in order to make the plan work. Bank managers see thousands of applications and they will see straight through it. And of course, you'll be kidding yourself and invalidating your business plan as a useful document, as well as wasting your time. Furthermore, if your franchisor has built up a good relationship with a particular bank, you'll want to help maintain it. If anything, err on the side of caution.

Many entrepreneurs say, with the benefit of hindsight, that when planning a business you should halve the income you anticipate and double your expected expenses – any discrepancy in your favour will be a bonus. Others insist that they would never have secured funding without a few white lies, and that whatever you ask for, the bank will give you 20% less. Ultimately, it's your call, but remember that your business plan should plot your progress, and skewing it for any purpose will limit how much it can help you.

Your business plan should cover the outlined areas in detail, but you'll need to strike the right balance between being concise and being overly verbose – the latter will irritate rather than impress. Potential investors need to be able to see key information easily and clearly. Where appropriate, use bullet points and break up the text; bite-sized chunks of information are far easier to absorb. Don't leave anything out, but at the same time keep it brief; people can always contact you if they need more information.

OUTLINE FOR A STANDARD BUSINESS PLAN

- What your franchise business will do.

- Who your customers will be.

- Why people will buy your products.

- Evidence that this market exists, and its potential.

- Evidence for why your business will survive when others don't; analysis of the competition.

- Who you are and why you're going into business.

- Why you believe you've got the skills and expertise to run the business; your qualifications and experience.

- Details of any other directors or key management.

- How you'll fund the setting up of the business.

- How you'll repay any money you borrow.

- What your ongoing costs and overheads will be.

- Sales and revenue forecasts for the first 12 months of business.

- Details of suppliers and contracts.

- Your goals for the first 12 months and beyond.

Budgeting for the year

When working out your costs you need to plan for the first 12 months. That landmark first anniversary might seem a long way off when you're sitting there with an idea and a pile of research, but it's essential to consider not just your start-up costs but the ongoing overheads for the first year. Many companies break these down into one-month, six-month and first-year budgets.

This will help you to plan your business finances, assessing areas such as how much money you have and how much revenue you need in order to generate your target profit. Budgeting will also provide a good measure of whether your business plan is along the right path, or whether it needs adjusting. The figures that you work out for your first year's budget should go into a budget plan towards the end of your business plan.

Expenses

For a full budget, and to judge how viable your business is, you'll need to balance revenue forecasts against costs (we'll come to forecasting later). It's crucial to work out and keep track of how much you're spending, not just the sales you hope to make. Without expenses, any forecasts or even sales prove very little about how profitable your business can be.

Start-up costs

Begin by looking at all your initial start-up costs. All the costs of getting your franchise business up and running go into the category of start-up expenses. Depending on the type of franchise you are starting, they may include:

- initial stock
- equipment
- rent deposits
- down payments on property
- down payments on equipment
- shop-fitting costs
- utility set-up fees.

This is just a sample list and you probably won't have trouble adding to it once you start listing your costs.

Operating costs

Your operating costs are those expenses that your business will incur on an ongoing basis; essentially, what you'll need to pay out each month. They may include:

- your salary
- staff salaries
- telecommunications
- utilities
- stock
- storage
- distribution
- promotion
- loan payments
- office supplies
- maintenance
- professional services (eg accountancy fees)
- management services fee.

Again, this isn't a complete list and outgoings will vary from month to month. With respect to the management services fee, this will vary from franchise to franchise, depending on the level of service that the franchisor provides – this can be calculated as a turnover percentage, although some franchisors choose to operate on a fixed-fee basis. However, once you've completed your own lists you should have a fairly good idea, even if they're ballpark figures, of what revenues and/or funding you're going to need to support your business on a monthly, six-monthly and yearly basis.

> I believe that one of the reasons that our business has been so successful is in part due to the excellent support we have received from the EKW Group. We were swayed by the rapport we had built with EKW's business relationship manager. He was approachable, generous with his time and very knowledgeable. We leaned heavily on his knowledge to help us establish our business, and genuinely felt that we could ask him any questions.
>
> *David Blenkinsop, Seven Hills Optical Ltd*

Making revenue forecasts

Sales forecasting is notoriously difficult and is the point where many business plans fall down. This is because either the business owner is hopelessly optimistic or the plan succeeds only in proving that the business isn't viable because of the number of sales needed to generate a profit. Similarly, the cost that goods would need to be priced at is unrealistic or the cost of keeping the business going until it breaks even is unsustainable.

Your biggest difficulty is not having any previous sales history as a guide. You will have the benefit of the franchisor's experience of how other franchisees in the network have performed and how their location, territories and customer groups compare with yours. And don't forget to look at the direct and indirect competition. This is where your market research can help, providing you with examples of sales figures for businesses operating in a similar market. However, this won't give you an entirely accurate picture, as it's highly unlikely that you'll perform at a similar level for perhaps up to a year.

The simplest way to forecast is to start by working out what you hope to be selling within six months. Work this out per unit per day so you have a gross sales figure and multiply that by the number of 'opening' days in a month. Next, look to scale proportionately from month one, where you're unlikely to have many sales, upwards to month six. You can then extrapolate that scale over 12 months for an annual sales forecast.

In many professional services businesses your sales will be limited by the number of sales calls or visits you can make and the rate at which you convert sales calls into quotes, and quotes into orders. There's no point creating a plan that requires you to be on the road 26 hours a day; it's impossible.

You must also be very aware that sending one of your customers an invoice is not the same as getting the cash in the bank. That might come 30 days later if you're lucky. On the other hand, it might be 60 or even 90 days. Your profit-and-loss account, which works on the invoices you've raised, will look great, but your bank manager may still be telling you that you've reached your overdraft limit.

Carl Reader, head of franchising at Dennis & Turnbull, is a leading expert in franchise accountancy. He is always looking for new industry developments, such as online accounting and bank feeds, to help his clients stay one step ahead.

Steven Frost, Smith & Henderson

These issues of cash flow are critical in small businesses, especially in their start-up period, and their management should be an important part of your plan.

Forecasting cash flow needs to be as detailed as possible. The greater the detail, the more accurate the forecast. Record the customer payments that you get each month, and also factor in any other sources of income, such as the sale of assets, or bank interest. You need to offset these with a record of your outgoings each month, including elements such as tax, loans, stock, materials and rent. This combination of income and outgoings will give you as accurate a cash flow forecast as you can get.

After working out your forecasts, redo them three times using a pessimistic, optimistic and realistic outlook. Next try putting a real-time calendar next to your 'month one', 'month two' and so on, taking into account the seasonal peaks and troughs in trade that you anticipate and that are suggested from your research. Depending on the type of franchise you are considering, assess whether there are likely to be huge seasonal variations.

Putting it all together

Once you've worked out your outgoings (both initial start-up and ongoing) and your revenue forecast you can put the two together to produce a clearer analysis on paper of the viability of your business and when it will break even.

Begin by compiling month-by-month expenses and sales forecasts. In the same way that you accounted for peaks and troughs in sales, look out for those months where you expect expenses to be higher. For instance, if you have to cater for the Christmas rush you may buy far more stock in September, October and November than in other months of the year.

Again, prepare three projections: pessimistic, optimistic, realistic. Also try to account for the fact that the price at which you can purchase stock will, hopefully, decrease as your sales levels increase. However, that's a calculation you'll probably want to reserve for your optimistic forecast, unless you already have such an agreement in place with suppliers.

> ❝ I switched to d&t because it was one of the few accounting firms savvy enough to accept working with online software, but I stayed with them because they give such lovely service. ❞
>
> *Dr Mohammad Al-Ubaydli, Dennis and Turnbull client*

While your calculation will inevitably vary from month to month (something you'll need to be aware of when managing cash flow), the point where your sales equal your expenses is where you 'break even' and, hopefully, go on to generate profit. This level of detail should give you a much more powerful overview not just of how viable your business should be, but of what funding will be required and when. It will also enable you to identify when you may need assistance with cash flow or credit.

Having this information at your fingertips won't just impress investors and the banks, it should also put you on firmer ground when making buying decisions, for example, when it comes to actually sourcing stock.

BREAK-EVEN POINT CALCULATION

Break-even point (£) = Fixed costs ÷ Gross margin percentage

Example: A business buys portable fans for £10 each, marks them up and sells them for £20. Its monthly expenses (fixed costs) are £12,000.

The break-even point will be £24,000, or 1,200 units.

£12,000 ÷ (10/20) = £24,000

SWOT analysis

SWOT analysis is a method for describing your future company in terms of the factors that will have the most impact on the business. Its name comes from the initials for the words of the elements used in the analysis:

- Strengths
- Weaknesses
- Opportunities
- Threats

Strengths and weaknesses are internal factors, such as the quality of your product or the skills of your management, whereas opportunities and threats are external factors, which may include the development of a whole new market, or the arrival of new competitors.

You should carry out a SWOT analysis to identify key issues that may arise as your business starts and grows. For example, it can be useful to include a couple of worst-case scenarios and how you would deal with them. Weighing threats against opportunities is not a reason to indulge in pessimism. Rather, it is a question of considering how you would overcome, bypass or restrict potential damage.

A SWOT summary and a description of your approach to it should be included in your business plan. It will cover how you intend to:

- build on the strengths
- minimise the weaknesses
- seize the opportunities
- counter the threats.

One last bit of advice

It's helpful to get someone to review the business plan for you. Your franchisor will do this, but you may also want to get the viewpoint of someone independent from the business.

For further information on business planning, check out our sister guide, *Start Your Own Business 2012*.

THINGS TO REMEMBER

- Don't write your business plan just for your funders: use it as your main guide for the direction that your business will take.

- Include all the necessary detail, but don't overload it. A good plan is thorough but succinct.

- Be realistic with your sales forecasts. It's better to underestimate than to overestimate.

- Have three different trading forecasts – pessimistic, optimistic and realistic.

11.0

THE START-UP PHASE

IN THIS CHAPTER

One of the questions you'll ask yourself when considering becoming a franchisee is, quite simply, how to get started. It's worth remembering that a franchise is a hybrid between working for an established corporation and starting a business from scratch. Therefore, aspects of both will be evident in the running of your franchise company. You'll need to assess your own skills, strengths and weaknesses and match these to a suitable franchise opportunity. Likewise, the franchisor will need to assess your abilities and financial status and decide whether you are the right person to join the group of franchises, known as a network.

After you have signed and trained, next comes the exciting – and daunting – task of getting your franchise ready to open for business. Whether you have gone for a service-oriented franchise or a customer-facing one, there are some vital matters to consider before you can be fully up and running. You may need to source some equipment, recruit staff and build up relationships with suppliers for the long term.

In this chapter, we'll discuss:

- how long it takes to get your franchise up and running
- your first day and beyond
- how to buy equipment
- hiring staff
- setting up accounts with suppliers
- how the franchisor can help.

A guide to timelines

Once you've decided to start a franchise, have been selected by a franchisor and have signed the agreement, how soon can you expect to start training and then be ready for your first day of business? There are many variables that will influence how quickly you can get up and running.

The rate at which you get your franchise up and running will depend to an extent on your levels of motivation and how keen you are to get the business started. Factors can include finding premises, raising finance and training. And if you need to recruit staff, buy equipment and source stock, then you'll need to factor in more time. It can be difficult, therefore, to give a precise timeline, due to the number of variables involved.

However, most new franchises can be operational within two to six months of submitting the application, although this estimate can be affected by the number of other new franchises waiting to be trained, and the time taken in arranging finance and finding and preparing suitable equipment. Whatever the particular circumstances are of the franchise you have signed a contract to join, you will need to know what the timeline is likely to be, not least because you will have to finance yourself during this preparatory stage.

Finding premises

If your choice of franchise requires you to find premises, this can take several months, depending on how easily you find a location, and the amount of work required to get it ready for business. You also need to take into account the amount of time you have available for property hunting, your geographical flexibility and the time needed for property negotiations. While allowing for all these variables, the average time between submitting an application to Burger King and opening a new restaurant, for example, is approximately 12 months.

If you need premises for your franchise, securing the site you want will require a certain amount of patience. Most franchisors will offer some help in finding a location, which could help to reduce the time needed to find somewhere suitable.

Finance

Raising finance is another process that can take a lot longer than you might think, depending on your needs. You'll need to have enough money to cover the franchisor's initial fee, the cost of preparing the business for opening (such as recruitment, equipment and premises) and the cost of running the business until you start to make a profit. Of course, much of the finance that you need can be borrowed from the bank (see Chapter 8), so the sooner you can arrange this, the better.

Training

Part of your initial investment will go on training, and the level of training you receive and the time taken to do it vary enormously from one franchisor to another and from sector to sector. For a retail operation, for example, you may be required to observe the day-to-day running at another franchisee's premises so that you can become fully immersed in the business operations. If your chosen franchise provides a service, you may need more extensive training in order to become as familiar as possible with the industry.

You may initially receive remote training by phone or email before attending hands-on training at the franchisor's headquarters or some other venue. Depending on your needs, many franchisors will offer additional, optional training sessions. If you are new to starting a business, you would probably be wise to take up this offer. Some of the more popular franchises have a waiting list for training, so you'll need to factor in this time. On the plus side, your franchisor will be as keen as you are to get your business up and running, so the training will be well organised and mapped out.

> The initial training was vital for me as a non-accountant and I took every last ounce I possibly could from the course, often asking the trainers to stay late to give me extra support . . . which they were happy to do.
>
> *Renee Mackay, TaxAssist*

Your first day

What can you expect on your first day as a franchisee? As the day draws closer, it's natural to have mixed emotions – excitement and happiness at the prospect of starting your own business, and apprehension and fear from not knowing what is involved on a day-to-day basis until you are up and running. Of course, your business plan will tell you what needs to be done, but when you first start out you'll frequently ask yourself: 'What do I do now?' Plan, plan, and plan again. You won't be able to predict and plan for everything that might happen, but with enough planning under your belt, you'll boost your confidence and be better able to cope with unforeseen circumstances.

Just what your first day is like will also depend very much on the type of business you have chosen. For example, if you decide to go for a retail franchise, you'll need to ensure that your shop is properly stocked and that you are ready to receive customers. With a retail operation, you may even be able to drum up interest and potential business as you prepare the shop for opening.

You may start your first day still feeling overwhelmed by the amount of information you have taken in during the training period, and you shouldn't be surprised if you forget some of it. The run-up to starting your own business – whether a franchise or a company started from scratch – can be one of the most nerve-wracking and testing times of your life.

During your training you may have relied heavily on your franchisor, but it's important as you strike out on your own to have confidence in your own ability to run the business. Your franchisor will still be there to help and support you, but you'll need to take control of the day-to-day operations. If you need extra help, don't be afraid to ask – after all, one of the benefits of starting a franchised business is the fact that you are not going it alone.

Bigger franchises often send a small team of experienced franchisees to help new franchisees during their first, critical week of operation. This will enable you to master the day-to-day operations and to spot any weaknesses with which you may need more help. Signs Express, for example, which provides signage products, offers franchisees a four-week training course, after which they return to their territory to set up their production unit. Once the new franchisee is ready to start trading, head office sales and marketing teams will make several visits to assist with direct mail, web and e-marketing, PR and sales development, while the technical support and national accounts teams are on hand to assist with quoting and technical queries.

> ❝ **You work in an existing ZipYard franchise, learning all the processes and systems, so you understand every aspect of the business. Then when you're ready to open your own shop, the training manager stays with you until you're confident to manage alone.** ❞
>
> *Juliet O'Connell, The ZipYard*

THE START-UP PHASE AT A GLANCE

- ■ If you want to start a franchise, you'll need to make the first move and deal with the franchisors direct.

- ■ All franchisors will have a brochure or information pack that you can pick up at an exhibition or request in the post.

- Part of your initial investment goes on training, and the level you receive varies enormously from franchisor to franchisor and from sector to sector.

- You may receive remote training initially by phone or email before attending hands-on training at the franchisor's headquarters or other venue.

- Bigger franchises often send a small team of experienced franchisees to help the new franchisee during their first, critical week of operation.

Buying equipment

Depending on the type of franchise you choose, you may need to invest in certain types of equipment, which could range from printing machines to IT equipment to cleaning tools. If you've visited several different premises of franchised businesses you should have noticed that they look very similar in terms of how they are fitted and equipped. Franchisors are building a brand, and to do that they need all of their franchisees' businesses to look the same, and deliver the same range and quality of products and services, as far as possible, so that the customer has a similar experience regardless of which franchise they visit.

In many cases, you'll find the franchisor operates what is known as a turnkey scheme, which means that all the equipment necessary for running the business is supplied for you and included in the overall price. This is true for Domino's Pizza, for example, where shop-fitting and equipment-sourcing services are provided to franchisees as part of the franchise package.

If this is not the case for your chosen franchise, there are certain things to be mindful of. You may be tempted to go for more than you need when it comes to fitting out your business, but stick to what your business plan says and err on the side of caution. Even when your franchise package does not include equipment, your franchisor should give you advice on what is needed and where you can source it, and may well be able to help you negotiate discounts.

When buying, know what you want and what is required by your franchise specification. You must seek the best price and, for every purchase, ask yourself whether you absolutely need it, whether your customers would notice if you didn't have it and whether you'd definitely only make more money by having it. You'll soon find the nice-to-have luxuries don't pass this test.

Be economical, but don't go for the cheapest options on the market. The old adage 'you buy cheap, you buy twice' can certainly ring true when it comes to electrical goods and shelving units, and you could end up spending more in the long run if the equipment isn't up to scratch.

For larger items of equipment, you may consider buying outright, depending on the amount of money you have available, or leasing, which would help to free up capital to spend on other parts of the business. Bear in mind that you'll spend a lot more money on premises, initial stock, equipment and staff than the first few customers will pay for their purchases or your services, so at the beginning, on paper you'll be cash flow negative.

Hiring staff

As your franchise grows, you may need to consider taking on employees. As a franchisee, your staff will be your greatest asset. You'll rely on them to project a good image of the business as well as to help you run it on a day-to-day basis. Taking on staff is a big commitment and has financial implications. You must ensure that you have sufficient cash available and that you can take on the new responsibilities that hiring staff entails.

Be aware of your legal responsibilities. If you hire staff, you'll need to provide holiday and sick pay and carry out a health and safety check on your premises.

Successful recruiting

The key to successful recruiting is to do as much research and preparation as possible. In many cases, your franchisor will be able to offer support when it comes to interviewing and hiring staff – at Signs Express, for example, the head-office operations team assists with recruiting staff. But the onus will be on you to get the process rolling and to make the decision as to whom you recruit.

While it may be tempting to place an ad and sit back and wait for applicants, this is not the best way to recruit staff. Your business plan should have not only included an idea of how many members of staff you need, but also taken into account what you can afford.

Once you've established exactly how many staff you need you'll have to decide what you can afford to pay them. You'll need to strike a fine balance between being practical and not stretching your budget too far, and being realistic about what you need to pay to attract the right kind of talent.

FINDING THE RIGHT PERSON

Start by drawing up a detailed job description listing the duties and responsibilities of the position and the personal attributes, the skills and experience required of candidates. The more closely you define the position, the more likely you'll be to get applicants who match your requirements.

Once you've established the requirements for the position, prioritise them into primary and secondary criteria. This will give you a solid matrix against which to compare applications and interviews, so that if any legal objection is ever raised you'll have clear written evidence that the process was fair and above board.

This may seem an onerous process for recruiting for the position of a shop assistant, for example, but as well as protecting you legally, it should also serve you well in finding the right person and make your life easier. And once you've done it for the first time, you can use the same process again.

Advertising for staff

Once you've got a detailed job description, making out an advertisement should be easy. List all the job requirements, criteria for applicants and information about your business, and also state the salary or wage you'll pay. Some people advise against this, but by listing what you're prepared to pay you'll ensure that you won't waste time vetting applications from candidates who are expecting to earn more than you can afford to pay.

Just as important as what you detail about the job role is the information on how you want people to reply. Be specific. Ideally, you want everyone to reply in the same way so that you can make a fair and direct comparison of applications. The best way to do this is to use application forms, but you may not have the time to draw one up or you may feel they are not personal enough. If you want CVs, then ask for a personal letter as well. Try to tailor the applications to the skills of the role. For example, if you need someone who has a good phone manner, it might be that you ask people to apply in that way.

If IT skills are important, then applications by email only might be another way of vetting. Remember that how a business presents itself in the staff recruitment market is also a part of its brand image.

Your franchisor may in consequence have very detailed staff recruitment systems and advertising pro-formas in place that you will need to follow.

Interviewing

Successful interviewing requires certain skills. If you've never employed people before you may find some training helpful, and this is an area where your franchisor can help. If you'll need considerable help, it's worth checking at the outset that your franchisor can support your needs. Interviews must be planned extremely carefully. You have only a short period of time in which to elicit all the information you need from a potential recruit. You need not only to ascertain whether they have relevant skills and experience, but also to gain an accurate impression as to how well they fit the kind of environment you're trying to achieve in your business.

After drawing up your short list of applicants, contact the prospective interviewees and give them clear instructions about your location and how to get there, what they should bring with them, whom they should ask for and how long the interview is likely to last.

Set some time aside to do the interviews and make sure that there will be no interruptions such as ringing phones or other matters vying for your attention. To ensure you're not interrupted, put a sign on the door along the lines of 'Interview taking place – do not disturb'. This may sound ridiculously basic, but it's amazing what a difference such a simple measure makes.

Be aware of your legal responsibilities. Recruitment has become embroiled in employment law in recent years, with a number of high-profile cases where business owners have been taken to tribunals on grounds of discrimination for not employing someone because of their race, gender, disability, sexuality or religious belief. Being morally resolute that such a repugnant thought would never cross your mind sadly isn't enough to keep you covered from claims of discrimination. It's quite possible someone might see a fault in your recruitment process and look to take advantage, or you might inadvertently cause upset by your reason for rejecting a candidate.

Dealing with suppliers

You might have exactly the right balance of skills that it takes to become a successful franchisee, but you'll also need the right supplies for your business to be up to scratch. You'll need to strike a fine balance between the goods you can afford and the quality you need in order to provide the best service possible. The relationship you establish with your suppliers will be crucial to maintaining your levels of quality, and the quality you are required to provide will be part of the specifications set by the franchisor for their brand.

As part of the franchise agreement, your franchisor may well specify which suppliers you must use. If this is not the case, do your research carefully and compare as many options as possible before agreeing to any provision of service. If possible, and depending on the type of franchise you are operating, visit the premises of companies you are buying from.

Once you've established a network of suppliers that you're happy with and can rely on, it's important that you maintain a good working relationship with them – and it's not just about paying your bills on time.

- Try to deal with the same sales representative or agent whenever you order. Building a relationship with one person is more likely to inspire trust and the odd favour when you need it.
- Keep a check on prices and review them against what other suppliers are offering.
  Even if you don't want to change suppliers you may be able to negotiate more competitive prices. Don't be afraid to do this – suppliers will understand your need to get a good price and will be grateful to have the chance to match it rather than lose your trade to a competitor.
- Remember not to judge a supplier solely on price. Ensure that levels of customer service, flexibility and, crucially, quality of product don't slip.

Franchisor support

You've narrowed down your search for a franchise, but how can you tell what level of support you'll get once you have signed up? As we have already discussed, many franchisors will offer support when it comes to buying equipment and recruiting staff, but just how far their support will go depends very much on the individual franchisor, the sector you have chosen and your own skillset. Having a clear idea of the level of support you will get is one of the advantages of paying a visit to existing franchisees before you sign up.

If there are areas where you feel you would benefit from additional support, it's important to ask the franchisor at the outset – before you sign anything – exactly what support they will make available to you. This is not just for your own benefit. As a franchisee, you'll be passing on the training that you received from the franchisor to new recruits, as well as drawing on your own experience, so it's important to set a good example from the start.

> Running a business is always going to be a rollercoaster affair, with challenges along the way, but the support and dedication provided by the Driver Hire team and network has meant that I know I'm not alone and can push forward with a positive outlook. Being recognised for the hard work is an added bonus and certainly helps to motivate me and the team.
>
> *Manjit Singh, Driver Hire*

STAFF, VENDORS AND EQUIPMENT AT A GLANCE

- Depending on the type of franchise you choose, you may need to invest in certain types of equipment.

- It can be tempting to go for more than you need when it comes to fitting out your business, but stick to what your business plan says and err on the side of caution.

- The key to successful recruitment is to do as much research and preparation as possible.

- Ensure that you maintain a good working relationship with your suppliers.

- Don't judge a supplier solely on price. Ensure that levels of customer service, flexibility and, crucially, quality of product don't slip.

JOIN *THE* SUPPORTERS CLUB

AT SANDLER,
we support business leaders with our guidance.

Worldwide, for nearly fifty years, Sandler is there alongside CEOs and MDs, all the way to the peak of their sales ambitions.

And that's the same dedicated, ongoing support you will have, as a franchisee in the Sandler network, to grow your business.

Call us on 01608611211
Email: shaun@sandler.com

Visit www.sandlerfranchising.co.uk

Sandler Training
Finding Power In Reinforcement

12.0

RUNNING YOUR FRANCHISE

IN THIS CHAPTER

You've had your first few customers through the door or closed your first few sales on the phone. Now comes the mammoth task of actually making work what you have been planning and preparing for all these months. Even with all the pre-packaging that comes with a franchise business, you'll still need to do a lot of work to run it successfully.

It's not unusual to worry about whether you have made the right decision or whether you are up to the task. You may worry constantly about why sales aren't coming in faster, or lie awake at night thinking about the equipment malfunctioning.

After the initial excitement and buzz of starting your own business, you need to be prepared for an inevitably slow beginning. The first few months are a matter of survival. But this can also be a great opportunity to hone your operation and make sure everything is running perfectly.

In this chapter, we'll look at:

■ preparing for a slow start

■ managing the relationship with your franchisor

■ managing your time and your money

■ issues of control.

Preparing for a slow start

At your initial training session you may have relied heavily on the support of your franchisor and existing franchisees, which will have given you a huge boost in confidence. As you launch your franchise, you'll put all this knowledge – together with any new skills you have learned – to the test. In the first few weeks of running your franchise, you'll become increasingly familiar with the systems in place and your franchisor will have less day-to-day involvement with your business. It can be a daunting juggling act, however, as you'll be responsible for a variety of tasks.

As your reputation in the area builds, so too should your customer base. You should have accounted for a gradual increase in trade in your business plan anyway. The key to surviving the first few months is to do everything you can to keep the cash flowing in, while keeping overheads low. If trade is slower than you bargained for, this will be a good reminder to get on with your marketing or to tap into the support network of your franchisor. Make sure you are using all the systems you have been trained in – such as marketing and sales programmes – to boost trade and attract customers.

More than anything, stay calm but focused:

- measure everything
- record everything
- stick to your identity and business plan, but try to identify areas where you can do better.

> It's entirely up to you how quickly you want to travel on the road to growing your own business. I learned, early on, to build my business around the times and days which are most convenient for me. That way, I find clients who are well suited for me to work with, and I'm always at my best.
>
> *Nigel Dunand, Sandler Training*

As a franchise, you'll be limited as to how much you can change shop fittings, for example, but subtle differences may make a difference. If you've been tweaking, experimenting and measuring the impact of different approaches you'll be in a far better position to make a decision than if you've been sitting on your hands. It can be massively difficult to accept that things are not quite going as well as you'd hoped. However, there are no assurances in business, no matter how much planning and preparation you put in.

Be open minded

The most important thing is to be open minded and to prepare yourself. The key is to look at the business basics and get to the bottom of the problem. Go back to your business plan and hold it up to your franchise. Is the business you're sitting in a true reflection of the plan?

If, when you compare your actual business to your business plan, you see something different, then you may have found the answer. Did you get lost or sidetracked somewhere in the original vision? Are you differentiating yourself enough, and are you communicating the right messages? If you're not, then start to reverse those problems and get back on track.

Above all, don't be afraid to ask for help. After all, as a franchisee who has been trained to run a fully equipped business, your support doesn't end there. Most franchise companies offer their franchisees ongoing help in the early days of the business and often put newcomers in touch with more experienced franchise owners for advice.

Managing relationships

The concept of franchising is based upon a good working relationship between the franchisor and the franchisee. In the early days of your business and as it grows, it's vital to keep as open a relationship as possible with your franchisor. Two-way communication is essential from the word go.

Identify any problems early on and discuss them before they escalate. It's likely that your franchisor will have already come across the same issues with other franchisees and will be able to offer some sound advice. Your franchisor should provide various means by which you can keep in contact. These can be personal visits, written communications such as email, telephone briefings and franchise meetings.

In the early days of your business, expect to have regular personal visits from the franchisor, who will be keen to check that you are complying with operating standards and rules, as set out in the franchise agreement and the operating manual for the business.

You can also expect to receive paperwork from your franchisor. This can include regular newsletters with information on how the franchised network is doing, together with updates for the operations manual. You'll also be expected to provide the franchisor with regular financial updates and other information specific to your franchise, so it's essential for you to keep all your paperwork up to date and share it at regular intervals.

Many franchisors also hold regular meetings with their network of franchisees. Depending on the size and sector, these could be held on a regional or national basis. In keeping with the ethos of two-way communication, these meetings will give you an opportunity to network with and learn from other franchisees, as well as giving your franchisor the chance to update you on any new developments taking place.

> **Since everyone in The Christmas Decorators is also their own boss and we have compatible goals, the franchise team works in a synergistic and supportive way which is really refreshing and different from other experiences I have had in the past.**
>
> *Trevor Grinsted, The Christmas Decorators*

Fear of failure

While the franchisor will be there to offer you continued support, once you have bought the franchise it becomes your business, and you risk failing just like any other owner-manager. Granted, the failure risks for franchises are much less than for a business started from scratch, but nonetheless, the risk is still there.

It's important to set up a system of best practice from the start to help you identify problems that could jeopardise the business further down the road. If you come up against a problem, make a note of it and report it to the franchisor – other franchisees may have come up against the same problem and there may already be an effective solution in place to deal with it.

Don't forget that the franchisor too could fail, which would have a knock-on effect on your business. As well as monitoring your franchise's performance, keep a close eye on any dealings you have with your franchisor. Do you feel that they are withholding information? Is the quality of support deteriorating or not what you were promised? Irrespective of contractual commitments to your franchise, your franchisor's job is to ensure that you and your business are better off trading within the franchise than going it alone. If that isn't how it feels, then raise any issues with your franchisor before the relationship goes sour, not afterwards.

Managing your time and your money

Time management is crucial when you are running your business. Being responsible for so many different details means that your time will be precious and you'll need to spend it wisely. Discipline, planning and flexibility are the keys to success when it comes to time management. It is too easy to become distracted when you are working for yourself with no one to report to. Granted, you'll need to provide feedback and regular reports for your franchisor, but you'll be your own boss on a day-to-day basis. Time spent planning and preparing saves time in the long run and will increase your efficiency. Be flexible and regularly challenge every task associated with running your business.

Keeping up to date with your paperwork is also key to running a successful franchise. You'll be expected to give your franchisor business performance updates on a regular basis, together with financial breakdowns. Little and often is the key. Being disciplined about keeping financial records is important, and it can take time to get used to this, so the sooner you establish a routine for doing so, the better. Do not attempt to do all your paperwork for the month in one day, as by the end of the day you are more likely to be tired and make mistakes.

> Enjoy it and work hard. Plan your time carefully because there are a million different jobs to do, from sales and marketing to accounting, credit control and invoicing. Make sure you get your invoices out on time and keep a watchful eye on your cash flow. Lastly, network as much as possible.
>
> *Stuart Fisher, Recognition Express*

Monitoring your cash flow and forecasts

Monitor your cash flow and compare figures to the forecasts in your business plan. Keep referring back to your business plan and review the situation in relation to your forecasts and projections. Believe the figures (they won't lie) and use them to make informed decisions about your business. It is important not to underestimate the working capital needed to run the business from day to day while it is growing.

Problems with cash flow can be mistaken for poor profitability, especially in the early days, but careful planning and monitoring can help to prevent unpleasant surprises and reassure your franchisor.

How you market your franchise will ultimately play an important part in its success. In Chapter 13 we'll cover the basics of small-business marketing but the truth is that no one is better placed to market your business than you. If you communicate your passion for your product or service to your customers, you'll get them interested in the first place.

Coping with control

Franchising provides you with plenty of support, but it isn't exactly the business equivalent of a blank canvas, as is the case for normal entrepreneurs. Franchisors have their own criteria for how each of their outlets should look and operate.

However much it feels that you're the ultimate boss on a day-to-day basis, you'll always be working to someone else's vision, not your own. The amount of freedom afforded to franchisees varies, but you'll almost certainly be briefed on how the company wants to be represented, from staff uniforms to what suppliers to use.

In time, it is possible that you'll start to resent this amount of control, as well as having to pay ongoing fees. It's important to remember that some degree of consistency is necessary in order for a franchised operation to succeed. While you may feel further down the line that some restrictions are harder to bear than others, your franchisor should have a system in place for franchisees to contribute ideas that can be incorporated to benefit the franchised operation in the future.

RUNNING YOUR FRANCHISED BUSINESS AT A GLANCE

- ■ Keep the cash flowing in, while keeping overheads low.

- ■ Don't feel you have to face problems alone – seek support from your franchisor if necessary.

- ■ Keep up to date with your accounting and paperwork.

- ■ Consistency is necessary if you want your franchise to succeed.

EXPERT OPINION

In business for yourself, not by yourself

What is franchising?

Nigel Toplis, Managing Director of Recognition Express, ComputerXplorers, The ZipYard, and Kall Kwik, and past chair of the British Franchise Association, details the questions you should ask and the process you need to go through before you take the plunge into the franchising deep end.

Franchising is neither an industry in its own right nor even a business. It is, though, one of the fastest-growing and most consistently successful methods for distributing products and services.

It's a crazy mixture of conformity and individuality that combines the best elements of big business and small operations.

To be successful, a franchisee must comply with the franchise system, and yet such compliance will enable the franchisee to be more fulfilled.

The 2012 NatWest/bfa Franchise Survey highlighted the following:

- Market turnover in excess of £13.4 billion

- Over 594,000 people employed

- Approximately 40,100 units in UK

- 929 active franchise systems.

In Britain, there is a latent but massive and increasing desire to run our own businesses, and this goes across culture, race, age and social background.

There is no template for being a successful franchisee – except perhaps the following:

- willingness and propensity to work hard

- acknowledgement to follow and adopt the franchisor's system

- a desire to succeed.

'In business for yourself, not by yourself' really does capture the essence of franchising.

A franchisor will always be on hand to provide knowledge and expertise on all the key areas of business, which franchisees can take as much or as little advantage of this as they require. Some have referred to the relationship of franchisor and franchisee as a 'marriage'. It is the ideal option for both entrepreneurs and those less keen to take a big leap into the unknown.

Support

Due to the scale of this support, franchisees come from a wide range of backgrounds and previous experience. Running a franchise is amenable to a variety of transferable skills, including project management, marketing, operations and sales, and the franchisor is there to help if you need to boost any skill sets.

Opportunity

Franchisees can often choose where their franchise is based and many can be run from home, meaning more time to spend with the family and no daily commute. This is a huge benefit for many franchisees, especially parents. Franchising is also ideal for people who have lots to offer, but who would find the structure of regular employment unsuitable, such as single parents or people with disabilities.

For young people too, franchising is an excellent way to launch their careers. Franchisee Alex Newman, was in his twenties when he took on his franchise.

> Buying a Recognition Express franchise has given me a unique opportunity to become a business owner at such a young age. The market potential is massive, our product range extensive and the range of companies we access is huge.
>
> *Alex Newman, Recognition Express, Coventry*

Rationale

There is a good quote from the book *Growing Pains* that accurately differentiates between running your own 'independent' business and a franchise, stating that running your own business is

> **about as easy as navigating unchartered waters in a leaking rowing boat with an inexperienced crew while surrounded by a school of sharks. The crew might be glad to know that others before them have made the voyage successfully and to hear (and learn) of the lessons that other voyagers learned in the process.**

Franchising is very much a two-way street where the franchisor can achieve faster expansion of his or her operation, make more money and gain a higher return on capital employed.

For this the franchisee gets a proven business system to include marketing, goodwill, training, support and trademarks to become a successful business person in their own right.

Selecting a franchise opportunity

Key questions to ask when considering a franchise:

- **Why do I want to run a business?** Personal ambition, getting just reward for effort, attaining greater job security, learning new skills, building a capital asset and working with the family are all well documented reasons.

- **What am I good at?** Sit down and evaluate your strengths and weaknesses, your likes and dislikes. You should look upon a franchise as a long-term tenure, more a vocation than a job.

- **What sort of person am I?** It will help if you are positive, outgoing and energetic, if you like solving problems and see yourself both as a self-starter and a team player.

- **What can I afford?** Be sure you can afford both the initial fee and time spending training and thus not working as well as any shortfalls over the first months of trading.

If you think the venture is going to cost you £100,000 and you only raise £80,000 be very, very sure before you beg and borrow (usually from family) to go ahead.

Once you've identified a business that:

■ interests you

■ uses your skills/experience

■ you can afford

■ matches your aspirations

the next step is to find the right franchisor.

Ten questions you should ask:

1. Do they have a solid trading history?

2. Are they financially sound?

3. Do they have a history of success?

4. Is there a genuine head office support structure?

5. What do they actually provide by way of support?

6. If the franchisor supplies product, what are the terms and conditions?

7. What is its position in the market?

8. Are projected cash flows realistic? Can they prove so?

9. Does the company have a finance facility with the banks?

10. How tough is their interview process?

You should now be in a position where you have decided to become a business owner, you know the type of business and industry you want to be in and you've chosen the franchisor to get into bed with.

Next do a business plan (possibly with the help of a good accountant) which explains what you hope to do, how much money you need to do it and how you propose to pay the money back. Finally approach the bank!

The magic of franchising is that it combines an individual skill set, ambition, drive and energy with the tools, training, branding, support and proven business system of the franchise.

Remember, you're in franchising for yourself but never by yourself.

Further information

Nigel Toplis is Managing Director of bfa award-winning Recognition Express (established 1979) – the badges, signs, clothing and promotional gifts franchise – and its major shareholder.

He was previously MD of print giant Kall Kwik, where he subsequently merged its back-office operation with that of Prontaprint to form On Demand Communication.

In 2012 Nigel again took the reins at Kall Kwik bringing the business back into his group. In addition to Recognition Express, Nigel franchises ComputerXplorers, which provides ICT education to 3–13-year-olds, under a master franchise arrangement from the American owner; in October 2010 he launched a third franchise – The ZipYard – a high street operation specialising in garment alterations.

Nigel has written two books on franchising, was previously Chairman of the bfa and is a Fellow of Lancaster University.

(*Source: 2012 NatWest/bfa Franchise Survey)

ComputerXplorers

is part of the world's largest education franchised network

ComputerXplorers offers quality technology education to children from 3 to 13 years in: School Clubs Summer Camps Nurseries Primary Schools

Outstanding Opportunities:

- 11 million children
- 58,000 schools, nurseries, etc
- 20 years of experience
- Fantastic business opportunity
- High profit margin

Your profile:

- Are you a good communicator?
- Can you follow a system?
- Would you call yourself a 'people person'?
- Do you agree that hard work is essential?

Our support and strategy:

- Extensive marketing support and collateral
- Centralised marketing programmes
- Integrated business planning
- Proven profit margins
- Ongoing training and support
- Business-to-Business
- Franchisors who know franchising

"A priority for improvement in our school has been the development of learning experiences for pupils which are meaningful and equip our young people with skills for life. We recognise that these experiences are often best delivered when working in partnership with others. The ComputerXplorers courses are delivered by a highly professional team. Every effort is taken to ensure effective delivery of learning opportunities which motivate and engage our young people and planning has included opportunities for parents and staff to become involved. ComputerXplorers has given our children access to resources and equipment we as a school simply could not do and has provided advice and support for staff should they wish it."

Head Teacher

Total Franchise Package Price: £29,500 plus VAT

For further information contact Janet Matthews
T: 01530 513308
E: jmatthews@computerxplorers.co.uk
www.computerxplorers.co.uk

ComputerXplorers

13.0

ATTRACTING AND KEEPING CUSTOMERS

IN THIS CHAPTER

The risk of a franchise failing is substantially lower than for other start-up businesses, but that doesn't mean you can afford to be complacent.

Once your franchise is up and running, its success will depend on your marketing and sales strategy. Marketing is the means by which your business identifies, anticipates and then satisfies customer demand, and sales is the way you'll increase turnover. Marketing will help you to understand who your potential customers are and reach out to new ones.

In this chapter, we'll discuss:

- building a marketing strategy
- how to measure the success of your marketing plan
- the pros and cons of advertising
- top tips for marketing your franchise
- ways to increase your sales.

Building a marketing strategy

Once you've completed your initial training as a new franchisee, you'll be full of enthusiasm for the products and services you are about to offer. It's at this time that the reality dawns on you that you are required to master many skills and wear different hats, two of the most important of which will be marketing and sales. You may not feel confident or comfortable in this role, but it is one you'll need to get good at, and quickly too.

Successful marketing is about accumulating knowledge and is an art as well as a science. But you shouldn't find the process daunting; embrace the task of keeping up with the changing demands of customers and finding new ways to get them through your doors or on the end of a phone.

There are no hard-and-fast rules for creating a marketing strategy. It's up to you to set your own goals. However, as a general rule, you need to ask what you want your franchise to achieve in one year's, two years' or even five years' time compared to where it would be without a marketing strategy.

> **I set myself stretching but realistic targets for client acquisition and set about marketing the business like crazy. My two mainstays are the shop itself and networking, which between them bring in the majority of new clients, with the national website (and TaxAssist Support Centre) and my social media presence also adding new clients for me.**
>
> *Renee Mackay, TaxAssist*

Depending on your past employment history, you may have previous sales and marketing experience, along with tactics that may or may not have worked well in the past. What all new franchisees bring to the table is the experience of being sold to, and this may substantially colour how you feel about being marketed to, and how you feel about being labelled as a salesperson.

Many of the basics of marketing will already have been provided within the franchise system and structure you have chosen. This ensures that many of the common marketing challenges associated with stand-alone, independent businesses are removed. These include:

- Where to advertise? Franchisors already have a format that works for you to follow.
- How to use social media? Franchisors may have a central page on Facebook for the brand and an active Twitter account.

- What makes the ideal customer? Franchisors have already profiled this for you.
- What are the best price points? These have already been tested and refined.
- Building a recognised brand. The franchisor has already spent time and money on this.

While your franchisor may have given you some training on tried and trusted sales techniques that they are sure will work all the time, as a new franchisee you are likely to come up against the following challenges:

- painfully long selling cycles
- bad sales habits eroding margins
- prospects demanding – and getting – costly price concessions
- being part of a bidding war
- struggling to differentiate yourself in a competitive market.

> I get sent regular new business leads from Card Connection's head office, and when I have interest like this I always aim to visit the retailer the following day. I believe that providing this level of service is one of the keys to running a successful business.
>
> *Gabriel McGeown, Card Connection*

Some tips for your marketing plan

You'll still need to market the business on a day-to-day basis, and prove that you can attract and retain customers and generate repeat sales. Here are some tips to remember when devising your marketing plan.

- Start by setting clear objectives: where do you want your franchise to go?
- Set clear financial targets for these objectives.
- Define your target market and identify your potential customers.
- Understand the brand and the values you have bought into and need to communicate.
- Plan your promotion strategy.
- Set a budget.
- Devise a schedule.

- Decide how the strategy will be measured: for example, increased sales, direct responses, coverage in local press.
- Implement the programme according to the schedule.
- Monitor and evaluate results as an aid to future marketing decisions.

> For the coming Christmas we will be better prepared with a larger, fully trained team to help between 40 and 50 clients. The last year has been analysed, a steep learning curve has been traversed and changes have been made so that the coming Christmas runs much more smoothly, with a higher profit margin.
>
> *Trevor Grinsted, The Christmas Decorators*

Measuring success

If you've got several marketing or PR strategies happening at once it can be difficult to measure which ones are actually bringing in the customers. After all, you're not going to advertise in a newspaper and then ask each customer who walks through the door if they've popped in because they saw an advert in the local rag. If you're not sure which marketing technique is giving you the best return on investment, then why not try them one by one, then calculate any increase in customers or turnover for that period.

Of course the success of certain promotions, such as vouchers or discounts using codes, is easy enough to measure because you can count up how many customers make use of the offers. However, it's important to remember that you need to bring in more custom as a result of the promotion than you spend on your marketing. It's no good offering discounts and doubling your footfall if you end up making a loss on your products. Be sure to check your marketing and PR ideas with your franchisor. It may be, for example, that local radio advertising has already been tried and found to be a very expensive mistake. Avoiding such pitfalls is one of the advantages of buying into a franchise.

For each piece of marketing you do, set clear key performance indicators (KPIs) that will help you to assess whether it's proved worthwhile.

Promoting your products and services

One way of attracting new customers is to run special offers or promotions. Shops, for example, traditionally have end-of-season sales, but there are other ways to draw people in off the street, to suit all manner of franchises. But do remember that these should be suitable to the franchise.

> **The main growth in year one came from canvassing – approximately 50% of my customers came this way. I made sure that all my friends knew what I was doing. I gave my customers good service, called in unplanned on problem lawns and made a fuss of them.**
>
> *Steven Hook, Greensleeves*

Offers and the way they are presented will have an impact not just on your brand, but on the brand you've bought into, which is shared by all the franchisees. Whatever you do, do it with your franchisor's support. Limited special offers run on a daily or weekly basis can help to keep your business looking fresh and feel like you're offering an incentive or weekly special rather than selling end-of-line or old stock.

TEAM PROMOTIONS

If you're in retail, approach local clubs, groups and companies used by your target customers and ask whether you can put up a poster or distribute promotional material in exchange for providing them with a small discount.

You'll find most will welcome this as a way for you to attract customers. In other kinds of franchise, different sorts of strategic local partnerships may be worth exploring. Talk to your franchisor.

You should make the most of the local area around you. Keep an eye on your diary and what's going on in the neighbourhood. If there's a bandwagon you can jump on, leap onto it. If your town or local community is campaigning for an issue dear to your customers' hearts, put a poster in your window.

> **I recently noticed that the local landlord fairs had dried up due to government funding cuts. I decided to team up with a local events company to run them privately, along with the assistance of local authorities who promote the events to all of the private landlords in their respective regions.**
>
> *Stuart Wright, EnviroVent*

If you can help local schools, help them. Make the most of festivities and celebrations. It should go without saying, for instance, that if you're running a bar franchise, Guinness should be in your window for St Patrick's Day and champagne for Valentine's Day.

It is common knowledge that it is far easier to up-sell and cross-sell to existing customers than it is to find and sell to new ones. This is because they are familiar with your brand, your service and your products. Creating customer loyalty is more about managing the process of good service. In short, it is about creating customer delight. Customers are delighted with your business when their expectations are exceeded. So aim to under-promise and over-deliver in all that you do, and always follow through on what you say you'll do. It goes without saying that if you don't deliver on your promises, you risk doing untold damage to the brand and your business prospects.

Advertising

According to Sarah Cook, founder of marketing specialist Coconut Creatives, advertising is just one of many marketing options that you have when it comes to marketing your business. But you really shouldn't be dependent on it. Your franchisor may well be using a few, or all, of the other marketing methods listed here:

- direct mail
- internet
- email marketing
- public relations (PR).

> **Customers often send us photos of their weddings or special days, which we display on a digital photo frame in the shop.**
>
> *Juliet O'Connell, The ZipYard*

THINGS TO REMEMBER

- ■ Have a clear and defined marketing strategy before you start spending your budget.

- ■ Think carefully about what kind of promotions you offer and apply them to your slower days or times.

- ■ Explore with your franchisor how to use strategic partnerships.

If your franchise involves using newspaper or magazine advertising, there are certain tips, says Cook, that you can follow to maximise its potential.

- ■ Advertising on the right-hand side of the page can turn an unsuccessful advertising campaign into a successful one. This has been tested again and again. Your eyes are drawn to the right-hand page as you flick through a publication, so more people will see your advertisement if it's on the right-hand page.
- ■ Make it clear very early on that you have no intention of paying the full rate for advertising. Most advertising rate cards are far too high and you can always negotiate.
- ■ Don't make the mistake of advertising in publications or on various forms of media just because your competitors are doing so. Don't think that all your competitors are there because their ads are producing great results – most of them won't have a clue whether their advertising is working or not.
- ■ If your advertising isn't working, find out whether this is a common experience with other franchisees in your network, or if it's just you. If it's common, raise the problem with your franchisor. If it's just you, try to work out why. Consider using posters in as many places as possible, and make sure to ask people where they found out about you.

Social media marketing

Social media presents an interesting – and low-cost – marketing opportunity for most franchises, but is not something you should undertake without prior agreement. If the franchise has active social media accounts on Twitter, Facebook and LinkedIn, or a blog, it may well insist on retaining control of brand messaging. Some franchises now use social media to share news, link to articles, advertise new products or offers, or to share information about new franchisees. The brand approach to social media is something you would need to establish at the outset.

Hypothetically, marketing via your own Facebook, Twitter and LinkedIn accounts could help you to target your network of friends and acquaintances as well as people in your region with special offers on a particular day of the week. Doing this would be a form of effective permission-based marketing, would ensure the likelihood of repeat sales and would help to build your franchise's profile. As a sign of how things may develop, McDonald's is one brand that manages a corporate Facebook page, but then allocates a tab for local content for US users. Users can enter their zip code (the equivalent of a postcode in the UK) to see content that is directly targeted for an outlet in that region.

In the UK, music group franchise Monkey Music is one franchise that manages its own Facebook timeline – a chronological wall of brand highlights or announcements. It features news from its franchisees around the country and comments from parents who take their babies and pre-school children to the franchise's classes. Ultimately, though, you need to be absolutely clear about the ground rules, and any social media activity is unlikely to be permitted without agreement and specific guidelines from the franchisor.

TOP TIPS FOR MARKETING YOUR FRANCHISE

You will need to know about methods your franchisor has built into your business format; which ones they don't use and why.

Sarah Cook, founder of marketing specialist Coconut Creatives, also has the following advice when it comes to marketing a franchise.

Use direct response advertising

There are two types of advertising – direct response advertising and brand advertising. Understanding the distinction between the two will immediately save you a fortune. Companies like Coca-Cola and large car manufacturers use brand advertising to build and increase awareness of their brand. Unless you have huge amounts of money that you are happy to lose, avoid brand advertising at all costs. For a small business it is a complete waste of money. The only type of advertising you ever want to consider is direct response advertising, the purpose of which is to produce a clear response.

Testing and measuring

It is absolutely essential to test and measure all of your advertising. If you are going to go for direct response advertising, you need to be able to measure the response, otherwise you'll not know if the advertisement is working.

At the very least you need to know how many people responded to the advert. You then need to compare that figure to the cost of the advertisement and you can immediately work out how profitable the advertisement was, or whether you should stop running it. One reason why radio and television advertising can be so high risk is that it's very difficult to test it on a small scale. Never invest in radio and television advertising unless it's money you can afford to lose.

Use fun and exciting headlines where possible

Be adventurous with your headlines. Test different versions to see what works best. There are no rules – except what works.

Remember AIDA

A classic formula used by advertisers is well worth remembering. The formula is AIDA. It stands for: **A**ttention: grab the reader's attention; **I**nterest: create an interest in your product or service; **D**esire: convert that interest into a strong desire to contact you and find out more; **A**ction: give your customers a reason to act now – for example, a free consultation or a buy one, get one free promotion. Follow this formula in every advertisement that you write or produce, and you'll greatly increase your chances of success.

Benefits, benefits, benefits

One of the principles that should drive all of your marketing is communicating the benefits of your business.

Successful selling

How you build sales in your franchise business depends to a large extent on the type of business you choose and on the extent and quality of your franchisor's training. Mail Boxes Etc., for example, covers the art of selling in great detail as part of its training for franchisees.

> I am a cruise expert, and offer a very personal service to my customers, who come back to me time and time again because of my service, my advice, my recommendations and my in-depth knowledge of the cruise industry. I will match customers to cruises and will very often offer bespoke packages to ensure the customer gets exactly what they want from their holiday.

Martin Spence, GoCruise

Establish a sales system

Shaun Thomson, chief executive at sales management training firm Sandler Training, says that sales is a series of skills that can be learned, developed and grown. He says:

> **As with most things in franchising, the first step is simple: you must have a sales system in place. Ideally, this will be taught to you by the franchisor. By having a sales process that can be replicated, you'll have a system to follow that will allow you to improve and highlight those areas that need attention.**

This means that the sales process can be broken down into simple steps and all stages can be practised, improved and mastered. Having such a system in place will also help as you grow your franchise and add other staff to your business. You'll be able to train them and mentor them on the sales process, as you'll all be talking the same sales language.

The basic skills you need are communication and people skills, regardless of the type of franchise you are operating. Every sale you make, whether it is face-to-face or on the phone, is an opportunity for you to get to know your customers. You can build on this to find out if existing customers are happy with your service, encourage them to do more business with you and ultimately get new customers on board.

Effective selling techniques

As mentioned above, you'll need to have a sales system in place, which ideally you can formulate with help from your franchisor. This will provide you with a basic structure that you can use to monitor and measure results, allowing you to make adjustments as necessary. Put yourself in your customers' shoes. People are most interested in themselves. They're not interested in your fantastic features and benefits or how many outlets your franchise has. So don't simply sell the features and benefits of your franchise – ask yourself what it is that your customers really want.

The amount of sales you make is proportional to the amount of information you gather, not the information you give out. One of the greatest skills you need to master in a sales environment is to be an effective listener. If you ask questions, you'll find out what your customers want and you'll be able to target your products or services more effectively.

Define your ideal prospect. It's a lot easier to go out to find clients when you know exactly what you're looking for. Also, if you have a detailed profile of your ideal customers, it helps when asking for referrals. But remember that not everyone who passes through your doors or makes a phone enquiry will be a potential customer. If people are not going to say 'yes' to a sale, then the next best thing is to get a 'no'. It will save you time and trouble, and avoid you spending resources on people who are not going to buy from you.

Continually assess your own sales techniques. When you come out of a sales meeting or put down the phone, take a few seconds to think about the interaction that has just occurred. If you could have handled things better, ask yourself, 'If I could have done one thing better, what would it have been?' and rehearse it with yourself for the next time.

> The Greensleeves offering is very simple. They believe in customer service and so provide excellent service at good prices. I am a strong believer in customer service – you cannot treat customers like cash machines, and because we deliver such a high standard, this is what brings in repeat business.
>
> *Steven Hook, Greensleeves*

Generating repeat sales

It almost goes without saying, the first and best way to generate repeat sales is to get it right the first time. Customers will return if they have received a professional, efficient and customer-friendly service. Building rapport and being able to deal with queries will ensure you are somebody the customer would go to if purchasing again.

While it may not be appropriate for low-value items, if a customer has purchased a service or a higher-value product from you, find out whether they are happy. Create a plan to follow up with after-sales support at a sensibly scheduled time. How long you leave between sale and follow-up may depend on the product or service the franchise offers. In addition, their feedback can help you or the franchise to improve your offering.

In order to market to existing customers you need accurate records of who they are and how to contact them, as well as what they've purchased from you in the past. You may also want to keep personal notes from previous conversations, which can help to maintain rapport or could even suggest likely future needs. Maintain contact according to the prescribed approach of your franchise, but this may involve tailored emails detailing new offers or services, as well as any discounts you are permitted to promote.

Becoming known in your local community may also help as your customers become used to seeing your name or the name of your franchise at functions and events in your region. Finally, keep an eye on what competitors might be offering. If customers are likely to switch because of price, offers and discounts, or because somebody is offering a better service, you need to be aware of it – and respond.

ATTRACTING AND KEEPING CUSTOMERS AT A GLANCE

- There are no hard-and-fast rules for creating a marketing strategy – you'll need to set your own goals.

- Under-promise and over-deliver – you'll exceed customer expectations.

- It's essential to test and measure your advertising.

- Listen to your customers and react to their needs.

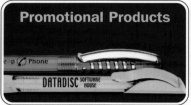

14.0

GROWING YOUR FRANCHISE

IN THIS CHAPTER

The fact that you've chosen to start a franchise suggests you're an incredibly motivated person, but once the doors have opened and the regular customers start flocking in and the orders come in on the phone, how can you ensure that you maintain that level of enthusiasm?

The start-up process is incredibly demanding, both physically and psychologically. After all that hard work you clearly need to slow down the pace slightly, but you can't sit back and hope the franchise will run itself. For one thing, you have a commitment to your franchisor, as set out in your franchise agreement, and you also have personal goals outlined in your business plan.

In this chapter, we'll look at:

- future opportunities
- managing staff
- managing yourself
- time management.

Future opportunities

Your biggest concerns as you grow your franchise, and turn your attention perhaps to expansion and purchasing other locations or territories, are likely to be keeping control of your finances and increasing profits and managing your time.

As a franchisee, certain systems will already be in place in your business, such as brand identity, a marketing strategy and the range of products or services you are expected to sell. While this means you have something to rely on, compared to first-time business owners, it can be a challenge mastering the franchise system and applying it consistently on a day-to-day basis. You may experience issues with quality control and there could be conflict in the franchisor/franchisee relationship as your franchise grows. The franchisor will be keen for you to maximise and increase sales: income for franchisors in franchised businesses is ordinarily linked to turnover, and franchisors will take a percentage of this as part of their income. As a franchisee, however, you'll be focused on creating and improving profits, which is where you'll be making your money.

Building a franchised business is a delicate balancing act where you aim to keep a tight rein on costs so that your overheads don't run out of control, while at the same time you strive to grow turnover to meet both your own and your franchisor's expectations. In your first year, you may feel impatient of the continuing control imposed by the franchisor. Communication between franchisor and franchisee will be vital as you build your franchise. If, as a franchisee, you have expectations that are not congruent with what the franchisor can deliver, you'll make the job of building your own franchise that much harder. It's an obligation on the franchisor's part to ensure they do not over-promise in any way, and it's an obligation on the part of the franchisee to acknowledge the different parties that are in it together and that it's going to be hard work.

You'll naturally become an expert in your business, so much so that you may consider branching out into other ones and purchasing additional outlets, but finding appropriate locations could be a challenge. Of course, you'll need to have demonstrated to your franchisor that you are a good candidate for running multiple outlets, and you will have to finance these new outlets. However, raising more finance from the bank should not be that difficult, particularly if you have a successful track record from your first franchise to back you up.

You may also identify sales and marketing opportunities that you are not allowed to take advantage of, as these fall outside the remit agreed with your franchisor. While this can at times be frustrating as you seek to grow the business, you need to remember the rules of franchising, and that it's important to have consistency across the franchise network. In some cases, you may be able to contribute ideas about ways of improving franchises at regional or local franchise meetings.

Not every franchise opportunity works out, and you may find after a year or two that franchising is no longer for you and you don't want to continue the business. However, you'll need to continue to commit to the business under the terms set out in your franchise agreement. The franchisor, too, will need to keep within the conditions set out in the agreement.

This is why agreements often have a fixed period, such as five years, to allow for sales of franchises, for modernising and refitting premises or for buying new equipment for use in the business. If, as a franchisee, you are considering renewing the contract for another five years or longer, you may be asked to invest further to ensure your facilities are brought into line with market trends.

Staff management

There's simply no avoiding the fact that a business is nothing without the service provided by the people running it. Unfortunately, while it's not hard to find people, it is difficult, especially in a retail franchise, where staff turnover is at its highest, to keep hold of good staff members.

To do that, and to keep your team motivated and bringing in the sales that keep your business healthy, you'll need to be familiar with the qualities that make for effective leadership and develop a management style that works. From employee number one, you'll also need to ensure that you have access, ordinarily provided by your franchisor, to the myriad of detail in HR legislation.

The minute you employ another person, you go from being a humble business owner to being a boss, a manager and the point from which authority and company culture flows. If you're not used to it, that can be quite a culture shock. Some people react by becoming too authoritarian; others try too hard to be their employees' friend and end up losing respect. To run a motivated, disciplined workforce you'll need to strike a balance between the two and lead by example. You'll have guidance from the franchisor in terms of training employees and monitoring their progress.

If you have decided to expand by purchasing additional outlets, you'll need to hire people who will accept your style and be able to train other employees in that same style without your presence. Turnover of employees is expensive and time consuming, so finding the right managers who can train to your standards and translate your vision should be high on your priority list before you even consider taking on a second location.

The value of networking

Once you've established yourself as a franchisee, you may find people more willing to confide in you and share their experiences with you, as you'll be able to offer them advice in return.

Networking should be an ongoing process. Many franchisors hold regional and local events where you can meet other franchisees and share experiences, as well as keep up to date with franchise developments. Try to mix with other franchisees and franchisors at these events, where you can get advice and seek support. As a franchisee, you mustn't think that useful advice or guidance can come only from other franchisees in the same sector. The principles of running a franchise are the same from one franchise to another and you'll be surprised at how friendly and open to communication people can be when they have the same goals as you do. The opportunities for franchisees from different networks to meet are currently limited, but the bfa is trying to build local franchise networks around the country for this exact purpose.

> Regular conference calls, here in the UK, are a chance to think aloud, share our experiences. Just the other day I talked with Andy, down in Exeter, about networking with chambers of commerce. Pooling our knowledge. There's always someone you can reach, who's been there before.
>
> *Nigel Dunand, Sandler Training*

Managing yourself

In the same way as you might set targets for staff, and key performance indicators (KPIs) to measure performance and flag training and resource needs, you need to do the same for yourself. If you see that you're not performing as you'd like, take stock. Don't be too harsh on yourself, though, as it'll almost certainly be the case that you're doing too much and need to delegate more.

Again, sharing experiences and networking can keep you motivated. Running any business can be a lonely experience, but with a franchise you have access to local and regional support within the network, so make use of this. Having people to share your experiences with can really lift the load and renew your determination. More than anything, though, make sure that you appreciate what you have achieved as well as what's left to do. If you want to maintain a successful business, you have to dedicate just as much time to your own self-development as to your franchise.

Your personal development

It can be hard to measure your personal development when you're your own boss. Granted, in your first few months of business you can expect your franchisor to pay regular visits to check that things are running smoothly and to answer any questions you may have, which will help with your personal development. But as you become more confident as a franchisee, these visits will become less regular. And just because your franchise turns over a tidy sum at the end of each month, that doesn't mean you're as effective as you could be as a leader. That's where the focused and planned development of your knowledge and skills through training can benefit you.

Running a franchise, much like running any other kind of small business, requires you to be multi-skilled. The role of franchisee can involve everything from buying stock and dealing with customers to ensuring consistency with other franchises, business planning and taking care of the accounts. Regardless of whether you have a hands-on position in all of these roles, you need to be at least familiar with what they entail.

If you employ someone with more experience than you and see them following certain processes, swallow your pride and ask them about it. They'll appreciate you showing an interest and you'll get valuable insight. Ask questions of your accountant. You may not be a whizz with numbers, but you still need to understand the basics of a tax form or balance sheet.

Time management

With so many hats to wear in your role as franchisee, managing your time effectively is absolutely essential, and this is where many people fall down. It's absolutely critical that you grasp the principles of strong time management from a very early stage.

The most important aspect of time management is to list and prioritise everything you need to do. This will allow you to recognise the difference between what's important and what's urgent. Running a franchise will involve various 'to do' lists. There are your long-term goals, such as growing turnover and improving your margins, nurturing and expanding your customer base and developing your own skills as a business owner. Next come your monthly goals, which could be setting sales targets, recruiting new staff, trying a new supplier or getting your accounts in order. And of course there'll be daily and weekly objectives to meet as well.

If you're running a retail franchise, certain times of the day will be busier than others and dictate when you can and can't focus on administrative or planning responsibilities. Whatever your role, you need to set aside enough time to get on with these tasks, as they are just as important as serving customers when it comes to running a successful establishment.

Here are a few tips for prioritising workloads and making sure you don't neglect important aspects of running your business.

- List all the tasks you need to do, and then prioritise them in order of what is most urgent and important.
- Don't underestimate the amount of time interruptions can steal from your schedule. When allocating time for a particular task, build in room for interruptions.
- Don't be afraid to turn off your phone or email and ask not to be disturbed when you really need to concentrate. If having no distractions helps you to get a task done more quickly, you may end up with extra time to deal with clients, customers or staff.
- Break large tasks up into manageable chunks. It's tempting to run lots of little errands instead of getting stuck in to a big, important job. However, completing it one stage at a time will make it seem less daunting.
- Build room into your schedule to deal with unexpected problems or events. If nothing unforeseen crops up, you'll end up ahead of schedule.
- Make sure no more than half your time is allocated to top-priority work. All those little jobs that aren't so time-sensitive will start to mount up if you don't crack on with them.
- If possible, delegate. You may think the franchise will fall apart if you don't oversee everything, but perhaps your time can be more profitably spent.

GROWING YOUR FRANCHISE AT A GLANCE

- Communication between you and your franchisor is vital, particularly in the first few months.

- Staff-management skills are important to master as your franchise grows.

- Make time for yourself. If you want to maintain a successful business, you have to dedicate just as much time to your own self-development as to your franchise.

- With so many hats to wear in your role as franchisee, managing your time effectively will be essential.

- Sadly, not every franchise opportunity works out, but you'll need to commit to the business for the length of time set out in the franchise agreement.

> Kumon is ideal when you have a young family. Most of the work is done at home, when I can pick it up and put it down when my own children dictate! It enables me to keep my children at home with me rather than having to put them into full-time childcare. I carry out my enrolments in the evenings when my husband is home to look after the children and put them to bed. Apart from my Saturday morning class, we have the luxury of spending all our weekends together.

Vicky West, Kumon

15.0

BUYING ADDITIONAL FRANCHISES

IN THIS CHAPTER

Most successful entrepreneurs are never happy with limits and like to continually test themselves by taking on new risks and challenges, such as expanding their business. Once you've been up and running as a franchisee and are starting to reap the rewards of all the hard work you've put in, you too may be tempted by thoughts of acquiring more franchise units to expand your business. You'll be in good company too. According to figures from the latest NatWest/bfa Franchise Survey, more franchisees own multiple units than in the previous year, with more than a quarter operating more than one unit – the average for a multiple unit franchisee is under three units.

In this chapter, we'll look at:

- why expand?
- when and how to consider expanding
- what to watch out for
- the different choices available.

Why expand?

Put simply, owning multi-unit (more than one) franchises rather than just one is likely to mean that you can expect to make more money. You may also be attracted by the idea of building a 'mini-empire' or be seeking a further challenge once you have got over the initial excitement and rollercoaster ride of becoming a franchisee.

Additionally, you can benefit from economies of scale in your business, across areas such as payroll and accountancy. And owning a bigger business means you can provide more career opportunities for your employees. You'll find that banks are likely to look more kindly on you too, as they typically lend franchisees almost all of the costs required to buy an additional outlet, provided you have a strong track record.

What it takes

As we've discussed previously in this book, starting a franchise is a lower-risk option than starting a business from scratch, as you are working with a proven business model and can benefit from additional support. As a franchisee, however, guaranteeing success means being prepared to put in the hard work, invest in training, assess your strengths and weaknesses and ask for help where necessary. And the same goes if you wish to purchase any additional franchises, in different locations or territories.

The more prepared you are to work hard and commit yourself to making your initial franchise a success, the better your prospects of being able to expand by buying additional franchise units, often referred to as multi-unit rights. You'll need energy, drive and enthusiasm – and plenty of it!

This is because franchisors have very strict standards when it comes to granting these rights – the quality of a franchisor's network is only as strong as its weakest franchise owner. Of course, running one successful franchise often means it's easier the second time around, but you must still be able to demonstrate a successful track record in running a business, including the ability to manage and motivate your staff, handle sales and cope with day-to-day responsibilities. You'll be expected to come up with a host of good reasons for wanting to expand, and answers to how you are going to meet the new demands and challenges that will be thrown at you.

In some respects, if you want to expand, you'll have to go back to square one. You'll have to assess your financial situation and stump up the additional finance needed to purchase these new units, conduct research into your proposed territory and assess the strength of the competition.

When is the right time?

It's difficult to put a finger on when is the right time to expand. You'll need to have built up a successful track record in your existing outlet and it would be unwise to even consider expanding unless you were absolutely comfortable with your skills and abilities as a franchisee – and this can take a lot longer than you think. You'll also need to take into account some practical considerations, such as whether you have enough money to expand and the resources to do so, such as additional employees.

Some franchisors prefer that you start additional outlets later rather than sooner, so as to have time to assess whether you do indeed have the right skills to expand. As a reward for waiting, they may offer you a second franchise at a reduced rate. Others will give you more practical help to assess your readiness for expansion. Multi-unit franchisees at Domino's Pizza, for example, typically work their way up through the business and then receive additional management training from the franchisor so they can hire their own store managers. This means the transition to another franchise can be made more smoothly. In its network, 60% of franchisees now own more than one store and 40% own at least three. At McDonald's, the average number of restaurants per franchisee has risen from two to four.

Some things to consider

Ask yourself the following. Choosing to expand equates to relinquishing some control over your original franchise: is this the lifestyle that you want? You'll certainly be freed from many of the day-to-day responsibilities, but in some respects you could find yourself even more busy than before.

Your management skills will be tested now more than ever before, as running a multi-unit franchise is quite different from running a single operation. You can't be in more than one place at the same time, so you'll need to ensure that your employees will be able to deliver your service or product to your same exacting standards. And since you can't be everywhere at once, you'll need to be where the problems or the opportunities are.

> The two centres are only six miles apart so it works well from marketing and word-of-mouth points of view. I have many students who 'bunny-hop' between my centres, so it provides families with flexibility and this continues to prove a good selling point. Running two centres with two children is a challenge, but one I enjoy!
>
> *Vicky West, Kumon*

Consider the sector you chose for your franchise in the first place. Does it lend itself to a multi-unit model, and if so, have other franchisees successfully expanded from one to several franchises? If not, what have been the potential obstacles? In the UK, hotel and catering franchisees are those most likely to be running multi-unit businesses, while those in the transport/vehicle services sector are least likely, according to figures from the latest NatWest/bfa Franchise Survey. The statistics reflect the natural differences in the sales process between a low customer-spend retail business, where customers buy the product not the person, and business-to-business high-value sales, where clients buy the professional skills of the individual franchisee. If it's you and your skills that clients buy, it's more difficult to grow beyond your own capacity to deliver.

If multi-unit ownership is on the cards, examine your finances. Do you have enough capital to expand? Many franchisees use the profits from their existing franchise to fund their expansion – if you choose this route, what will you live on in the meantime?

EXPANSION: KEY POINTS

- It can present you with a new challenge and an opportunity to make money.

- You can benefit from economies of scale.

- You will have to be prepared to give up some control of your existing franchise.

- You'll need to invest further in time management.

What to watch out for

Franchisors may sometimes be wary of allowing you to expand the business to more than one or several units. They may believe that if you are making a lot of money, then you'll be less inclined to work hard, harming potential profits in the long term. And some franchisees face numerous challenges with just one franchise, let alone several. For some, the transition from running a small franchise to being in charge of several can be more than they anticipated.

Remember, too, that franchising is a two-way process between you and the franchisor. You'll also need to do your homework and consider how well equipped the franchisor is or will be to run multi-unit franchises, and if they have existing ones already, ask yourself how successful they are. Does the franchisor have the necessary financial resources to help support you as a multi-unit franchisee? A good franchisor, for example, will want to help you out with things on a practical level, such as with sourcing new sites or gaining planning permission.

Multiple choice

When it comes to expanding, there are a few options you can pursue. You can buy the same franchise from an existing franchisee in a different area, for example. You may hear about such opportunities at regional meetings held by your franchisor or through a newsletter sent to existing franchisees. Be very wary of franchises that appear to have changed hands many times over. For any business to have had several owners is often not a good sign, and implies that it may have been in trouble. Be sure to get accurate financial records of the history of any potential franchise purchase before going any further. You must ask the existing franchisee questions, but also need to quiz your franchisor.

In a small number of franchises in the UK, you could opt for what is known as an 'area franchise', where you buy the rights to an entire area and then establish franchises within that area. The number of franchises you'll be expected to set up varies – in some cases the contract will specify that a certain number must be set up within a certain time, in others the number you open is left entirely up to you. Be careful and ensure there is enough profit in the business, and that there will continue to be enough profit, to support unit franchisees and the franchisor.

Master franchising

As you research and think about buying an additional franchise, you may come across 'master franchising'. This is the term used to describe securing exclusive rights to develop an international franchisor's brand and trading system in the UK. Many franchisors from the US and across Europe have set up operations in the UK by granting master franchise rights. Your role would be to oversee the expansion in the UK, either by setting up owned outlets, or by recruiting a sub-franchised network or by doing a mix of the two. Sub-franchising involves become a franchisor in your area and earning a management service fee from your sub-franchisees' turnovers.

As a master franchisee, you'll be expected to recruit, train and support franchisees at a local level. As with other franchises, the cost of a master franchise depends on a number of factors, such as location, market potential, brand size and reputation and, ultimately, the perceived value set by the franchisor and agreed by you as the master franchisee.

As a rough guide, to set up an established international franchise in the UK you would be looking at spending several hundreds of thousands of pounds. This might seem like a considerable investment, but, like most franchises, this is an investment that will become an asset over the long term – assuming, of course, that the business develops in line with expectations. Under the terms of your franchise agreement you may be able to sell this on at a profit, and at the very least, if the master franchise performs in line with expectations, you may generate a solid income.

When thinking about expanding and becoming a master franchisee, there are factors to take into consideration, the most important of which is probably the working capital required, as you'll need a substantial outlay in order to ensure a successful franchise launch and achieve the kind of market penetration required to establish this type of franchise growth.

To become a master franchisee, you'll need all the skills required to expand your franchise and that little bit more, as more investment and working capital are required than if you were buying additional units. You'll also be responsible for ensuring that all franchisees' obligations are met and you'll need to supply support and training on a regular basis. In short, you will be setting yourself up as a franchisor, enabling other people, your franchisees, to start their own new businesses under your brand and business system. You need to know what you'll be letting yourself in for.

EXPANDING YOUR FRANCHISE

. . . the pros

- You can benefit from economies of scale.

- You're likely to make more money.

- It will help you to develop additional skills.

- You may get greater job satisfaction overseeing a small empire.

- It's easier to raise finance.

- The different businesses can often complement each other.

. . . the cons

- You'll need exceptional management skills.

- You'll need to be comfortable delegating to staff.

- You'll have to make yourself available at your different franchises, which can be tiring and time consuming.

- There will be more paperwork to complete.

- Your work–life balance may need to be put on the back burner for a while.

- Much of your success will depend on the level of support you get from your franchisor.

The following companies are all accredited members of the bfa that have chosen to support this publication through advertising. In this section you will find useful examples of the different types of franchise businesses operating in the UK. There are also helpful case studies of franchisees to give you a better idea of the type of business you would end up running should you choose to buy this type of franchise.

AUTOMOTIVE

Driver Hire Nationwide
Snap-on Tools
Mac Tools

COMPANY PROFILE

Driver Hire Nationwide

An experienced company . . .
Over the last 25 years Driver Hire has become the UK's largest specialist supplier of transport and logistics staff. It is also one of the most successful and respected management franchise brands in the UK. We are regular finalists in the bfa Franchisor of the Year Award, one of three winners in 2012 and outright winners in 2006.

A growing market
Driver Hire operates in a huge market – the UK recruitment industry is estimated to be worth almost £20bn a year. Its franchise network supplies thousands of satisfied customers each year, from multi-national freight companies to builders' merchants, parcel carriers and local authorities. What's more, when the UK economy is experiencing uncertain times, Driver Hire's core service of supplying temporary staff is ideally suited, giving flexibility to people looking to control their workforce costs.

A growing business
Driver Hire recently won the backing of Lloyds Development Capital to support its continued growth. Financial backing from a proven investment company is a positive endorsement for the business and will help to create further development opportunities for the Driver Hire group and its franchisees.

The franchise package
As you'd expect from a leading franchise, Driver Hire is dedicated to its franchisees and provides a comprehensive support package, helping you to plan, launch and develop your business to its maximum potential.

The support package
The support package includes:

- the benefit of the Driver Hire brand, which is acknowledged as a market leader

- support from a 50-strong head office team, all dedicated to helping you succeed

- an intensive two-week foundation training course

- a wealth of marketing and promotional material aimed at attracting customers and candidates

- an industry-leading website incorporating a jobs board and a personalised microsite to promote your own office

- a National Accounts team delivering nationally negotiated contracts with key customers

- a centralised customer invoicing system

- Driver Hire's unique, industry-leading computer software package

- valuable customer and business intelligence provided on a regular basis

- a central compliance team helping you to maintain business processes and quality standards

- a range of networking opportunities aimed at improving skills and knowledge by sharing best practice

Throughout the lifetime of your Driver Hire franchise you will be allocated an Area Development Manager (ADM) to provide sales support to you and your staff. In the first few months of trading – whilst you find your feet – intensive support will be provided by your ADM and head office staff.

Financial returns

The established Driver Hire business model translates into success for its franchisees. In 2011/2012, 40% of all franchisees achieved annual sales of over £750,000 – more than twice the UK franchise average turnover, according to the latest NatWest/bfa survey. Sixteen Drives Hire offices surpassed the magic £1 million mark.

Low fixed costs mean that franchisees who follow the system and operate their business effectively can take home 10–12% of turnover and build a significant capital value as their business grows.

Investment

Even though Driver Hire already has a thriving UK network there are still some great opportunities for new franchisees to join us. It currently has a number of key UK locations, including start-up territories and franchise resales. Entry-level investment for a start-up is £30,000 for the franchise licence fee and additional capital of £10,000 is recommended for set-up costs and fees. The price of a franchise resale will vary according to the profitability and trading history of the individual business.

People like you
No two franchisees are the same, but to be truly successful with Driver Hire, it goes without saying that you'll be ambitious, hard working, committed and self-motivated.

You'll also be a good relationship builder – Driver Hire is a sales-focused organisation, so you will have lots of direct customer contact.

Good organisational skills are vital, together with the discipline to work within a structured environment where legislative compliance is of paramount importance. You'll also need basic IT skills and a reasonable understanding of finance.

However, you won't need any previous experience either in recruitment or in the transport sector – Driver Hire's training provides you with all the required knowledge and skills to get your business off to a flying start.

The next step
If you'd like to achieve your personal goals by sharing in Driver Hire's success, call Kasia Baldwin, Franchise Marketing Manager, on 01274 361073 or email franchise@driverhire.co.uk.
Web: www.driverhirefranchise.co.uk

CASE STUDY

Driver Hire Nationwide

Franchisee: Manjit Singh
Location: Enfield

Manjit's first experience of running a business was his investment in an independent wine shop – more commonly known as a 'corner shop'. Whilst this gained some success, he reached a point where he needed guidance on moving the business forward and therefore decided to sell up and look at various business-to-business management franchise opportunities – in order to access a business model where advice and support were readily available.

Building your business

Manjit Singh opened the Driver Hire Enfield office in April 2007 with nothing more than a database of lapsed clients and candidates in a second-floor office within a business complex. With the support of the Driver Hire head office team, neighbouring Driver Hire franchisees and one other member of staff, his first week of trading billed three clients just over £1,000. In the space of six months and with a lot of hard work, the Enfield office under Manjit had a record turnover week – billing just over £15,000.

'In my first year and a half of trading the growth we achieved was more than I could have initially imagined. Going from a turnover of £0 to £450,000 in year one had me planning grand things to spend the profits on!' comments Manjit.

Challenging times

When the credit crunch started in September 2008, Manjit initially didn't experience any signs of a downturn in business. However, by April 2009 the impact became apparent. According to Manjit, thoughts of leaving the business were setting in. 'By May 2009 I achieved my lowest weekly turnover since opening, and I made my first monthly loss in December 2009. I started to seriously consider walking away with what cash reserves I had left – and if I was lucky enough to find a buyer, maybe even my franchise fee.'

Road to recovery

At this point Manjit turned to his franchisor for support – something he couldn't have done when running his 'corner shop'. When faced with challenging times, the value of the old adage 'being in business for yourself but not by yourself' becomes apparent when working within a franchise model.

Manjit recalls: 'After a number of discussions with Driver Hire franchisor directors, the message I got was that I had the right attitude to recover and take the business to bigger and better things. They also highlighted that while some other offices had seen revenues fall there were many offices that were in fact growing their business. This was a turning point – for me, proof that Driver Hire's core business was sound and that there would always be demand for its services. It was this that gave me the reassurance that I was looking for to continue, to work with my franchisor to come up with a recovery plan.'

He adds: 'It was time for me to make use of all the tools, systems and support mechanisms put in place by my franchisor, instead of trying to battle through on my own.'

For Manjit this included:

- attending all regional meetings and conferences
- holding regular meetings and working closely with his area development manager
- building good working relationships with neighbouring Driver Hire franchises
- sending out bespoke mailshots, assisted by the Driver Hire marketing team and press officer
- using the Driver Hire league tables as a motivator for the office team
- making operational changes in his office: job roles, bonus structure and tactical pricing.

Onwards and upwards

With hard work and as a result of using the Driver Hire network and support structure, Manjit saw his business start to improve and grow once again. In the financial year 2010/2011 Driver Hire Enfield achieved a turnover in excess of £1 million, and in 2011/2012 that figure rose again to £1.6 million in a tough business climate. This has meant that Manjit has also been able to expand the team to further invest in his business's future growth.

Rewards

In September 2011, the hard work and effort was recognised and rewarded. Manjit – for his excellence in franchising – made it to the regional finals of the bfa Franchisee of the Year

Awards. Driver Hire was also proud to award Manjit and his team the Rose Bowl Award for endeavour at its annual winter conference, which was held in Edinburgh in January 2012.

Manjit adds: 'Running a business is always going to be a rollercoaster affair, with challenges along the way, but the support and dedication provided by the Driver Hire team and network has meant that I know I'm not alone and can push forward with a positive outlook. Being recognised for the hard work is an added bonus and certainly helps to motivate me and the team.'

COMPANY PROFILE

Snap-on Tools

Industry leaders

Snap-on Incorporated is a leading global developer, manufacturer and marketer of tool and equipment solutions for professional tool users, including high-quality hand tools and tool storage, workshop equipment, information and management systems.

Snap-on is very proud of 90 years of one-to-one relationships with professional tool users. The company sells its products and services in over 150 countries worldwide, consistently delivering high-value-added products and services. Its customers include automotive workshops and their technicians, manufacturers, users in aerospace, commercial aviation, the marine industry, construction, agriculture, mining, oil and gas industries, together with military forces worldwide.

Operating in more than 130 countries with over 22,000 products, Snap-on has more than 4,800 franchisees worldwide.

In the UK, Snap-on's head office and distribution centre is located in Kettering, Northamptonshire. It has a network of more than 430 franchisees and was voted the British Franchise Association 2007 Franchisor of the Year.

In 2008 it was awarded the coveted 'Business Superbrands' status, and in 2011 it ranked 203rd, confirming it as one of the strongest business-to-business brands in the UK.

In 2011 Snap-on was ranked 6th in the Franchise Direct Top Global Franchises, reinforcing how dominant its brand and franchise are.

Be in business with the best . . .

Snap-on is looking for highly motivated individuals with the determination to succeed in a competitive environment. An ideal Snap-on franchisee devotes considerable time and attention to making their franchise a success and must be capable of building long-term relationships with their customers. Snap-on has built its business on service, and its franchisees understand that service is integral to their success.

Franchisees call on their customers every week, at various places of business including:

- main car dealerships

- independent repair garages

- body shops

- bus companies

- truck repairers

- haulage contractors

- auto electricians

- motor-cycle workshops

- plant hire/forklifts

- council depots

- agricultural engineers

- tyre and exhaust depots

- quarries

- marine yards

- airports.

A business on wheels

Franchisees operate from mobile stores which provide the necessary tool-display area to encourage impulse buying at their customer's place of business. They deliver a personalised, professional service associated with the Snap-on brand. Every franchisee also has an 'office on wheels,' as each Snap-on van is equipped with its own personal computer system.

Why Snap-on?

There are some unique features to the Snap-on franchise that set it apart from most of the market today:

- an award-winning franchise system

- no franchise fee

- established company

- comprehensive product line

- no advertising fee

- financial assistance

- no management fee

- ongoing training and support

- franchisee business software

- credit assistance programmes.

Compare these features with any other franchise, and you will agree that the Snap-on proposition is unique. These features, coupled with the legendary product quality, make Snap-on's franchise offering second to none.

Training and support

Training is essential to getting a new franchise off to a good start. Snap-on sees training as a process, not a one-time event. You will be assigned to a field group of approximately 12–16 franchisees, with your initial training covering:

- product knowledge

- policies and procedures

- sales training

- franchisee computer sales system

- credit programmes

- record keeping

- van display.

And it doesn't stop there!

Over the following weeks, your field manager will accompany you on your route to help train you in the day-to-day aspects of the business. You will continue to be assigned to your field group and will attend regular meetings to hear about new products, sales aids, promotions and sales programmes. Working with your field manager is like having your own personal trainer!

Financial information

Snap-on is a $2.6 billion, Standard and Poor's 500 company headquartered in Kenosha, Wisconsin and employs approximately 14,000 staff worldwide. As the market leader of tool and equipment solutions, Snap-on Tools provides you with an opportunity to invest in a financially strong company with an outstanding reputation for quality, service and innovation.

Snap-on has a range of finance packages available to qualifying candidates.

Who's ideal for us?

We look for integrity and professionalism and a contributive, co-operative spirit. An ideal Snap-on franchisee will possess the willingness to devote their full time and attention to making their business a success, along with an ability to deal effectively with customers, suppliers and the community.

A successful Snap-on franchise requires hard work, planning and the development of personal relationships with customers. As a Snap-on franchisee, you will enjoy a professional and respected position in the tool industry, with excellent income potential.

You will need the communication skills to talk to people at all levels, the ability to sell on a one-to-one basis and the drive, enthusiasm and sheer determination to be successful.

If you believe you have the qualities to make a success of your own business, we would like to hear from you.

Territories/locations

We have opportunities in most areas of the UK and Ireland.

If you've ever wondered what it would be like to lead the pack, to represent the best of the best and to have the time of your life while you're at it, you owe it to yourself to find out more about the Snap-on franchise opportunity and be in business with the best.

CASE STUDY

Snap-on Tools

Franchisee: Tim Adkin
Location: Scarborough

You don't need to know much about the product to start a Snap-on franchise. Improbable? In reality this was a positive advantage for Scarborough-based franchisee Tim Adkin when he started his business 13 years ago. 'I found that not being familiar with the product meant I had to use other selling methods. I quizzed my customers about the items they picked up and they told me the features and benefits of the various tools. It's an excellent technique, as the technician-customer ends up selling it to himself, and it certainly built my fund of product knowledge.'

Tim was never particularly interested in the automotive world – he'd rather watch *The Apprentice* than *Top Gear*. It was the joy of selling that brought Tim into the franchise world.

From market stall to mobile store

A market trader for 14 years, Tim always had a burning desire to sell and to make money. Leaving school with no qualifications, he set up his own market stall selling Marks & Spencer seconds, which for quite a while made him a really good living.

Over time, boutique shops started to open in the town and impacted on his sales. He kept the stall going as long as possible but the downward trend meant that something had to change.

Tim's wife, Sandra, offered a solution – she would run the market stall so that he could enrol at college. First came an HND and then he graduated with a business degree. Not bad for someone who couldn't wait to leave school as a teenager!

Tim realised that the stall had no future and closed it down. Determined to use his newly acquired qualifications, he applied for sales jobs with various multi-national companies. 'Despite being shortlisted I was unsuccessful. My disappointment in not being selected was tempered on seeing an advert to run a company store for Snap-on Tools.

'I knew Snap-on was a good brand and a class product sold directly to vehicle-technician customers from a mobile store, but little else.'

Potential profits

The company-store programme at that time allowed would-be entrepreneurs like Tim to join Snap-on and earn very good money on a salary and commission basis. Half of his commission was 'reserved' for the day when he chose to convert to franchisee status, although, as Tim says, 'To be honest I didn't really relish this prospect as I perceived a franchise to be too restrictive.'

The potential profits changed his mind. 'This was the carrot for me. I love wheeling and dealing – nothing appeals to me more. Selling is what gives me the buzz! What amazed me is that I became accustomed to working within Snap-on's constraints and programmes, and I'd even go so far as to say I fell in love with the whole business.'

Dream orders

One part of the Snap-on programme that Tim found to be most effective was the 'needs list'. Needs lists were first used in the days of the Great Depression, starting in 1928. In those difficult times, when customers didn't have any money, Snap-on salesman invited them to make a list of those products that they would wish to own when money became available.

In those days they called them 'dream orders'. Tim continues today gathering dream orders from his customers: 'My customers only have to pick something up and it's on their list, but we have a laugh about it and it still works, despite them being wise to my technique! I have a great relationship with my customers and this makes them easier to sell to, because I know what makes them tick.'

Tim likes the financial benefits his franchise provides. He lives and works in a great part of the country and likes nothing more than going cycling at the weekend, enjoying a few pints en route. Also a keen diver, he's just booked a holiday in Croatia, staying on a chartered yacht!

His 13-year-old daughter, Callandra, likes horse riding and her younger sister, Coralie, enjoys playing the piano and is looking to go on a surfing course. Tim says: 'We feel we can give our kids the best in life – what could be better than that? Sandra is very much a part of the business too. As well as running our house and looking after the children she does all my paperwork and even drives another van for me, running errands and taking urgent orders to customers.'

Tim says: 'Snap-on offers a great support system, and there is always help there if I need it. I feel that the best thing they gave me was the confidence to go out there on my own and sell tools with only a small amount of product knowledge. It just proves that you don't need a background in the automotive business to make it at Snap-on. It's long hours and hard work, but the benefits for me and my family are beyond measure and I always tell people that.'

COMPANY PROFILE

Mac Tools

Mac Tools is a full member of the British Franchise Association and part of Stanley Black & Decker, an $8+ billion global organisation, and owner of the world-famous Stanley and Black & Decker brands.

If you have the desire and passion to work for yourself, available cash of £15,000 and the ability to build relationships, you can be a part of this exciting story.

Your investment and rewards

As a Mac Tools franchisee – as with any franchise – your success depends on the investment you are prepared and able to make. That investment will be both personal (time and effort) and financial.

The total franchise package costs £50,000. Unlike in many other franchises, the bulk of this cost is starter stock that you will sell on at a profit, and includes everything you need to get started.

Opportunities

Existing Mac Tools franchisees are typically earning gross profits ranging from £50,000 to £75,000 from one territory, and there are various territories available across the UK.

The opportunity is there for you to build the goodwill asset value of your territory and sell it on as a going concern to an existing or new Mac Tools franchisee.

Your life as a Mac Tools franchise owner

This is an exciting opportunity for you to be your own boss and work from home; to fulfil that dream of owning your own business.

Mac Tools provides you with a professionally equipped van, which is stocked with a wide and world-class range of products for you to sell. You will be allocated a territory, and a database of all the known automotive-relevant outlets within it, which will give you a minimum of 300 potential customers from the day you start. You will then be able to sell directly to customers by calling in to their workshops on a regular and reliable basis.

There is no charge from Mac Tools for ongoing royalties so you keep 100% of your profit.

What you can expect from Mac Tools

Mac Tools provides a full support team. The following are some examples of the help you will receive.

Your Mac Tools licence

- Allows you to operate under the highly reputable Mac Tools brand.

- Gives you a proven system to help you build your own successful business.

- Provides access to the comprehensive and innovative Mac Tools branded product range.

- Allows access to Stanley Black & Decker's first-class Facom, Britool and DeWalt brands.

- Gives the ability to build your territory into a valuable asset and sell it on as a going concern.

Comprehensive training

- You will be flown to the USA for product, sales and business training at Mac Tools' 'Tool School' in Columbus, Ohio.

- You will receive market-specific and business-planning training as part of your UK induction.

- You will spend time with your franchisee support manager and current franchisees in the field.

- Ongoing training, development and support will be provided.

Professional marketing support

■ Promotional flyers, catalogues, information leaflets and online support will help you to drive sales.

■ There are regular regional meetings where you'll meet other franchisees and receive training and can take advantage of new products and promotions.

■ You can attend the Toolfair exhibition, which offers an opportunity to meet other franchisees and buy the latest tools.

■ You will have access to exclusive sponsorship and brand-recognition deals.

What does Mac Tools expect from you?

■ Experience is an advantage, but attitude is essential.

■ Previous sales and business experience and a basic knowledge of mechanics' tools will help.

■ Self-motivation.

■ People skills.

■ Reliability.

■ Financial stability, clear credit history and liquid capital of £15,000.

■ Full driving licence.

"Over 30 years and still going strong, what more can a franchise offer?"

Name Badges

Promotional Products
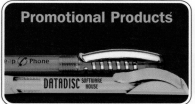

Display Posters

Business Gifts

Corporate Clothing

Signage

Continuous Support

- Extensive marketing tools & collateral
- Centralised marketing programmes
- Integrated Business Planning
- Proven profit margins
- On-going training and support
- In-house procurement service
- Top owners achieving £1M plus p.a.
- Franchisors who know franchising
- Equipment supplied and installed
- Weekly communication
- Regular regional meetings
- Bi-annual Conference

Sally Findlay Recognition Express, Mid Surrey

"The support has been first class with excellent material and an ever-improving range of centralised marketing programmes.

Jan Chidley, Franchise Owner for Hull and East Riding had been out of the workplace for some 18 years and was apprehensive about starting her own business.

"The support I've received from Recognition Express has been exceptional, so much so that at the end of my first year I had achieved all my financial targets and made the transition to Business Owner. The business is going extremely well."

Alex Newman was a senior employee at Recognition Express and took the plunge to become a franchisee

Says Alex: "Buying a Recognition Express franchise (Coventry) has given me a unique opportunity to become a business owner at such a young age. The market potential is massive and we have seen a range of companies use our products from small to medium businesses to international groups. Almost every business or organisation uses some of our range."

Full Franchise Package available for £35,000 plus VAT

For further information contact:

Sue Toplis
t: 01530 513300
e: stoplis@recognition-express.com

www.recognition-express.com

bfa FULL MEMBER

PROUD TO FRANCHISE
LOCAL BUSINESS I NATIONAL SUPPORT

Recognition EXPRESS

Unique Solutions in Promoting Your Image

BUSINESS SERVICES

BCR Associates
Sandler Training
Business Doctors
Recognition Express

COMPANY PROFILE

BCR Associates

Be part of it: enjoy life as a BCR associates business owner
Running your own business requires hard work, determination and entrepreneurial flair. BCR Associates franchisees all share a common goal – to develop a thriving, flourishing business that will deliver a comfortable income – whilst also addressing

the importance of an improved work–life balance. There is also one other significant trait that is prevalent throughout BCR's franchise network: passion – the passion to succeed, and a passionate belief in the solid business proposition BCR Associates offers its clients.

As a franchisee you are able to access the proven business model BCR has established in the business cost-reduction sector, helping your clients to achieve enhanced profitability by cutting overspend on essential running costs.

We're different
The fact that you will be trading in a recession-proof sector (indeed, BCR Associates' business thrives during tough economic times) is reassuring in itself, but add to that the unique 'win win' concept – **clients pay nothing** to have their essential services reviewed but **receive 100% of any savings** achieved – and it is quickly apparent that BCR Associates' offer differs dramatically from that of others operating in the same field.

BCR Associates has saved its customers an incredible £1,410,505 over the past 12 months. At best, your clients will benefit from trimming unnecessary costs affecting the bottom line, and at worst they receive a totally free business health check. Using the specialist resource based at head office, you will be able to negotiate the very best deals on the market for your clients – deals that are often only available exclusively via the BCR Associates procurement team.

Once you've decided that BCR Associates is the right business for you – and we've confirmed that you have the appropriate competencies and skills, combined with the vision and enthusiasm required to operate under our reputable brand name – you will join a network of like-minded, high-calibre franchisees. The transition from training to trading has been specifically designed to ensure our franchisees can hit the ground running within a relatively short time frame, courtesy of our 120-day integrated fast-launch programme. Initially you will receive one week of intensive training delivered by the experts at head office, which will equip you with the core knowledge needed to kick-start your new venture. We will also provide you with the necessary marketing collateral to support the business.

As we don't impose geographical territories on our franchisees, you will be able to begin contacting your existing business network immediately, to introduce them to the benefits of the BCR Associates cost-reduction service. Once you have established some leads and gathered the relevant information to carry out a cost review, you will return to head office for further detailed training about the cost-reduction areas we work in. Although you will have acquired the skills to coordinate a cost review, you will be safe in the knowledge that there is always access to the specialists at head office to provide additional guidance if necessary.

Following the initial cost review for a customer, you will action any changes and manage the account on their behalf. On average, BCR Associates customers can expect to achieve a 27% reduction on running costs. After the savings have been made you will receive commission from the suppliers, but you don't need to worry about chasing money, as all invoicing is handled on your behalf by head office – enabling you to focus on what really matters: building a successful business. Of course, once you have realised the initial savings for your customer you will have the perfect opportunity to cross-sell other cost-reduction services. And with 9 out of 10 customers staying loyal to BCR Associates, and the residual income our business model offers, you will continue to earn an income for the lifetime of that client.

Looking ahead

In time you can expect to see your business grow and deliver a healthy income while you get to enjoy the benefits of a more balanced, flexible lifestyle. After just two years one of our franchisees has a client base of 240 and a five-figure monthly income . . . but don't just take our word for it! We encourage you to talk to our franchisees yourself to get their honest take on what running a BCR Associates cost-reduction franchise is really like.

If you are interested in finding out more about the BCR Associates franchise opportunity, visit bcrassociatesfranchise.co.uk, call us on 0844 880 9838, or email franchise@bcrassociates.co.uk.

CASE STUDY

BCR Associates

Franchisees: Nigel and Pip Collins

Having built a career in the mortgage industry, when the housing market plummeted Nigel saw his income disappear overnight. Nigel and his wife, Pip, lost everything, including their house, but in the early part of 2009 Nigel learned about the BCR Associates franchise opportunity. 'I arranged a meeting with the two founding directors and was very impressed with the business model. What particularly attracted me to the proposition was the simplicity and universal attraction that the proposition offered – "no cost or risk to the client".'

Support

Nigel and Pip set their business up in an office in their house.

After a week of intensive training they left with the information and collateral required to contact their existing business network and introduce the benefits of the BCR Associates cost-reduction service. Once they had established potential customers they returned to head office for further technical training to get the knowledge required to carry out a cost review. 'The training at the outset was excellent. I was given a thorough overview of the cost-reduction industry and Pip received full training on the bespoke customer relationship management system.'

In addition to the 120-day fast-launch training programme, the experts at head office are on hand at all times to guide franchisees through any questions or issues they have. 'I know there are always specialists in all areas to speak to should we need any expert advice. For example, I had an issue with an energy contract for a customer and with the deadline looming I was unable to beat the quote the client had sourced elsewhere. I spoke to the energy technical specialist at head office and through his in-depth knowledge we were able to identify a competitive price. Without his assistance and technical input we would not have secured the deal.'

No looking back

'Thinking back, it wasn't always easy; at the beginning we had to move house three times in six months and the stress of that made it difficult to focus our full attention on the business. However, we have built a loyal customer base which now brings in a five-figure monthly income. We thoroughly enjoy our work and are delighted with the decision we made to become franchisees – there is nothing more satisfying than saving our customers thousands of pounds off their cost base and earning good levels of income at the same time.'

Advice

'I would have no hesitation in recommending a BCR Associates franchise. I would say though that it is important you discover if it is the right franchise for you. Make sure you do a lot of research and visit competitors. You'll then have all the information you need to make that life-changing decision.'

If you are interested in finding out more about the BCR Associates franchise opportunity, visit bcrassociatesfranchise.co.uk, call us on 0844 880 9838, or email franchise@bcrassociates.co.uk.

COMPANY PROFILE

Sandler Training

You are now leaving the beaten track
Have you just paused? Unsure about entering uncharted territory? Or do you instinctively choose the road less travelled?

Sandler helps businesses to reach the summit of their sales ambitions. That needs boldness, because it's not a well-marked route. The well-marked route is where everyone else is. Sandler – and the businesses it helps – knows that all the normal, signposted roads would just lead them to form an orderly queue, behind their competitors.

The beaten track is for the easily beaten. Freedom – and success – comes when we're bold.

Businesses that choose to leave the beaten track need more than a map and a compass. They need someone who knows how to negotiate the terrain, off-road; who will know when to encourage them to be bold. They need a guide.

Since you are still reading, then maybe that guide could be you.

Sherpas, not shepherds
Sheep love the beaten track; the comfort of the herd; the unambitious reassurance of the low-lying pastures; the whistles and barks that mean they don't have to think where to go.

With Sandler, your clients are not sheep. So they don't need a shepherd.

Your clients are bold business leaders – they have made brave choices and taken risks as they lead their business. They don't want hand holding – they want someone to show them the hand-holds – where to reach; how high to stretch.

As a Sandler consultant, you'll be alongside, guiding their progress and giving ongoing support – like a Sherpa, not like a shepherd.

Growing sales: sales people need not apply
Your clients are rarely sales people – so they don't expect you to be a salesperson, either. Your clients are more likely to be called owner, partner, MD, CEO; to be entrepreneurial and ambitious; to be thinking strategically about growing their own business. Just like you.

And you can guide these business leaders, because you will have done everything you ask them to do – first. You'll be sure that it works, because it has worked for you. And then you'll show them again, working alongside, so they can see for themselves.

Sandler's (off the) track record

Over 50 years ago, David Sandler took the first steps towards developing what has become the Sandler Selling System. He systematically set about taking every well-trodden, steeped-in-tradition, ritualistic – and failed – stage of selling and finding an alternative way.

Today, the Sandler method is used worldwide – to guide and grow clients' businesses, from global corporations to financial services partnerships.

Ongoing support

Just as Sandler's clients enjoy ongoing support to the summit, so will you. From initial training, and an assessment of your learning style, Sandler structures a framework for your personal development – guided by the UK coaching team, backed by the Sandler Selling System.

The 10-day initial programme is reinforced with close support to meet your needs – from the setting up of your new venture to building your own client base.

David Sandler gave us the best-selling system. Staying the best means innovation, constant learning and reinforcement. Sandler franchisees meet regularly as a UK network – and visit colleagues in the US – to share experiences, learnings and knowledge. And to congratulate each other in their shared successes.

It's this pride, individually and collectively, that keeps Sandler at the top, and that ensures that you are supported on your own path to success.

Pre-selling your sales

With high-profile brand communications and thought-leadership in the national business press, Sandler UK works on your behalf to pre-sell your services. You'll be involved too – using the Sandler toolkit to create your bespoke website, and digital marketing to stimulate your client leads.

Together with your clients, you'll build the Sandler brand – to drive your business growth, and to maintain a valuable asset on your balance sheet.

Still feeling bold. . .?

Sandler UK franchisees succeed from diverse backgrounds and industries, from corporate to entrepreneurial, from engineering to HR.

Determination, drive and boldness are the common traits.

The rewards, like our methods, are uncommonly good.

To discuss your business opportunity within the Sandler UK network, call Shaun Thomson on 01608 611211, or email ukinfo@sandler.com.

CASE STUDY

Sandler Training

Franchisee: Nigel Dunand
Location: West Midlands

Nigel Dunand has been successfully growing his Sandler franchise from his base in Longbridge, Birmingham for five years, guiding business leaders – chief executives, managing directors – to, in turn, grow their own businesses.

His award-winning results have far exceeded his early estimates. 'It would have been too lofty, too presumptuous, when I started, to expect this size of business.'

Now, with the example of those he meets elsewhere in the Sandler network, Nigel is in no doubt of the potential for continued growth. 'Here in the UK, we are starting to believe what our colleagues in the US have always told us – that we can reach a turnover of £2 million.'

To grow like this needs support. That support, says Nigel, comes from a range of sources. Firstly, from the wealth of knowledge and experience that is available in the Sandler learning materials. 'I can't imagine getting here if I had tried to create this, on my own. An entire system, backed up with development materials in every form of media. It's all there. Why would I try to replicate that? I would need to repeat the 50 years it has taken to build it.'

And even if you tried, Nigel asks, how would you know it would work? 'Proven. That's what you get with Sandler. It's a proven road map. You use the methods to build your own business, and you share the same methods to guide your clients – to grow theirs.'

Secondly, there is the support of the network. After the formal early stage of coaching – from the team at the UK centre – there is the ongoing support from colleagues. 'Regular conference calls, here in the UK, are a chance to think aloud, share our experiences. Just the other day I talked with Andy, down in Exeter, about networking with chambers of commerce. Pooling our knowledge. There's always someone you can reach, who's been there before.'

Nigel takes full advantage of the opportunities – formal and informal – to build his expertise. When he attends the regular conferences in Baltimore, the US home of Sandler, as well as taking in the agenda, he always pre-arranges dinner dates with other franchisees. 'Just a few of us, maybe with my former mentor, and a couple of others I haven't met before. I try to pick someone who's, like, a year ahead of where I am. The only condition is that you stay curious, that you remain eager to learn.'

And it's this personal characteristic – curiosity – to which Nigel attributes his success. 'Always ask others for their stories. You need what I call "intellectual humility". It keeps you fresh. When we're guiding our clients, we're always looking for stories to share. Ways to enrich the Sandler material with our own, everyday experiences.'

'If you want hand holding, you won't succeed. Sure, the Sandler materials are always there, as a constant guide. And you are well trained. And the support is there. These are like hand-holds. You've still got to reach for them. You have to put yourself out there, be bold. We're showing business leaders how to grow their businesses. You've got to have the entrepreneurial spark, yourself, to be credible.'

Part of that entrepreneurial make-up is the need for freedom. 'It's entirely up to you how quickly you want to travel on the road to growing your own business. I learned, early on, to build my business around the times and days which are most convenient for me. That way, I find clients who are well suited for me to work with, and I'm always at my best.'

For Nigel, the difference offered by his Sandler franchise is clear. 'I hadn't run my own business before. Now I'm a successful entrepreneur. I used to have a career in industry, managing engineering operations, not growing sales. Now, CEOs and MDs look to me – to help their businesses grow. Sandler transforms mere mortals, like me, into business gurus.'

COMPANY PROFILE

Business Doctors

The consulting market in the UK is worth £8 billion, is one of the largest in the world and is growing exponentially! Even in tougher economic times, consultancies find that their fee income still increases. As a vital component of the modern economy, business consulting is a booming sector in the UK.

Businesses used to be able to turn to Business Link for local business advice and help, but with the demise of this service they are now particularly in need of Business Doctors.

Business Doctors is not a consultancy. It is a prestigious management and career franchise business.

Entry levels

Business Doctors has two entry levels: regional franchise manager and local area franchisee.

Regional franchise manager

As a Business Doctors regional franchise manager, your role would be to manage licensed Business Doctors and, harnessing their skills and availability, fully develop your regional market. Together, you and your team would offer a highly competitive,

Business Doctors Franchisee:
Steven Cleaver

comprehensive business support and advisory service to small and medium sized enterprises (SMEs) across the region, and dominate the regional SME consulting market in your territory.

Local area franchisee

As a local area franchisee you would deliver packaged business advisory and support services to SMEs in your locality. Working in concert with your regional and national franchise manager, additional business opportunities might also be available to you.

The Business Doctors franchisee provides clients with:

■ instructive assessments

■ personalised advice

■ hands-on facilitation

■ coaching and mentoring – provided with a personal touch

With a premier training programme in place (see below), you can join the Business Doctors franchise and become a qualified business 'health' advisor as well, enjoying a high social status and income.

Georgie Cox: Business Doctors

Training and support

You will receive comprehensive training in all aspects of the Business Doctors franchise.

Training and support include:

■ a thorough induction into the Business Doctors market-place, business operations, proprietary systems, and the proven marketing and sales strategies that have been successfully used by existing Business Doctors

■ the Business Doctors franchise operations manual, on loan to franchise owners for the duration of their trading licence, which outlines the franchise's business practice

■ assistance from the Business Doctors professional support team to launch your franchise, whether local or regional

■ ongoing support service

■ transfer of Business Doctors' skills, knowledge and procedures.

To join Business Doctors, no consulting experience is needed because training in all aspects of the operation will be provided. However, you will need to have:

■ the motivation and capacity to learn how to become a premiere business advisor.

- the professional experience and business acumen to develop your own Business Doctors franchise.

Business Doctors is looking for people who:

- are business minded

- have managerial and/or sales experience

- have well-developed people skills

- have great communication skills

- have the initiative, commitment, competence and determination to succeed.

It is also important that candidates have a strong client-care mentality, and are able to respond well to problems.

The best franchisees have the wisdom to apply the proven model. In time, their diligence and Business Doctors' transferred expertise will enable them to enjoy the many rewards inherent in a Business Doctors franchise.

Territories/locations

Business Doctors is seeking to establish franchise territories throughout the United Kingdom. Not all locations will be suitable, so it is essential that any chosen area be carefully assessed. Business Doctors retains the final decision on territory.

Business Doctors founders Matthew Levington and Rod Davies

Tel: 0845 219 7077
Fax: 0845 223 2957
Email: info@businessdoctors.co.uk
Web: www.businessdoctors.co.uk

CASE STUDY

Business Doctors

Franchisees: Michael Gulliford, David Sherfield
Location: Edinburgh and West Lothian, East Midlands, Ipswich and Chelmsford

Business Doctors' national presence has grown once again with the opening of a further three offices.

Michael Campbell will be operating the second office in Scotland, covering Edinburgh, West Lothian and the surrounding areas. Mike Gulliford will be

heading up Business Doctors East Midlands, covering Nottingham and Derby, while David Sherfield will be working with businesses in Ipswich and Chelmsford for Business Doctors Eastern.

Business Doctors director Rod Davies says: 'These three new signings all come with exceptional business pedigrees and we are incredibly proud to bring them on board. We feel confident that they will all make superb additions to the network, and these are exciting times at Business Doctors, with some fantastic teams coming together.

'Our expansion across the country is really gathering momentum now and things are developing at quite a pace – we are almost running out of pins for our map! The speed at which we are growing proves that there is a great hunger in small and medium-sized businesses across the country for the kind of expert, friendly, practical support and advice we offer.

'And with a number of territories still available, we're very keen to hear from anyone with great business experience looking for a new challenge, who believes they could make a good addition to the team.'

For more information, go to www.businessdoctors.co.uk or call Business Doctors on 0845 219 7077.

CASE STUDY

Business Doctors

Franchisee: Simon Halliday
Location: North Manchester and Lancashire

Experienced businessman Simon Halliday is launching an office for Business Doctors to provide advice and assistance to small and medium-sized businesses in North Manchester and Lancashire.

Simon has successfully owned or managed a number of businesses – everything from family firms to listed companies. His senior management background includes stints with Care Shop, Verna Group and Prism Medical, plus, at the corporate end, Boots and Iceland Stores. His sector experience takes in healthcare, logistics, manufacturing, wholesale and retail, and he's come up against most business issues in the course of a long career.

Simon says: 'No matter what the size or nature of your business, there are proven processes that lead to long-term growth and prosperity. What Business Doctors does is work alongside businesses to help them adopt these methods in a way that I have seen be hugely successful with all companies looking to get on the right track to success.

'By setting up a Business Doctors office in Bolton and servicing the North Manchester and Lancashire area I'm hoping to put something back into my local area, working with young businesses or older businesses seeking to adapt to new times.'

To find out more about Business Doctors visit www.businessdoctors.co.uk or call 0845 219 7077.

COMPANY PROFILE

Recognition Express

From badges to business gifts

From branded business gifts and corporate promotional products to personalised name badges, staff awards, signs and branded corporate clothing, the range is huge and the market massive. Recognition Express is renowned for its high level of ongoing franchisee support, advice and programmes in the areas of marketing, sales, product sourcing, technology and business planning.

One of the most successful business-to-business franchises in the UK, Recognition Express operates in a market now worth over £3 billion per annum and has become the UK's leading supplier and manufacturer of corporate and personalised products to businesses.

Recognition Express has a proven record of trust and success:

- bfa Franchise of the Year 2003
- over 30 years' experience and profitability
- continued growth and business development
- top franchise owners, turning over £1 million plus per annum
- full bfa member since 1980
- Europe's number one industry provider.

Centrally designed, managed and implemented direct marketing programmes form the backbone of the marketing system and are complemented by high-quality collateral, marketing tools and ongoing training designed to drive business growth, client contact and brand awareness.

Nigel Toplis, Managing Director adds: 'It's you who makes the key decisions in your business but you are not on your own – we are always on hand with help and advice, business planning, financial planning, training and marketing – including an appointment-generating system that directly assists franchise owners to get in front of customers – and much more.'

> **I have always found Recognition Express to be a model franchise. It is an outstanding example of a company which takes ethical franchising seriously. The benefits are shared by Recognition Express, its franchisees and its customers. And that is why it is successful.**

Sir Bernard Ingham, bfa President

The franchise package

The Recognition Express franchise package costs £35,000 (plus VAT), so each prospect requires a minimum of £10,000 personal funding, with the rest to be raised via bank finance. A territory covers around 9,000 businesses and the package includes all the hardware, samples and templates you need to get started, as well as full central-office support, initial and ongoing training, a comprehensive marketing launch programme (including appointment-generating system) and access to a network that can fulfil any order.

Franchise contact: Janet Matthews

Recognition Express Ltd, Unit 2, Cartwright Way, Forest Business Park, Bardon, Coalville LE67 1UE

Tel: 01530 513300
Email: stoplis@recognition-express.com
Web: www.recognition-express.com

CASE STUDY

Recognition Express

Franchisee: Stuart Fisher
Location: Harrow

Stuart Fisher took the plunge and became a Recognition Express franchise owner in early 2008. Stuart, 48, had been a qualified accountant his whole working life and his previous 11 years had been spent as finance director for an exhibition and conference company. He is married to Beverley and has two children, Laura and Leo.

Invest
Why did he invest in a Recognition Express franchise? Says Stuart: 'I had always fancied running my own business in some shape or form, and following a failed management buyout I decided to research purchasing my own business.'

Following the research, Stuart felt that buying a business was far too risky for a man with a wife, mortgage and two kids. 'I then started looking at franchises and, not knowing much about them, I went up to Birmingham for the National Franchising Exhibition,' he says. 'I knew that I wanted to move away from finance and do something completely different.'

Stuart came across Recognition Express, and after having a chat with Nigel Toplis, the company's managing director, he thought the franchise had a good connection to the business he'd been involved in previously. 'After discussing it with my wife, who thought I was having a mid-life crisis, I took a bungee jump out of my comfort zone and purchased a franchise with Recognition Express in December 2007. My first proper trading month was January 2008.

'I started the business from home to save on overheads and it was a major culture shock for all the family. The kids actually see me in the mornings before school. I used to be out of the house at 6.30am and not back home until 7pm. The downside is having your office in your home, so you can't switch off. I'm forever checking or replying to emails and preparing quotes.'

Helpful

How helpful has the franchisor been? Stuart says: 'I can honestly say that the organisation does everything it says it does on the label: comprehensive initial training with refreshers if needed; great support from head office in terms of technical, marketing and sourcing enquiries, and a very helpful network amongst the other 45-plus franchise owners.

'In addition, there are quarterly meetings with Nigel Toplis, which I have found hugely valuable in helping me to focus my business in the right direction. He is a great sounding-board for new ideas and opportunities. Recognition Express is providing me with the base on which I can build a successful franchise business and achieve my personal and business goals.'

Stuart's advice to new franchisees? 'Enjoy it and work hard,' he says. 'Plan your time carefully because there are a million different jobs to do, from sales and marketing to accounting, credit control and invoicing. Make sure you get your invoices out on time and keep a watchful eye on your cash flow. Lastly, network as much as possible.'

CASE STUDY

Recognition Express

Franchisee: Jan Chidley
Location: Hull and East Riding

Women in franchising

Jan Chidley, 47, was born in New Zealand and first came to England at the age of 21 for a working holiday. Having been a full-time mum for 18 years, providing stability for her children while the family travelled, Jan decided in June 2008 that it was now her time and she set up Recognition Express Hull and East Riding.

Jan takes up the story.

'I had a business back in New Zealand with my father, growing apples. We sold it and I decided I wanted to do something in the UK now that my family are nearly all grown up. I like the idea of doing something that is my own business but where I am supported.

'My husband, Chris, is the CEO of a large, nationwide franchise, Driver Hire, and I could see the benefits of being a part of a franchise.

'Nigel Toplis and the team are very supportive, there is a wide range of good-quality products and hence a broad range of potential customers, and the business model is sound.

'My husband Chris was aware of Recognition Express and had met Nigel on several occasions. We both felt that Recognition Express was the right sort of business for me.'

Although Jan is the sole franchisee, husband Chris has been a big support, along with the Recognition Express head office staff.

'The business is growing nicely each month and we are picking up new customers all the time. We are building up a good, loyal customer base,' explains Jan.

'I have added a member of staff, who is already an asset to the business, so I am now able to spend more time winning new business and it also allows more time with existing customers.'

Asked what advice she would give to other people thinking of starting their own business, Jan is very clear:

'It is hard work, with a lot of commitment required, but if you get it right it is extremely satisfying. It is all about meeting people on a regular basis, forming good relationships and being able to deliver the end product.'

'Having my own business gives me flexibility around my home life. However, it is important to remain focused on the business and to continue to put in the time required to keep things on the up.'

But would she recommend franchising to other women?

'I would. Whilst you have to do your homework before signing on the dotted line, you should be buying into a proven business model. For busy women this can be an appealing option.'

It takes someone special to make special things happen

Could your passion for education be the inspiration that helps children in your community fulfil their true potential?

It takes a special person to run a **Kumon maths and English study centre**. If you are committed to the ideal that, with the right guidance, every child has the ability to develop the skills needed for a happy and successful future, we'd like to meet you.

As a Kumon Instructor you will benefit from:

- Job **satisfaction** and flexible working hours
- Full training and **support**
- A **successful** career through running your own business

We currently have fantastic opportunities to take over established study centres or start up new centres within your local area. For more information or to attend a FREE Information Session please call 0800 854 714 or visit kumon.co.uk.

For more information visit
kumon.co.uk
0800 854 714

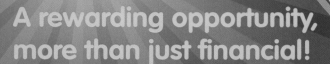

CHILDREN/ EDUCATIONAL SERVICES

Banana Moon Day Nursery
Tumble Tots and Leaps and Bounds
Kumon
ComputerXplorers

COMPANY PROFILE

Banana Moon Day Nursery

About Banana Moon Day Nursery
Banana Moon Day Nursery was started in 2006, as a result of difficulties encountered by one of the directors when trying to place his own children in what he considered to be a good-quality day nursery. It soon became clear that the standards he required could not be met by any of the childcare businesses he visited, and as a result he decided to open his own nursery.

Initially this was done by securing a franchise in an existing day nursery network, but it soon became apparent that the nursery had outgrown the franchisor and was in fact leading the development of the franchise in terms of business modelling, legislation and codes of practice, so it was decided to take the business out the franchise network and go it alone under the Banana Moon Day Nursery brand. During this period a second nursery was opened to serve increasing local demand, and within just a few months the nurseries were being recognised as the best in Warwickshire.

Why franchise?
The founders of Banana Moon Day Nursery have always remained convinced that franchising is an excellent route to business success.

It is imperative that the franchise model is thoroughly tested and well defined and that the franchisor has sufficient skills and experience to provide the necessary support to any new franchisee starting out. This experience enables the franchisor to know that what a franchisee expects, wants and does not want from their franchisor. Banana Moon Day Nursery is able to offer franchisees the highest level of support, which, coupled with a well-proven business model, will provide every franchisee operating their own Banana Moon Day Nursery the very best opportunity to succeed in a large (and growing) business sector with a profitable and enjoyable long-term future.

Have you ever thought of building your own business, but not known where to start?

Do you have energy and enthusiasm, and do you want to earn a sizeable income?

The great news is that Banana Moon Day Nursery is now offering franchises to selected applicants, enabling you to build your own successful day nursery under the highly respected Banana Moon brand.

Banana Moon has developed a unique system that is loved by parents and children alike, but the key to its success lies in extremely high standards across all of its nurseries; its systems for safety and security are second to none, ensuring a safe, caring and fun environment that parents love to recommend to their friends and families.

Training and support

As a franchisee you will receive all the training, support and guidance necessary to get your business up and running quickly and painlessly, reducing the risks normally associated with business start-ups as you will be following Banana Moon's own proven system.

The franchisor will work with you to develop a tailored business plan, and help you to identify premises, employ staff and find customers. Most importantly, it is committed to ensuring that your business succeeds, and will always be on hand to help you grow your business.

Investment will be required and building any new business requires hard work and dedication, but running your own Banana Moon Day Nursery is hugely rewarding in so many ways – and not just financially.

The Banana Moon Day Nursery franchise is a successful business model that has been created, tested and refined to ensure that the very highest levels of childcare can be provided. The model offers consistency across different locations throughout the UK and worldwide.

The Banana Moon concept is in essence quite simple. However, there are certain crucial factors that have ensured its rapid growth and continued success. In order for franchisees to replicate that success it is imperative that the quality standards are maintained and the current business model, including all of its operating systems, is adhered to in its entirety. It is for this reason that a franchise will be awarded only to candidates who demonstrate a commitment to maintaining and upholding these standards. It is by doing so that Banana Moon Day Nursery can be sure that its franchisees will enjoy similar levels of success, ensuring that the financial and lifestyle aspirations of each franchisee can be met and exceeded and that the brand continues to grow throughout the UK and beyond.

Your business

As a previous franchise owner, the franchisor has the experience and knowledge to know what is required to run a successful franchise business and, in particular, to run a nursery.

Banana Moon franchises are not the standard business in a box. Its ethos is to be the best and to provide the pinnacle in childcare. Whether it be through systems in place, security, marketing or continuous support, you will be investing in the best. Installed CCTV security system, bio-metric entrance recognition, full nursery set-up, with a marketing support campaign that no competitor can match – this is just a snapshot of the full Banana Moon franchise.

Put the fun back into business . . . call us today to discuss the full wealth of benefits and understand the reason why Banana Moon is the market leader in franchising in the booming business sector of children's daycare.

Is it for you? When considering working together, it is very important to both you and Banana Moon to make the right decision. Therefore, there is a process in place that enables the franchisor and prospective franchisees to find out about each other and to ensure that each feels comfortable with any decisions they make.

CASE STUDY

Banana Moon Day Nursery

Franchisee: Mohamedraza Virji
Location: Solihull

Mohamedraza contacted Banana Moon Day Nursery with regard to opening a large children's day nursery purely as a business investment. After visiting many other nursery franchises on the market and being disappointed with what they had to offer, Mohamedraza was delighted to find a nursery franchise that gave the complete package.

Banana Moon at Solihull opened in January 2012 in a fantastic, 6,000 sq ft, three-storey building in Cranmore Boulevard, Solihull.

'Banana Moon stood out from all the other nursery franchises that we had visited. There was never any "hard sell" from the team; we found them highly professional and very approachable with all aspects of opening a children's day nursery. I have no experience whatsoever in childcare, but they give you the complete A–Z to make you successful. Today I feel that it is a superb business investment, yet it is also rewarding to see small beautiful lives take their first steps in our own nursery.'

CASE STUDY

Banana Moon Day Nursery

Franchisee: Susie Glenister
Location: Lower Sundon

Choosing to take voluntary redundancy from her 15-year career in law enforcement, Susie approached Mark Bates at Banana Moon Day Nursery with regard to investing in a children's day nursery franchise.

Susie secured her territory on paying her deposit and Banana Moon got to work looking for property. Banana Moon soon found a beautiful barn conversion set in fantastic rural surroundings.

Banana Moon at Lower Sundon near Luton opened its doors in November 2011. Now many parents and children are enjoying the fantastic facilities available.

'I was sold with Banana Moon after my first visit, with their team's support, advice and experience, which was and is second to none. They do exactly what it says on the tin – from finding property, getting planning approval, training and so on to opening the doors. Since opening in November I have been inundated with interest from parents wanting a "first class" nursery in my area.'

COMPANY PROFILE

Tumble Tots and Leaps and Bounds

Tumble Tots is a structured, active physical play programme for children from six months to seven years. It has been designed to develop children's motor skills of agility, balance and co-ordination during their formative years. At the same time, through the programme children develop self-confidence, independence, self-discipline, self-worth and sense of security and identity.

The international success of Tumble Tots has been built upon a commitment to developing children's physical and social skills and positive personality traits within a loving and caring environment. During each weekly session, Tumble Tots provides challenging and structured physical activities, where children fully explore and develop their physical capabilities and social skills. In addition, action songs and rhymes contribute to language development. All Tumble Tots children have an equal opportunity to realise their potential, and tasks are varied according to the different ages and stages of a child's development. Sessions are stimulating and exciting, as formats are changed regularly.

Tumble Tots has been operating a successful franchise network since 1979. If you're interested in becoming your own boss and helping children to develop and have fun, then this business opportunity could be for you! Tumble Tots franchisees have benefited from the established company model and have not only discovered the financial rewards, but also the personal satisfaction of loving the work that they do with children. The business model is a mobile one in which franchisees provide the Tumble Tots programme at various centres within their agreed territory each week. Tumble Tots is a registered trademark and franchisees generate their income through the weekly session fees.

All children are required to join and become members of the National Tumble Tots Club. The annual membership fee includes personal accident insurance for Tumble Tots members while attending sessions. Tumble Tots (UK) Limited arranges a comprehensive insurance policy covering all aspects of the business.

Start-up costs

The initial investment in a Tumble Tots franchise is approximately £13,500 (excluding working capital and vehicle). This includes a designated territory, a license to run the Tumble Tots programme, technical training for the franchisee and their staff, and business and marketing support from an experienced team of Tumble Tots personnel. The investment also includes a 25% payment towards the specially designed comprehensive equipment (the balance being paid in monthly instalments).

Leaps and Bounds

Leaps and Bounds by Tumble Tots (UK) Ltd has been developed for pre-school settings – a progressive physical and movement programme for children from walking up to five years. The programme is designed to complement the indoor and outdoor physical activities currently provided in pre-school settings. The programme was designed in consultation with Patricia Maude MBE of Homerton College, University of Cambridge.

Leaps and Bounds is a skills-based, weekly 30-minute programme that aims to build children's confidence in physical activities and skills for life. Children are encouraged through a sequence of tasks to develop skills including: locomotion, agility, balance, climbing, co-ordination and language development through the use of action songs and rhymes. The programme also helps develop children's skills of confidence, movement vocabulary, movement memory, and movement quality. The range of equipment has been chosen specifically to help develop children's gross and fine motor functioning.

Using bright equipment, large and small, with illustrated visual aids to assist the younger children in following instructions, Leaps and Bounds offers identifiable learning objectives, supported with teaching points and extension activities. Our own highly experienced, trained team of instructors delivers the programme.

The sessions are 30 minutes and are split into three age groups, (walking to 2 years, 2 to 3 years, and 3 years to school age) and take place at pre-school settings, either indoors or out. With each session including no more than 10–12 children; there is lots of opportunity for individual encouragement and attention. Each physical play activity is linked to a learning objective and is 'progressive' in its structure. The walking to 2 years programme underpins the Early Years Foundation Stage and also prepares them for the 2 to 3 years programme which is in line with curriculum guidance for the Foundation stage and guidelines in the Birth to 3 Matters Framework (Sure Start). So parents can be sure that the activities are in line with national curriculum objectives.

An avid supporter of the programme is Olympic gold medallist turned broadcaster Sally Gunnell OBE. 'It is great to see how involved children are in the activities and how much fun they're having. We know if children begin to enjoy physical activity from an early age, they will keep it up in later life,' she says.

The Leaps and Bounds franchise opportunity starts from an investment of £11,500 which includes the licence to operate the Leaps and Bounds programme in a designated territory, a full set of equipment and comprehensive training.

We would welcome the opportunity to discuss the Leaps and Bounds franchise with you. If you would like more information about the Leaps and Bounds programme, please contact us. Call 0121 585 7003 or email anne.griffin@leaps-and-bounds.co.uk.

If you would like to discuss the Tumble Tots franchise please contact us on 0121 585 7003 or email franchise@tumbletots.com.

CASE STUDY

Tumble Tots

Franchisee: Nicky Miller
Location: Wilmslow and Macclesfield area

Tumble Tots franchisee Nicky Miller was working as a leader for Tumble Tots when a franchising opportunity came up. 'I had thought about running my own business but wanted to have the risk reduced by using a formula that was proven to work. I felt it was more secure and less of an uncertainty when dealing with a large sum of money.'

Before joining Tumble Tots, Nicky had had a number of varied jobs, from chauffeur/PA to managing a chain of curtain shops and running the interior section of a garden centre. All of them involved dealing with the pubic, which is what she enjoys. 'I had a five-year break when I had my daughter and had taken her to Tumble Tots, so when I wanted to go back to work it seemed like a great idea to join the Tumble Tots team.'

When a resale opportunity came up in a nearby area, Nicky raised funds for her new business by taking out a bank loan secured on her house.

'I worked in the new area to get to know the staff and understand a little bit more about the business before the sale was completed. It was really nice to meet the children and parents and introduce myself. I didn't need any training for running the Tumble Tots classes, but I did attend the course for Gymbabes and Gymbobs at head office. I had a lot of support from the previous licensee and this continued even after I had taken over.'

'I didn't realise how much of my time would be taken up as the previous licensee made it look so easy!' says Nicky. 'I found that having the office at home I was always in 'work mode', but the advantages are that I can work at any time and fit it around my family.'

Nicky says that being a Tumble Tots franchisee has changed her life such that she enjoys her job and gains a lot of pleasure from knowing that her work makes a positive difference to the children and parents who attend the sessions.

'I didn't want to do a job where I would just turn up, work, and then go home, which is fine for some people, but it was never going to be enough for me.'

What advice does Nicky have for someone thinking of buying their first franchise? 'As long as you have plenty of enthusiasm and energy, enjoy a challenge and have a positive frame of mind, can be organised and disciplined with your time, have a good, supportive family and friends who will help you, then you will be fine and should go for it!'

Nicky plans to continue to improve her business skills, carry on enjoying her job and to do more marketing.

Would she do it again? 'Yes, I certainly would – I didn't know how hard it would be and if I was to do it again, I would do things a little different and get to know the business side of things as well as the classes. When you're working for yourself it involves a lot of roles, from book-keeping to marketing, staff management, customer services and then running the classes. For me, that's the best bit. I love being with the children and seeing the parents each week. It is such great fun and I never get tired of it.'

CASE STUDY

Leaps and Bounds

Franchisee: Maeve Larkin
Location: County Antrim, Northern Ireland

Maeve Larkin chose franchising as a 'safe' option for owning her own business. 'I wanted to be my own boss, but I just wasn't sure that I would have the experience or all the business acumen that would be necessary. Therefore having a source of information and a team of experts to speak to when I needed to seemed to be the right solution for me.'

Prior to starting her franchise, Maeve was a personal assistant to the vice president of sales and marketing in a bus-manufacturing facility. She has a degree in business studies and wanted to find a job where she could use her knowledge. Maeve was lucky enough to have savings that she could use to buy the franchise.

Maeve attended an initial two-day training course on the practical side of the business, and a one-day course on the business side of things. Within six months of starting the business, another day's training was provided on sales and marketing.

'Ongoing, the team are always at the end of the phone or email and will help in any way they can,' says Maeve.

To begin with, Maeve experienced issues with work-life balance: 'I personally found it difficult to manage my time at home between running the business and family commitments. However, this is something I have learned to be stricter about – I have my set work hours and when the children come home from school, it is family time.'

'My life is much more flexible now,' Maeve continues. 'It is great being able to take time off when the children have school holidays and I don't have to worry about sorting out childcare any more, because I plan my working day around their school time.

'It has also allowed me to grow in confidence as a person, as I have had to make all my own decisions and overcome many challenges. This has definitely made me much stronger.'

Maeve advises that anyone looking to buy their first franchise should do their research on the franchise and speak to existing franchisees to get a good feel for the business.

'If you are sure you want to go out on your own, but don't have all the confidence or knowledge, then a franchise is the answer. It is a "security blanket" which you can use when you run out of the answers yourself.'

COMPANY PROFILE

Kumon

Passionate about education? Think you can make a difference?

Kumon is the UK's leading after-school education provider, offering maths and English programmes to children of all ages and abilities. Originating in Japan, Kumon's method of individualised learning has helped millions of children worldwide to fulfil their potential.

The company's founder, Toru Kumon, was a maths professor who, back in the 1950s, wanted to help his son Takeshi with his numeracy skills. He developed a worksheet programme for young Takeshi where he could learn at just the right level, building on his current abilities in order to become more advanced with his maths. The method was so successful that Mr Kumon extended the programme to the wider community, helping children of all abilities to achieve academic success.

Due to the increasing demand, Kumon is looking for new franchisees to start exciting business opportunities or take over already established study centres up and down the country. With an initial outlay of only £400 for the licence agreement and an investment of £2,600 for the marketing of your new centre, Kumon is certainly one of the lowest-costing business opportunities around.

As a Kumon franchisee, you will have an enthusiasm for working with children coupled with good business sense – teaching qualifications are always welcome but are not compulsory, as you will be trained to become a fully licensed Instructor. You will also benefit from Kumon's extremely generous support package, giving you every opportunity to become a successful franchisee and a valuable member of your community.

Kumon is looking for business professionals with a passion for education and the drive to establish a successful Kumon franchise. Study centres range from commercial premises to rented communal space. Opening hours can be set by you but it goes without saying, the more hours your service is available, the more students you can accommodate.

A job that 'has it all' – satisfaction, flexibility and remuneration – might not seem a realistic prospect, but perhaps it's time to think again. By starting a new career as a Kumon Instructor and running your own study centre, you would be helping children in your area to develop skills in independent learning and achieve their potential. You would also be working for yourself, managing the franchise business in your own time while earning a living. If you are looking for a rewarding career and understand the true value of education, then you could become a Kumon Instructor and own a franchise that would give you freedom, flexibility and solid financial rewards. Instructors come from many different walks of life, but what they all have in common is a passion for education and a desire to help children develop.

Kumon has more than 67,000 students at over 630 study centres in the UK alone – with over 4.4 million students worldwide. Despite the recent recession, its student base grew by 13% in the UK in 2009, making Kumon the most successful supplementary education provider in the country. Kumon's Instructors are extensively supported throughout their careers by dedicated staff, and the company boasts an impressive record of success spanning more than 50 years.

Al Shaw became a Kumon Instructor just over a year ago. He says: 'Being a Kumon Instructor has all the benefits of working for yourself, plus great support from an established organisation.'

Instructor of 13 years Rachel Reeve agrees: 'Every day I am impressed by the power and flexibility of the Kumon programme! It is very exciting to be able to help those students who are struggling with their school lessons, as well as challenging those students who are excelling in maths and English. I love the opportunity to be involved with the education of individual students over many years, often seeing them develop their skills from primary school to GCSE level and beyond.'

Ella Ritchie, who runs two Kumon centres, says: 'Kumon provided all of the initial training sessions, and I could contact staff members and experienced Instructors if I had any questions. Personal development is extremely important in the role of an Instructor, and Kumon provides regular meetings and training sessions. Instructors in my area also work together to provide a support network.'

Kumon recently opened its first permanent high street premises in the Harborne area of Birmingham. This has given the Kumon brand great local presence, and as a result of the Harborne success it has plans to establish more centres in prominent locations within the next few years. Again, Kumon is looking for candidates to become part of this exciting new venture.

For more details about becoming a Kumon franchisee in your local area, call 0800 854 714 or visit kumonfranchise.co.uk.

CASE STUDY

Kumon

Franchisee: Vicky West
Locations: Portishead and Nailsea

Vicky West always wanted to be a teacher. However, after studying for a BEd at the University of Exeter, she found that this was not necessarily the route she wanted to take. Having studied with Kumon as a child, and knowing the value of its maths and English programmes, Vicky decided to become a Kumon franchisee, and to help children to fulfil their true potential for learning rather than 'just gearing them through exams'.

Now aged 28, Vicky is married, with two young children, yet still has time to run two Kumon study centres in Portishead and Nailsea, both just to the west of Bristol. Vicky is also an active member of the community and has a great relationship with local schools.

Vicky says: 'After leaving school, I embarked on a BEd at Exeter, but after two terms I was unsure I wanted to be a teacher as I did not agree with the SATs system. I transferred to university in Bristol, where I studied accountancy and statistics, and while studying I worked for a chartered accountancy firm. After finishing my degree, I applied to Kumon to become an Instructor, and was invited to train. I used savings to pay for the franchise and set-up costs.'

As someone who knew about Kumon from an early age, becoming an Instructor seemed like a natural progression for Vicky – as well as a good business opportunity: 'My little sister and I were students at the Wells centre,' she says, 'so I knew about Kumon and its values. Given the reason I did not want to teach in schools, Kumon ticked all of the boxes for me. Kumon embraces my core values, and lets me focus on each child's all-round development rather than just gearing them through exams.'

Becoming an Instructor did have its challenges, but thanks to the support network Kumon offers, Vicky is now getting involved with many initiatives to market her centres. She explains: 'When I first started instructing with Kumon, my biggest challenge was building relationships with the local schools. Kumon was totally unknown in the area and none of the schools would distribute my leaflets. Over time, the schools have seen the results and now five out of the six local schools hand my leaflets out; many local teachers and head teachers also make personal recommendations to their students/parents. I try to attend all training days and I have always received a lot of support from office staff. I keep in close contact with the staff and ask for their help whenever I need it. In the recent past, they have accompanied me to open days, school assemblies, Portishead carnivals and student award ceremonies, as well as helping out with leafleting.'

To become a Kumon Instructor, there has to be a willingness to work with youngsters, and this is something that Vicky finds one of the best parts of the role. She enthuses: 'I adore working with children, especially listening to their stories. I love playing a part in building their confidence and helping them work toward and achieve their goals. I enjoy developing their abilities and also trying to instil a love of learning. My students make me smile every single day – and children say the funniest things!'

Has being one of the youngest Kumon Instructors in the UK helped Vicky relate to the children more? 'Definitely,' she says, 'especially when I refer back to when I was a Kumon student myself. I think my students see me as easy to talk to and many of their parents comment that it's nice for the children to have such a young team working around them. I can certainly relate to how difficult it is studying Kumon as a teenager, juggling this with schoolwork, commitments and attitudes that teenagers have.'

Having a young family and running two study centres must take its toll, so how does Vicky maintain that vital work-life balance? 'Kumon is ideal when you have a young family,' explains Vicky. 'Most of the work is done at home, when I can pick it up and put it down when my own children dictate! It enables me to keep my children at home with me rather than having to put them into full-time childcare. I carry out my enrolments in the evenings when my husband is home to look after the children and put them to bed. Apart from my Saturday-morning class, we have the luxury of spending all our weekends together.'

'The two centres are only six miles apart so it works well from marketing and word-of-mouth points of view. I have many students who "bunny-hop" between my centres, so it provides families with flexibility and this continues to prove a good selling point. Running two centres with two children is a challenge, but one I enjoy!'

During her time as a Kumon Instructor, there have been plenty of happy memories for Vicky, who would like to move into permanent high street premises in the future. She says: 'The highlight for me is the number of people I have met and worked with over the last five years. I have learned a lot myself and feel that so many people respect my judgement where their children's learning is involved; this is a nice feeling, as it is a subject close to the heart. I have a huge collection of letters from families thanking me for what I and Kumon have done for their children.'

COMPANY PROFILE

ComputerXplorers

ComputerXplorers is a home-based franchise offering a huge variety of programmes blending tangible education and technology skills – delivered in a fun-filled package for children aged 3–13 years.

As at July 2012 there are 15 franchises operating across the UK and Ireland in Bristol and Bath, Cotswolds, Dublin South, Solent, South East Wales, South East Scotland, South West Scotland, Bromley and Dartford, Northants, Middlesex, Wessex, Midlands Ireland, Birmingham East, West Surrey and North Yorkshire.

Each franchise has trained instructors who run classes that reveal the world of computers and peripherals to children in after-school clubs, summer camps, gifted and talented groups, pre-schools and nurseries. Sessions are strategically planned to cover a range of educational skills and subjects in a fun and inspirational way, appropriate for each age group.

ComputerXplorers offers each of its franchise owners a proven business model, extensive training and ongoing operational and marketing support. Every teacher employed by ComputerXplorers' franchisees is fully CRB (Criminal Records Bureau) checked and is trained to provide quality ICT education that puts an emphasis on fun. It is a combination that is proving successful for both franchise owners and schools.

Existing franchise owners come from a wide range of backgrounds, including the IT/telecommunications industry, retail, aeronautical engineering and even education itself. It is certainly not necessary to have experience of computers or of working with children to build a successful business in the sector. However, the franchise owners share a belief in the importance of IT education in today's world.

Nigel Toplis, Managing Director of ComputerXplorers, gives this advice to anyone thinking of buying a franchise, particularly one relating to children: 'Going into business and picking a franchise is a huge decision. However, if you are looking for a sector that is rewarding, interesting and satisfying, you should certainly consider a children's franchise.'

'Working with children can be hugely fulfilling and allows our franchise owners to run a successful business while making a real difference to their communities. At ComputerXplorers we have been delighted by the reaction we have received from parents, teachers and children,' adds Nigel. 'However, the most important advice I can give on buying any franchise is to ensure that you choose a franchisor that you can trust to offer you the ongoing knowledge and support you will need to allow your business to thrive.'

ComputerXplorers sets a standard for franchised businesses in the 21st century and dovetails with the requirements of many modern business owners, including:

- work from home

- modest entry costs

- flexible working hours

- low operating costs; high net margins

- appeals to both sexes

- huge existing market, which will continue to grow.

Most importantly, ComputerXplorers operates in the area of ICT and children's education – both of which are critical in today's world.

Mastering technology skills at an early age increases children's e-confidence and competence, and gives them a great head start in their education. ComputerXplorers runs classes that are fun and inspirational, and designed to enhance the learning skills of children of different ages and abilities. The classes are held in nurseries, pre-school settings, schools, after-school clubs and holiday camps.

Children learn best when they are having fun at the same time – and it's that premise which underpins the ComputerXplorers programme. Along with our lungs and mobile phone features, a lot of us use just 20% of the potential of the computer. Children today are surrounded by technology: digital cameras, Sky+ and Wii to name but a few, but they largely use computers for the most basic functions of accessing the internet, playing games or chatting with their friends. However, some children don't have access at home to a computer or connection to the internet, and tend to associate ICT with creating Word documents in science lessons or PowerPoint slides in English at school.

At ComputerXplorers, we show children a different side to technology – that it's fun when you know how! In groups of 10–12, children learn that computers are exciting learning tools, empowering them to make films, create animated slideshows, design their own video game or produce a comic, activities that satisfy and develop creativity while extending their knowledge and use of ICT. Problem-solving, critical-thinking and team-working skills are very useful by-products of participation.

Younger children can develop their confidence and build their academic readiness in core areas such as literacy, maths, science, music and art. Older children can improve their computer and software skills, and learn some exciting new computer-based subjects like clay animation, movie making, robotics and how to design their own video games.

One head teacher comments: 'A priority for improvement in our school has been the development of learning experiences for pupils that are meaningful and equip our young people with skills for life. We recognise that these experiences are often best delivered when working in partnership with others. The ComputerXplorers courses are delivered by a highly professional team. Every effort is taken to ensure effective delivery of learning opportunities that motivate and engage our young people, and planning has included opportunities for parents and staff to become involved. ComputerXplorers has given our children access to resources and equipment that we, as a school, simply could not do and has provided advice and support for staff, should they wish it.'

Successful franchisees will almost certainly have high energy and ambition, take pride in their involvement in education and be keen to deliver a high-value product to the market-place – but most importantly, they will have passion. Passion for business, for children and for technology.

Nigel Toplis adds: 'We are tremendously proud of ComputerXplorers and the excellent feedback from parents, teachers and, most importantly, the children. ComputerXplorers offers a very rewarding and satisfying career to anyone who would like to be their own boss and work with children, and we are still looking for potential franchisees across the country.'

Further information
Investment level: £29,500 + VAT
Business type: Children's computer tuition

Franchise contact: Janet Matthews
ComputerXplorers Ltd. Unit 2, Cartwright Way, Forest Business Park, Bardon,
Coalville LE67 1UE
Email: jmatthews@computerxplorers.co.uk
Web: www.computerxplorers.co.uk

CLEANING AND HYGIENE

Chemex

COMPANY PROFILE

Chemex

Chemex celebrates its 26th anniversary this year.

Reaching 26 years in business is no small feat for any company, especially one operating in a highly competitive industry that has seen many changes over the last few years.

You could be forgiven for looking at the latest fad or explosive new franchise opportunity – but starting off with a bang can often mean coming back down to earth with a bump. There are plenty of 'here today and gone tomorrow' business ideas, but can you really spot a good opportunity when you see one?

At Chemex, the UK's leading franchised cleaning and hygiene solutions provider, the medium- to long-term objective is to help each and every franchisee to grow a valuable business asset. The aim for new franchisees is to help them create a business that they can ultimately sell for a profit when they decide to leave the network.

There is no such thing as a 'standard' Chemex franchise. Each business brings something different to the company and the clients that it serves.

When looking at regional and national accounts, franchisees get support from board level and are encouraged to seek out opportunities that will help their businesses to grow. Regional sales managers will also coach new and existing franchisees in areas such as sales and marketing, lead generation, customer care and product application.

From day one, franchisees are encouraged to think about their exit plan and what they are hoping to gain from investing in a Chemex franchise. Most will realise that the only way to build a saleable asset is to employ staff and invest in premises.

In 2009, at a time when many SMEs were going out of business, Chemex maintained its position as an industry leader and stuck by its values, providing good-quality cleaning and hygiene solutions to industry. Partnerships formed with environmental health officers helped to distinguish Chemex from its many competitors and the launch of innovative products that helped to combat MRSA, norovirus and the H1N1 flu virus kept Chemex ahead of the game.

Overseas operations

At the start of 2010, Chemex International concluded successful negotiations with a long- and well-established Canadian company, Diachem Inc, granting it a licence to manufacture and sell Chemex's hygiene and cleaning products throughout Canada and in a few selected states in the USA.

Chemex, a blue chip and long-established franchise, already has five overseas operations, all Europe-based, so the Canadian link is the first 'long distance' partnership to be formed.

Diachem has a 100% share of the specialised automotive paint preparation market in Canada, supplying pre-treatment products and systems to all the major automotive manufacturers in both Canada and the USA.

With the worldwide downturn in the economy, Canadians and Americans are feeling the pinch, reflected by a decline in motor car purchases over the last 18 months or so.

Frank Butterworth, the owner and Chief Executive of Diachem and its sister company, Chemfil, recognised the changes in buying patterns and realised that with such a large investment in one industrial sector they would become very vulnerable, very quickly. Having all their eggs in this particular basket would lead to disaster.

On a visit to the UK in 2008, Frank and his wife spotted a van on the motorway that immediately struck a chord. The vehicle was liveried as Chemex International. A quick look at the company's website confirmed that the Butterworths' initial interest was justified, and they decided to investigate Chemex more fully upon returning to their home in London, Ontario.

They quickly realised the pedigree and franchising respect that Chemex commanded. Frank, being a trained chemist, also realised the quality of the products behind the brand.

Frank first contacted Ron Hutton, sales director at Chemex International, by email, explaining who he was, what his company did and what it aspired to. This simple approach led to long and frequent dialogue, culminating some three months later in a face-to-face meeting at Chemex's Smethwick headquarters.

Although the initial discussion was in terms of a master franchise, it soon became apparent that it would be more sensible, with the Canadian company's experience, to manufacture the products locally at its existing site in Windsor, south of Toronto.

Much discussion and negotiation ensued in the following weeks, with agreement finally being reached in mid-November for Diachem to represent the Chemex brand in Canada.

Mel Lusty, Chemex's chairman and major shareholder, together with Ron Hutton, the company's Sales Director, flew out to Toronto for a week's visit.

Time was taken not just to meet representatives of the new partners, but also to visit potential customers in the province.

Temperatures of minus 24 degrees Celsius and snow flurries producing near-whiteout conditions at times didn't prevent Mel and Ron from travelling between the numerous business and industrial centres, allowing many useful contacts to be made.

Diachem has acquired new, purpose-built premises for the production and distribution of its Chemex products and the company's 19 sales representatives, located throughout the whole of Canada, will soon be undergoing training in the products and the market application in which they excel.

The longer-term strategy is for the Canadian operation to build a four- to five-van 'pilot' over the first two years, moving towards the franchising concept thereafter.

CASE STUDY

Chemex

Franchisee: Graeme Stephenson
Location: Bath and east Bristol

Graeme Stephenson has swapped a career in the drinks trade for a new role as franchisee for Chemex, covering Bath and east Bristol.

And Graeme, who was made redundant 12 months ago, is looking forward to the chance to be his own boss. 'I've spent the last 30 years working for other people, and when my last role came to an end it seemed a perfect opportunity to make a fresh start,' he said.

'I wanted a business which offered me flexibility and the chance to work from home as well as the ongoing support and training a franchise offers.

'When I found out about Chemex it seemed like a perfect mix of a great product range combined with a strong advisory element, working with customers to make sure they are using the right products to meet the needs of their business.'

And Graeme, who most recently worked with drinks distributor Matthew Clark, is looking forward to using his licensed trade knowledge to help pubs, hotels and restaurants in his region.

'One of the biggest challenges facing all small businesses, but particularly the hospitality trade, is keeping up to date with the constantly changing legislation, especially regarding health and safety,' he says. 'Because I know the licensed trade sector well through my work at Courage and Matthew Clark, I know the issues business operators face and feel I'm uniquely positioned to help them tackle them. And with the ongoing training and new business support on offer from Chemex I'm confident that I'll make a success of the franchise.'

CASE STUDY

Chemex

Franchisee: David Sidwell
Location: Huddersfield and Halifax

David Sidwell is providing consultancy, training and hygiene solutions to nursing homes, leisure centres, sports clubs, restaurants, pubs and hotels in the Huddersfield and Halifax area, having invested in a franchise with Chemex.

David will be offering a tailor-made service to the area's nursing homes, restaurants, hotels, pubs and local sports venues, ensuring that they take advantage of the latest hygiene products and don't fall foul of health and safety laws.

'Whether it is entire hygiene systems for food preparation or large-scale laundry or dishwash systems, I can help and advise my customers to give them peace of mind,' said David. 'It is that confidence within today's maze of ever-tightening regulations for food production that is valued by customers, whether they are a chef in a burger bar or a superchef in a Michelin-starred restaurant.'

With more than 30 years' experience in sales management, dealing with national supermarket chains and other companies that are household names, David knows the importance of customer service.

'The quality of the products is first rate. They are market leaders – tried and tested,' says David.

After thoroughly researching the franchise market, David selected Chemex because of its reputation for products that were not just highly effective, but recession-proof too.

'We sell necessities, not luxuries and therefore they are better suited to riding out the downturn,' said David. 'There are over 600 products, many of which have been specifically developed and updated as part of the Chemex Hygiene Control programme to satisfy the changing food hygiene legislation. You can't buy them in the supermarket and they are incredibly powerful and effective.'

Melvin Lusty, Chairman for Chemex, said: 'David is an extremely positive addition to the network and I am delighted that he made the decision to join us.'

CASE STUDY

Chemex

Franchisee: Mario Erispé
Location: Chichester

Former call centre service manager Mario Erispé made the decision to become his own boss when he opted for redundancy after 18 years in his previous role.

'I was at a career crossroads when the option of redundancy was raised, as I was 51 and wanted to be my own boss,' Mario says. 'I'd had experience in retail sales at the start of my career and have extensive customer service training in my previous role, so I wanted to utilise these skills while being in control of my own destiny. Running a franchise seemed to be the perfect solution as it offered the freedom of running my own business with support and training on hand when I needed it.

'Chemex came highly recommended, with a great induction package and ongoing support, as well as a strong range of products,' Mario adds.

Mario is now targeting businesses in Chichester and the surrounding areas and will be targeting hospitality and healthcare companies, amongst others. He's confident the business will grow rapidly over the coming months, as Chemex offers more than just product sales.

'One of the key strengths of the Chemex service is the fact we offer a full, free site survey, as well as offering advice and training to our clients,' says Mario. 'It's more than just sales. We keep our clients up to date on changing legislation and new products to make sure that their cleaning regime is up to date and meeting their business needs.'

good food, good farming, good business

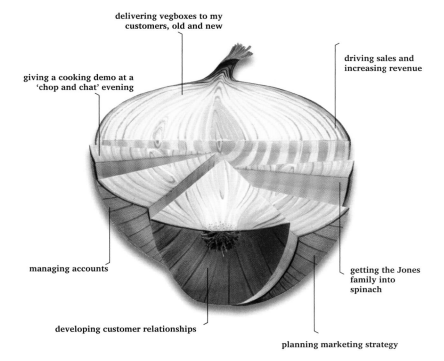

delivering vegboxes to my
customers, old and new

driving sales and
increasing revenue

giving a cooking demo at a
'chop and chat' evening

managing accounts

getting the Jones
family into
spinach

developing customer relationships

planning marketing strategy

franchise opportunities - uk wide
award winning vegbox home delivery company

Grab life by the onions! Spread the word about our delicious fresh organic grub! Become as essential to your customers' kitchens as salt and pepper! Yes, being a franchisee with the UK's leading and award winning organic vegbox home delivery company is about far more than just running a sound and ethical business. It's about building the kind of customer relationships that no other supplier can match, becoming a valued member of your community (as well as an expert on 1001 ways to use an onion) along the way. Like you we'll expect to see your business grow, so strong sales skills and a real determination to succeed are essential. Sure it can be backbreaking work and there'll be plenty of long hours too but you'll be building a business you can really call your own. So it might be tough, but it's as good for you as it is for your customers. Food for thought?

To find out more, email **franchise@riverford.co.uk**
or visit **www.riverford.co.uk/franchise**

DIRECT SELLING/ DISTRIBUTION

Card Connection
Riverford

COMPANY PROFILE

Card Connection

Card Connection is one of the UK's largest card publishers and is the market leader in the franchised distribution of greeting cards.

The company was established in 1992 and within a few years grew to be the largest and most successful organisation supplying greeting cards on a consignment basis. It became a full member of the British Franchise Association in 1995. In 2008 Card Connection was purchased by UK Greetings Limited, and is now a trading division of UK Greetings.

Using a proven system, franchisees place greeting card ranges in retail outlets on 'consignment'. This means that the stock and display equipment are installed on free loan to the retailer. This is one step beyond 'sale or return', as Card Connection customers never have to buy the stock in the first place, and pay only for what they sell. The award-winning merchandising service provided to retailers by local franchisees is second to none and has established the company's excellent reputation, especially within the convenience retail sector.

Card Connection franchisees have their own exclusive territories with an extensive customer base. All franchisees have access to a portfolio of unique products that generates immediate income from day one. Typically, franchisees call on retail customers on a monthly basis. Customers include convenience stores, sub-post offices, petrol station forecourts and staff restaurants in large offices. In addition, Card Connection supplies numerous national accounts, including the likes of Budgens, Londis, Spar, BP and Shell.

Card Connection operates throughout the UK, Ireland and Malta. It currently has 70 franchisees in the UK and Ireland, 20 of whom are 'Platinum' franchisees, with larger operations and a number of staff servicing a large territory. Through its network of franchisees, Card Connection services around 16,000 retail outlets countrywide.

Opportunities for new franchisees
Card Connection has limited vacancies for franchisees who are keen to run an expanding business. Ideally, successful candidates will have some management experience, as once established, they will be expected to employ a small team, operate a warehouse and have several liveried vans on the road.

Because the franchise networks in the UK and Ireland are complete, the available opportunities now consist of acquiring an already-established territory from an existing franchisee. These vary in price according to their level of development, but start at £20,000 (plus stock), with earnings potential in excess of £50,000 per annum.

Owning a Card Connection franchise allows you to buy into an established company and a proven business idea. Franchisees enjoy the flexibility of being their own boss, while having the experience and dedication of an established and highly successful organisation behind them.

For full income and goodwill price details, plus a map of the geographical territory of areas available, please visit our website: www.card-connection.co.uk

CASE STUDY

Card Connection

Card
Connection

Franchisee: Gabriel McGeown
Location: County Down, Armagh and South Tyrone

Ex-publican Gabriel McGeown became the Irish franchisee for leading greeting card publisher and franchisor Card Connection in 2008. Gabriel expanded his business quickly and, since then has bought part of the County Down area in addition to his existing Armagh and South Tyrone territory.

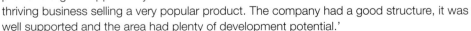

'After 31 years as a publican I was looking for a new challenge,' confirms Gabriel. 'I wanted to exchange the culture of working long hours behind the bar for a business that was more flexible.

'I saw the Card Connection franchise for sale in the local paper and, following some detailed research, realised it provided a great opportunity to run a thriving business selling a very popular product. The company had a good structure, it was well supported and the area had plenty of development potential.'

A full member of the bfa, Card Connection was established in 1992 and since then has grown to be one of the UK's largest greeting card publishers and is the market leader in the franchised distribution of greeting cards. Using a proven system, franchisees place greeting card ranges in retail outlets on a 'consignment' basis. This is one step beyond 'sale or return', as Card Connection customers never have to buy the stock in the first place, only paying for what they sell. The award-winning merchandising service provided to retailers by local franchisees is second to none and has established the company's excellent reputation, especially within the convenience store sector.

Card Connection franchisees have their own exclusive territory and operate from home, calling on their customers typically on a monthly basis. Customers include convenience stores, sub-post offices, petrol station forecourts and staff restaurants in large offices. In addition, Card Connection supplies numerous UK national accounts, which include the likes of Budgens, Londis, Spar, Shell and BP.

Although there is really no such thing as a typical day, Gabriel spends most of his working time on the road, his van packed with Card Connection greeting cards, aiming to visit between six and nine stores. 'The consignment system is very popular,' he confirms. 'New stores that I visit are very receptive to the Card Connection approach as it means they can offer more products to consumers at no extra cost to themselves. Many retailers are finding this particularly advantageous in recessionary times.

'Most retail outlets need to be visited at least once per month to deliver the supply of greeting cards and to ensure displays are kept looking fresh and up to date with seasonal products,' continues Gabriel. 'This is an important aspect of my work, as attractive displays encourage customers – which of course leads to higher sales.

'I deliver to small independent retailers and also to chains like Costcutter, Spa, Vivo and Musgrave,' he continues. 'I get sent regular new business leads from Card Connection's head office, and when I have interest like this I always aim to visit the retailer the following day. I believe that providing this level of service is one of the keys to running a successful business.'

Gabriel was recently named winner of Card Connection's Franchisee of the Year award for being consistently the top performer in average sales per retail outlet, growing his businesses' volume sales by 14% in the past year.

'I am delighted with how my Card Connection franchise has grown, even in these challenging economic times. The quality of the products, the merchandising service and the consignment system are really popular and it is largely this that has been behind my success so far. Each day my small team works hard, but we have the satisfaction of knowing, like anyone who runs their own businesses, that the rewards are ours to keep,' concludes McGeown.

Card Connection is part of UK Greetings, the largest publicly owned greeting card publisher in the world and has limited vacancies for franchisees who are keen to run an expanding business. Successful candidates would ideally have some management experience as, once established, they would be expected to employ a small team, operate a warehouse and have several liveried vans on the road.

Because the franchise networks in the UK and Ireland are complete, the available opportunities now consist of acquiring an already-established territory from an existing franchisee. These vary in price according to their level of development, but start at £20,000 (+ stock) with earnings potential in excess of £50K per annum. For further information see: www.card-connection.co.uk

COMPANY PROFILE

Riverford

Riverford, the nation's largest organic box scheme, has been delivering fresh organic produce direct from the farm to the door for over 15 years.

Grab life by the onions!
Spread the word about our delicious fresh organic grub and become as essential to your customers' kitchens as salt and pepper!

With your own organic food franchise through Riverford Organic – the UK's leading and award-winning organic veg box home delivery company – you will find out that it's about far more than just running a sound and ethical business. It's about getting out there, spreading the word about Riverford's organic produce at local events, building the kind of customer relationships that no other supplier can match and becoming a valued member of your community (as well as an expert on 1001 ways to use an onion).

You'll expect to see your business grow, so sales skills and a real determination to succeed are essential. Certainly, it can be back-breaking work and there'll be more than your fair share of early-morning starts, and late nights too, but you'll be building a business you can really call your own. So, it might be tough – but it's as good for you as it is for your customers. Food for thought?

Riverford grows the vegetables: you grow your organic food business
When Guy Watson started his business over 25 years ago (armed with just a wheelbarrow and 20 customers), he had a vision that's as strong today as it was then.

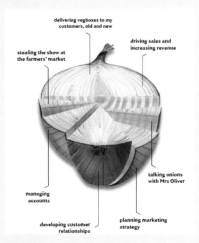

Guy wanted to make locally grown, organic food affordable and accessible to everyone and wanted to inspire people to reconnect with home cooking, rediscovering the simple joys of fresh, tasty, quality fruit and vegetables. He wanted to support the farmers who shared this vision, both here and overseas. Of course things have grown a little for Riverford Organic since then! At the last count customer numbers were over 65,000. But at heart, Riverford is still the same ethical, family-run firm that it's always been.

Beginning with Wash Farm in Devon, Riverford has expanded across the country, tickling the nation's tastebuds and helping families discover an ethical, healthy alternative.

To meet the growing demand, while maintaining its commitment to grow and deliver fruit and vegetables locally, Riverford set up a number of 'sister farms' which supply it with the very best in regional fruit and vegetables. The first was Sacrewell in Cambridgeshire, which now supplies households across the east of England. Next came Home Farm in North Yorkshire, delivering across the north and north east of England, and finally came Upper Norton Farm in Hampshire, which supplies central southern England.

On top of winning thousands of customers, Riverford has won more than its fair share of awards (everything from Best Organic Retailer and Best Ethical Business to awards for the quality of its produce). But perhaps most importantly of all, Riverford is helping to change the way that people look at food, reversing the tide of mass-produced fruit and vegetables in favour of a more sustainable (and tasty) approach that's simply better for everyone. With a history of success, a thriving network of farms and franchisees, together with a growing demand for the kind of mouth-watering fruit and vegetables and a customer focused service that only Riverford delivers, it's a great time to join the franchise.

Franchising with Riverford

Riverford needs franchisees for each of the farms to deliver its organic produce to local people by the most direct route possible. Franchisees are more than just delivery people. They manage their own area, look after their local customers and provide a personal service and link to the farm that customers just won't find at the supermarket. Riverford is looking for driven and enthusiastic people with a passion for food to join its growing success and operate new and resale territories across the UK. The franchise looks for people who believe in the product and who can communicate the Riverford story. You'll need to be well organised and enjoy building relationships while working in partnership with Riverford to continue growth.

Riverford franchisees deliver a friendly, reliable service to thousands of households around the UK each week and sell a whole range of fresh organic foods – from fruit to meat, eggs and wine – as extras to the vegetable boxes. Profits can be built by developing the customer base density and increasing the average spend, with some of the top-performing franchisees grossing over £600 per delivery round.

The farm offers its franchisees unlimited support, and its growing size means that sharing systems and ideas is easy. As Guy explains: 'Our idea is to retain the social, environmental and economic advantages of small, local businesses, while sharing the advantages that scale gives. This brings business benefits like sharing IT and finance systems, but even more importantly, we can share knowledge.'

Despite Riverford's growth, it is still a family-owned business that is motivated by traditional values.

If you are looking for a new challenge and have a passion for great-tasting organic produce, please get in touch:

Tel: 01803 762015
Email: franchise@riverford.co.uk

CASE STUDY

A Shared Destiny

To the backdrop of seagulls circling high, waves rushing over a long stony beach and the tourist hum and buzz of Brighton, Riverford Organic franchisee Stephen Spears, along with his small team of drivers, makes around 800 organic food box deliveries each week. Last year Stephen's turnover was over £750,000. And this June – during one of the wettest summers in living memory – he had his record sales week. So how did life start out for this ambitious franchisee?

Stephen says: 'My parents used to run a large garden centre with a £5 million turnover, but were then bought out by a conglomerate. I could never fit into the corporate mould, and so I started looking for something more suited to my personality, within the franchising industry.

'When I came across Riverford Organic, I loved their ethos and way of working as much as the business model they use. Riverford is an ethical and efficient company without being corporate, which I think is a great achievement when you consider that it turns over more than £40 million a year.'

Riverford has now been in business for more than 20 years, and franchising for 10 of those. What started out as one man – founder, Guy Watson – delivering a handful of organic veg boxes to a few local customers in Devon has since turned into a complex logistics operation involving four farms, 400 liveried vans, and 70 franchisees making around 50,000 deliveries each week.

'There's something refreshing about knowing that you're part of a business that has grown so much, yet never deviated from its core values,' says Stephen. 'Riverford is *still* a family-owned company that adheres to a mantra of "good farming, good food, good business". And being part of it has done more than provide me with an income: it's given me independence and flexibility, and has even turned me into a bit of a foodie.'

He adds: 'When I started looking at franchises, Riverford stood out amid all of the other opportunities: you really feel that it's a shared destiny, and that you're a part of something that isn't just about making money. I'm confident in the back up I get, and know that if anything happened to me that meant I couldn't run my business, Riverford would help me to find a solution. It's that kind of support not every franchise provides, and you would certainly never get if you set up on your own.'

However, even with the inherent benefits of training and support from a professional and knowledgeable head office team, running a Riverford business at the local level is still hard work. With morning starts as early as 5am, driving and delivering in all weathers, plus a good deal of physical work, there are considerations beyond the financial and ethical for prospective franchisees.

'It's true that it is quite labour intensive,' says Stephen. 'There are long hours at times, particularly when you start out, which is when you might be delivering and doing most of the admin work on your own, or as a couple. But if you don't mind that sort of thing, it's enjoyable.

'Also, as your business matures, you bring on more people. I have two drivers and somebody doing admin for me now. It's a cost consideration, but it lightens the load – and you really can't expand without employing people.

'Ultimately, the way I now have my business set up works well for me. It's been a fantastic year, and incredible that despite the wet summer we've had, which has decimated crops such as broccoli and spinach, June yielded my highest weekly sales figure ever. I took £17,000 of orders in a week – £200 more than my previous best. It's pleasing to know that I'm in a business that thrives even when you take into consideration all of the environmental and economic challenges there are today.'

FINANCE

TaxAssist Accountants
Dennis and Turnbull
EKW Group
Expense Reduction Analysts

COMPANY PROFILE

TaxAssist Accountants

TaxAssist Accountants is the largest network of accountants in the UK and specialises in providing professional book-keeping, pay-roll, tax and accountancy services to small businesses with a turnover of less than £1 million.

Each accountant runs his or her own business supported by the TaxAssist Accountants network – one of the UK's fastest-growing networks with over 37,500 clients. Franchisees trade with local businesses and are very much part of the community.

Founded in 1995 by a group of dedicated professionals, the TaxAssist Accountants franchise is based on a concept that was, and still is, fundamentally simple: to bring first-class professional services to the small-business owner.

TaxAssist recognised that there was, and increasingly is, considerable demand in the market-place for basic accountancy and taxation services for non-incorporated businesses and small limited companies. In addition, with the advent of self-assessment, TaxAssist Direct Ltd has enabled the demand for tax returns for the self-employed client to be met cost-effectively.

There are now over 200 outlets across the UK, 134 of which are shops. Through retailing accountancy services, the intention is to depart from the look and characteristics of traditional accountancy practices and to provide modern, accessible and welcoming locations for TaxAssist's clients, allowing them to access its services at their convenience.

TaxAssist's clients

The network supports over 37,500 personal tax payers and small-business owners, including sole traders, partnerships and small limited companies. In establishing a network that focuses solely on smaller businesses, TaxAssist targets a market that has a need for its services and operates from key shop-style premises or office-based locations, making it far more visible and accessible than its competitors.

Industry recognition

The British Franchise Association and HSBC named TaxAssist Accountants as the Gold winner at the Franchisor of the Year Awards for 2010; this was on the back of being named Silver winner in 2008 and 2009.

The 2010 awards aimed to highlight the outstanding business acumen, passion and achievement of franchise business across the UK, and TaxAssist faced tough competition from household names including McDonald's and Domino's Pizza.

In July 2011 TaxAssist Accountants was again recognised, this time by Accountancy Age, as one of the UK's Top 50 accountancy networks (the only accountancy franchise to be listed), being ranked as the 29th largest network in the UK, up on the 34th placing in the 2010 rankings.

Against a national trend that saw 15 of the Top 50 firms in decline and the overall UK fee income of the Top 50 fall by £80 million, from £9.87 billion to £9.79 billion, TaxAssist Accountants was one of just eight among the Top 50 to show double-digit growth, with its sales increasing by 16%, from £16.25 million in the 2010 rankings to £18.9 million in 2011.

The sustained growth that the network enjoys is testament to the strength of the business model, the support provided by the head office in Norwich and the quality of the franchisees within the TaxAssist Accountants network.

Are we compatible?

You, the franchisee, will be the principal of the business, employing accountants and thus leaving you free to focus on business development and managing your practice. Therefore you do not need any formal accountancy qualifications – full training is given, but TaxAssist does look for key abilities and attributes. High levels of commercial acumen and financial and business awareness are essential, as TaxAssist looks for franchise owners who are determined to build a sizeable business.

The franchise package

The franchise fee of £34,950 includes TaxAssist Accountants training and support.

Training is carried out in an informal atmosphere at the TaxAssist Support Centre in Norwich, by qualified personnel. The courses are residential and TaxAssist Accountants pays for all meals and accommodation.

Full training, support and guidance are given in the operation of your business under the TaxAssist Accountants brand name.

You will receive:

- an exclusive territory

- comprehensive training

- six-month nurturing programme focusing on business development, recruitment and client acquisition

- comprehensive operations manuals

- continuous guidance and support

- technical advice helplines, support website, support material and visits from the technical team

- access to specialist advice/in-field back-up

- regular contact with a franchisee development manager to monitor and discuss progress

- lead-generation service

- initial stationery and marketing materials, including your own personalised website

- national marketing and brand building

- first year's membership of a networking group

- telephone-answering service for first year.

The initial six-week training programme covers:

- in the first and second weeks – all aspects of accounts production and taxation for sole traders and partnerships

- in the third week – software training on taxation and practice management

- in the fourth week – social media and practice management

- in the fifth week – you will be working from home and you will be given relevant case studies to work through

- in the sixth week – sales, marketing and recruitment training.

To learn more about the TaxAssist Accountants opportunity please visit www.taxassist.net or contact the recruitment team on 0800 0188 297.

CASE STUDY

TaxAssist Accountants

Franchisee: Renee Mackay
Location: West Edinburgh

'Having been in business for myself for many years I knew the challenges faced by small business owners – having faced and dealt with just about all of them myself,' says TaxAssist franchisee Renee Mackay. 'As a result, although I am not a chartered accountant, I felt well placed to provide a service to the small business community in west Edinburgh.'

'It was also fair to say,' she continues, 'that I was looking for a change in the way I went about business, too. My previous business meant that I was running up and down the country, often leaving on a Sunday evening and coming home on a Friday night. I enjoyed every minute of it, but wanted a change, to travel less. I also wanted to build something for the future, an asset I could sell when I'm ready. And it was with this clearly thought through exit strategy I joined TaxAssist Accountants.'

Starting out

'I didn't really have to do much looking around because I already knew TaxAssist, the model and the people really well and so it seemed a logical step to me to join the network, which I did at the beginning of 2010.

'I already knew the model worked and so I was determined to stick to it rigidly . . . and that's just what I did.'

Renee made sure that she benefited to the maximum from her training. 'The initial training was vital for me as a non-accountant and I took every last ounce I possibly could from the course, often asking the trainers to stay late to give me extra support . . . which they were happy to do.'

Growing the business

'I went straight into a shop front, which opened in May 2010,' Renee says. 'I recruited my first member of staff straight away and so I needed to get clients on board quickly. I set myself stretching but realistic targets for client acquisition and set about marketing the business like crazy. My two mainstays are the shop itself and networking, which between them bring in the majority of new clients, with the national website (and TaxAssist Support Centre) and my social media presence also adding new clients for me.

'I've just finished my 10th trading month and recruited my 100th client this week. My fee bank is climbing steadily and this is balanced nicely with clients who need immediate work – good for my cash flow – and I have two members of staff.'

A fulfilling profession

Renee says that the past year has been the most enjoyable of her professional life. 'I didn't know I could work so hard, but I've enjoyed every minute. Each day is a huge learning curve and sometimes I wonder how much more I can absorb . . . the next day I get the answer: a lot more!'

'If I had to summarise my first year as part of the TaxAssist network in three words, they would be: exhausting, exciting, rewarding. I'd recommend it to anyone with the drive and determination to build something special.'

COMPANY PROFILE

Dennis and Turnbull

d&t is one of the few bfa-affiliated chartered accountants, looking after several hundred franchisees throughout the UK. It has a wide range of experience of various types of franchise business, from 'man in a van' operations through to multi-unit retail brands.

What sets d&t apart is that it truly understands franchising: 'Franchising accounts for a significant proportion of our business,' says Carl Reader, head of franchising at d&t. 'With over 40 national brands recognising us as network accountants, together with many independent franchisees benefiting from our services, we believe that we have a wide range of experience to deal with most franchisees'.

d&t's Services

Two main types of service are offered by d&t in the franchise market.

The first is a network accounting solution, where each franchisee in the network uses d&t to prepare their annual accounts. Liza Gratton, client relationship manager, says: 'This service is really beneficial for the franchisees. It allows the franchisee to have an accountant who truly understands their business, as we will already look after a number of similar businesses. They also benefit from a simple-to-use online accounting system,

customised for their business, and as it tends to be a large contract for us we are able to offer very competitive fees for the franchisee.'

The second is acting for independent franchisees whose network does not have a pre-agreed arrangement. Starting from just £35 per month, this service includes online accounting software, and the reassurance that the franchisee is getting the right advice: 'Franchise tax legislation is notoriously complex for the layman. Our role is to take care of all of the francisee's tax affairs, while maintaining our high levels of service and support,' says Emma Lowery, franchise tax manager. d&t also sticks by its service levels – it offers an unconditional 100% money-back guarantee.

Areas of support
Together with some partner businesses, d&t provides a full range of support in key areas.

Initial financial consultancy
Before offering any solution, it is necessary to fully understand how your franchise works. Whether you are just starting out, or are a fully established franchisee, d&t can review your systems to ensure that your finances are appropriately recorded and monitored.

Business planning
d&t's partners at Franchise Finance, another bfa-affiliated firm, are experienced in preparing business plans and finance applications for franchisees – with over 95% of applications accepted, they are undoubtedly the market leaders in the industry.

Accountancy and tax return preparation
The core service that d&t offers is the preparation of accounts, tax returns and other administration. By standardising the format and content of your accounts, the information prepared becomes comparable and relevant. What's more, d&t fully understands the tax legislation surrounding franchising, and the nature of franchise agreements.

Book-keeping, payroll and compliance

d&t is ideally placed to help you maintain your compliance affairs. Whether you use d&t's payroll bureau, its book-keeping team or any of its other compliance services, d&t can help you concentrate on your business rather than the administration.

Training

d&t training has a wide range of training methods available for franchisees across the country. It can provide you with training videos, webinars or, if you'd prefer a more hands-on approach, can offer group or one-on-one training. It's not just for the software – the training packages cover a range of financial and administrative matters.

Management accountancy and Virtual Finance Director

Qualified management accountants at d&t can help you to fully understand your financial position. They work with you to create a bespoke management pack for that can include reporting on performance vs budget, monitoring of key performance indicators and graphical analysis. You can also opt for a Virtual Finance Director service, where you can benefit from an outsourced finance director who fully understands your business and your franchise network – without the high salary.

Financial planning

Many franchisees are focused on the day-to-day, and neglect planning their personal finances. Whether it's for mortgages, protection or retirement, d&t can ensure that you have a robust plan in place. What's more, its holistic approach makes sure that any advice takes into account both personal and business circumstances.

Resale management

One of the benefits of franchising is that you can build a valuable asset that is yours to resell. d&t's partners at Franchise Resales, another bfa-affiliated firm, provide a structured process to help you maximise the value of your franchise at resale.

Appointing a new accountant can be a daunting process – and there is always uncertainty about the service you will receive. Here is what some of d&t's clients say.

> *Stagecoach Theatre Art's network of franchisees has used Dennis and Turnbull since 2007. The experience has been universally positive, and I receive regular feedback from franchisees that they are delighted to be using a firm that is responsive, efficient,*

properly resourced and – most importantly – gives clear advice and guidance in layman's terms. 〟

David Sprigg, Stagecoach Theatre Art

〝 *Carl and the team at Dennis and Turnbull do accountancy stuff really well! That should be no surprise; they have all the right qualifications. What sets them apart for me is that they care about the really important stuff – like me, their client. They care about understanding and helping my business, the franchise world that I operate in, and they care about me and what I'm trying to achieve. Did I mention that they are good at adding up numbers as well?* 〟

David Tovey, Dennis and Turnbull client

〝 *d&t is knowledgeable about franchise-specific tax legislation, has experience of how franchise networks operate and offers franchisees low, fixed monthly fees. Our franchisees who have already adopted d&t as their accountants also enjoy guaranteed turnaround times, a fixed price menu of fees, a personal relationship manager and, most importantly, a guarantee of 100% satisfaction. We have listed d&t as our recommended accountant for all existing franchisees, whilst all new franchisees who go with d&t get three months' free accounting paid for by EnviroVent as part of the franchise package.* 〟

Phil Harrison, Dennis and Turnbull client

〝 *I switched to d&t because it was one of the few accounting firms savvy enough to accept working with online software, but I stayed with them because they give such lovely service.* 〟

Dr Mohammad Al-Ubaydli, Dennis and Turnbull client

> *Dennis & Turnbull has consistently provided Smith & Henderson with a first-class service, expert advice and excellent value, always exceeding our expectations. Their head of franchising, Carl Reader, is a leading expert in franchise accountancy. He is always looking for new industry developments, such as online accounting and bank feeds, to help his clients stay one step ahead. I have no hesitation in referring our clients, whether they be franchisors or prospective franchisees, to Carl and his team at Dennis & Turnbull.*
>
> *Steven Frost, Smith & Henderson*

With several hundred franchisees using d&t throughout England, Scotland, Wales and Northern Ireland, the firm has proved that it can deliver its service nationwide to franchisees of all shapes and sizes – and its 100% guarantee means that you can be assured of its service levels.

Contact either Liza or Emma on 01793 741600 to find out more about how Dennis and Turnbull can help you, and to arrange a free initial consultation.

COMPANY PROFILE

EKW Group

accounting for your business

How can a bfa-affiliated accountant help you?
Whether you are a franchisee or franchisor, EKW Group is able to help you in a variety of ways.

The likelihood is that when you went into business it wasn't the producing accounts part of the business that excited you most. It was more likely developing a business, dealing with the public, living out a life-long ambition, developing a brand, or plainly and simply making money to give you and your family the lifestyle you want.

There are people out there who do get excited about producing accounts. EKW Group knows: it has lots of them, and that's what it does. EKW Group lets you focus on the reasons why you went into business.

About the EKW Group
The EKW Group, established internationally in 1935, is a leading accountancy firm, expert in helping independent franchisees and entire franchised estates to flourish.

Accredited as Sage Accountant Partners, EKW is also a registered Sage developer for true Sage expertise and also offers other products that fit the needs of individual franchises.

The EKW Group is an affiliate of the bfa. To become a bfa affiliate a business has to show evidence of its professional standing and submit evidence to show that its staff are qualified in the profession concerned and experienced in the application of that profession to franchising.

Accounting services offered by EKW
The EKW Group offers the full range of accounting services:

- accounting

- business planning

- formations

- outsourced accounting

- payroll

- registrations

- taxation

- VAT

- wealth management.

How EKW helps

For franchisors

EKW will provide a free evaluation of your network, tailoring its services to best support you and your franchisees.

EKW has access to the very latest accounting platforms – whether a traditional route such as Sage or a newer product that is completely web-based – and will provide you with instant analysis of the financial performance of your whole network, and each franchisee's accounts, wherever you are.

EKW will recommend the platform that supports your aims and one of its specialist franchise accountant/business advisors will come to meet you and discuss these with you and, from their experience, will be able to suggest solutions that have worked for other franchises.

Continued support, with EKW's large network of friendly advisors based throughout the UK and its specialist knowledge of retail systems, is offered to your franchisees. EKW can even relieve you of the responsibility of advising and training franchisees in financial reporting, leaving you to concentrate on developing the business.

The EKW Group is there to support your franchisees in setting up a successful franchise. The group is regularly asked to present at bfa seminars and help franchisees understand their accounting responsibilities. It acts for a considerable number of franchisees, offering a wide range of franchise services, and is the preferred accountant for franchise networks including Shell and Boots Opticians.

❝ **We are pleased to have worked with EKW over the past 25 years and, without doubt, their expertise and advice has provided considerable benefits to our retail network.** ❞

Nick Brown, communications manager, Shell Oil UK & Ireland

❝ **We're really pleased to be working with EKW, who have introduced great benefits to our brand partners here at Boots Opticians.** ❞

Michael Brocklebank, head of franchise operations, Boots Opticians

For franchisees

The EKW Group will provide a free evaluation of your business, and will tailor its services to best support and build your business. The group has access to the very latest accounting platforms, both traditional routes such as Sage and newer, completely web-based products, which give you instant analysis of your financial performance and access to your accounts, wherever you are.

EKW will recommend the platform that supports your aims, and one of its specialist franchise accountant/business advisors will meet with you and discuss your needs and, from their experience, will suggest approaches that have worked for other franchises.

The Group offers continued support, and through its large network of friendly advisors based throughout the UK and its specialist knowledge of retail systems, it will always be close at hand to offer support or listen to your ideas. EKW takes the number crunching away, leaving you to concentrate on developing your business.

EKW understands that, to help you with your business, it needs to understand your business. You will be allocated specialist advisors for each area in which you require help, whether this be your accounts, your tax or your payroll, and you will even have a separate allocated advisor for a complete overview of your business.

Tel: 0800 3898271
Web: www.ukfranchiseaccountants.co.uk

CASE STUDY

EKW Group

Client: David Blenkinsop
Franchise: Seven Hills Optical Ltd – Boots Opticians

Seven Hills Optical has just completed its first year as a franchisee with Boots Opticians. Franchisee David Blenkinsop says: 'I believe that one of the reasons that our business has been so successful is in part due to the excellent support we have received from the EKW Group.'

David says that he assessed a number of other potential accountants. 'We were swayed by the rapport we had built with EKW's business relationship manager. He was approachable, generous with his time and very knowledgeable. We leaned heavily on his knowledge to help us establish our business, and genuinely felt that we could ask him any questions.'

David finds accountancy quite technical, but, he says, 'The accounts team have never made it feel that way. They have been generous with their time, are happy to discuss situations in detail and have used their considerable expertise of handling franchised businesses to give expert options and then helped us make the best decisions for our business.'

The payroll team played a crucial role, handling some difficult situations on David's behalf. 'In my opinion they have offered different solutions to different issues that feel based on what is best for our business. The best part of the service we have received from the payroll team has been its ability to communicate often complex subjects simply.'

'I recently had an issue that occurred prior to the commencement of the business,' says David. 'I had expected that the contact at EKW would be reluctant to offer an opinion. However, I didn't feel cut adrift to resolve the problem myself and my contact took time to analyse the context of the issue and to explain the different options that I had and the people that I needed to speak to, to ensure that it was resolved.'

'It is perhaps this experience that has resonated the most,' David continues, 'as I believe that is how I operate my business. I never allow a customer to feel confused or undirected simply because something happened prior to my time with them. It is at such times that they need the most help, and they then see the true depth of service that a company has to offer.'

Tel: 0800 3898271
Web: www.ukfranchiseaccountants.co.uk

COMPANY PROFILE

Expense Reduction Analysts

When the recession bites hard, many organisations are under-prepared and begin to struggle with their financial targets. Our network of specialist procurement advisors enable organisations to save money and boost business performance through effective procurement, improved supplier management and smarter spending habits.

Expense Reduction Analysts

A business nation searching for effective cost reduction

Throughout the country, crisis meetings are being held to discuss how to survive the recession and reduce the impact that any 'double dip' may have. Sales teams are under increasing pressure as they are tasked with maximising revenue streams, just so that the business can stave off the threat of making redundancies. In these financially tough times every penny counts, so imagine if you had the answer to this global epidemic.

Across the UK, many organisations are benefitting from the services of cost, smarter spending, a unique business offering where professionally trained procurement specialists are brought in to investigate any 'profit leaks' and identify solutions. These advisors then take the process one step further and actually manage the changeover process, ensuring that the transition to the new supplier proceeds without a hitch. The client can rest assured that their procurement is in good hands, without having to invest their own time or resources.

In many cases, a dedicated consultant is able to identify savings with the current range of suppliers, eliminating the need to change to an alternative service provider. Such is the depth of knowledge and purchasing influence – as a result of the millions of pounds' worth of spend already under review – that the procurement expert can make a positive impact to the organisation's bottom line without jeopardising the quality of service being received.

Roy Bayliss, an Expense Reduction Analysts franchise partner, comments: 'We really add value to our clients' processes by streamlining their non-core costs, meaning that they benefit from substantial savings and improve the bottom line significantly, without increasing sales targets.'

The changing face of procurement

A recent McKinsey Global Survey revealed that reducing operating costs is top of the agenda for financial directors and chief financial officers (CFOs) in the current austere economy. The same survey revealed that many believe that:

- they are currently not getting the best prices

- managing these areas of expense is critical for improving their business

- lowering costs from suppliers is one of the biggest challenges they currently face within expense management.

Additionally, most CFOs feel that procurement is important to finance, but many lack the understanding or know-how to influence it, with many commenting that effective procurement is increasingly becoming a function of the finance department, in the same way that sales has become a function of marketing.

In reality, organisations are aware that reducing their costs is important to improving their bottom line, but because they are not procurement specialists they are not sure what to do. A cost, purchase and supplier management consultant is able to become a trusted advisor to the organisation, ensuring that savings remain competitive, while maintaining supplier relationships.

It is this process that makes many clients continue to engage procurement experts well after the initial contract has been fulfilled. In fact, many clients are realising the value that a trustworthy professional brings to their business, with many signing multiple projects across areas of their business ranging from stationery to marketing, fleet, insurance and logistics.

How your procurement consultancy can help suffering businesses

Simon Perkins became an Expense Reduction Analysts franchise partner in July 2010, after a career with a major parcel distribution company, says: 'The great thing about this business is that we are able to provide savings in over 100 areas of cost, purchase and supplier management. The experience within our network means that we never have to turn a client away. How many businesses can genuinely say that?'

In the current economic climate, the number one challenge that most organisations face is reducing their costs. Businesses are aggressively streamlining core expenditure, yet many of them are still overpaying by as much as 40% on their everyday operating costs. By engaging an expert in cost, purchase and supplier management, businesses are able to improve their bottom line far more quickly and easily than they can increase their sales, and with a safe pair of hands supporting them along the way.

Franchising opportunities with Expense Reduction Analysts

A franchise opportunity with Expense Reduction Analysts can provide you with your own procurement consultancy, successful in assisting other businesses to improve their bottom line.

To find out how you can become a fully trained procurement expert, contact our franchise recruitment team to book onto a free discovery day at our group office in Southampton.

Tel: 02380 829737
Email: franchiseteam@erauk.net
Web: www.erafranchise.net

CASE STUDY

Expense Reduction Analysts

Franchisee: Glenn Cotter
Location: Midlands

From RAF to ERA

'When I was looking at Expense Reduction Analysts, I was really nervous as I had no background in procurement or accountancy, which I thought was essential as a franchise partner. It couldn't really be further from the truth,' says franchisee Glenn Cotter. 'I was able to bring my skills that any person with a strong background could bring, which, when supported by world-leading training, really gave me the strong start I needed.'

Glenn Cotter joined Expense Reduction Analysts in March 2001, having previously been a squadron leader in the Royal Air Force.

'I really enjoyed my time in the Royal Air Force, but was after a new challenge where I could use my existing skills and build on them to deliver a better work-life balance – and with superior financial rewards too.'

Training for a six-figure income

'Expense Reduction Analysts is a fantastic opportunity that provides the autonomy and flexibility to manage my time and my business as I deem best,' says Glenn. 'It really is a refreshing change from the military. I am able to manage, control and make the decisions that drive my business forward, but I am never alone; the support, training and advice from Expense Reduction Analysts will always ensure that I have the best opportunity to make a success of my business.'

'I have found that many of my fellow franchise owners demonstrate the same skills,' continues Glenn, 'such as having the self-discipline that is required to manage your own business, having the drive and motivation to generate a six-figure income, as well as having a likeable personality and the ability to solve problems.'

A rewarding franchise opportunity
Glenn says that Expense Reduction Analysts is 'a really rewarding franchise'. 'I get to save large companies money, making a difference along the way. I never thought that I would be able to generate a six-figure income, which I have been doing consistently. I guess that is the real strength of the Expense Reduction Analysts franchise – you are expertly trained to become a leading procurement consultant, with the ability to win business and deliver huge savings to your clients.'

'In summary,' says Glenn, 'I really am enjoying the benefits of all my hard work, and I look forward to every day.'

CASE STUDY

Expense Reduction Analysts

Franchisee: St John Rowntree
Location: South East

'The lifestyle that I aspired to.'
'Being your own boss does have its own challenges,' says Expense Reduction Analysts franchise partner St John Rowntree, 'but it also gives me the freedom to choose my hours of work. I've been on more holidays since joining Expense Reduction Analysts, including trips to Thailand and the Caribbean; I've paid off my mortgage, bought a new Mercedes for cash, and a holiday home too – all within the last six years.'

St John joined Expense Reduction Analysts in June 2005, having previously been an operations director for a division of Federal Express.

'Prior to joining Expense Reduction Analysts I had been in corporate life for the last 20 years across a range of different roles. I enjoyed a number of them, but this franchise opportunity definitely works well for me, and it gives me the lifestyle that I always wanted.'

Using the franchise network's expertise
The range of expertise within the franchise network means that new opportunities provide a flow of new business. St John says: 'Whether it is specialist areas such as fleet and logistics, or something which seems quite simple, like stationery, each category we analyse has its own unique challenge. Whatever the project happens to be, there is a wide range of expertise within our organisation, so we never have to walk away from new business.'

He continues: 'Due to the volume of business we are putting forward, the relationship that we have with suppliers makes my role a lot easier. It gives my customers real value and ultimately helps me to sign more clients. I believe this is unique to Expense Reduction Analysts, as no other cost reduction franchise I've encountered has this kind of ability.'

Benefits of being your own boss

St John enjoys the benefits of being his own boss. 'Since joining I have, on average, earnings of over £100,000 a year. Last year it was almost £200,000. You certainly get rewarded for the time and effort that you put in, which without doubt was not the case in previous employment. I am delighted that I joined Expense Reduction Analysts and I wouldn't go back to working for somebody else again.'

Don't be a Guinea Pig!

Across the UK there are dozens of domestic lawn care franchises, all offering pretty much the same thing, or so it seems.
Our competitors recruit a 'man-in-a-van', we are looking for business people.

GreenThumb has pioneered lawn care in the UK since 1986 and is by far the market leader, with over 450,000 customers, 200 branches nationwide and a turnover exceeding £60 million per annum.

How are our competitors' guinea pigs faring?

	Competitor	GreenThumb
Area:	**Maidenhead**	**Kendal**
Customers after 5 months	165	471

Source: Business Franchise - Oct 2011

Area:	**East Yorkshire & Hull**	**Dartford**
Customers at end of year 2	350	1,600

Source: Business Franchise - July/Aug 2011

Area:	**Richmond**	**Shropshire**
Customers after 9 years	3,500	6,650

Source: Competitors Website Aug 2011

Why be a guinea pig for another lawn care franchise only to accomplish a fraction of what a GreenThumb franchisee achieves? With virgin territories and resale opportunities available, ranging from £31,700 to over £500,000+, there has never been a better time to talk to us.

Call 01745 586041 or go online at
www.greenthumb.co.uk/franchising for a franchise pack.

GreenThumb
LAWN TREATMENT SERVICE

www.greenthumb.co.uk

If you want to be a 'man-in-a-van' franchise treating lawns yourself, don't call us, speak to our competitors.

GARDEN AND LANDSCAPE SERVICES

GreenThumb
Greensleeves

COMPANY PROFILE

GreenThumb

GreenThumb is the United Kingdom's largest and best-known lawn care franchise, with more than 200 franchises nationwide and almost half a million customers.

Celebrating its 25th anniversary this year, GreenThumb was the first lawn care company to be established in Britain and continues to defy the downturn.

The company carries out an all-year-round programme of treatments, which start at just £15 per treatment, with the average price at around £25. Over 450,000 customers receive a highly professional service to feed and weed their lawn for less than it would cost them to do the job themselves. They can also benefit from a range of other services, such as scarification and hollow-tine aeration.

GreenThumb provides such a value-for-money service, with clearly visible results, that customers not only continue the treatments year on year but also recommend the service in their thousands to friends, neighbours and family.

While franchisees are taught how carry out these treatments, GreenThumb is not a 'man and a van' franchise.

It is a full management franchise and franchisees operate multi-van businesses serving the needs of thousands of customers.

What does GreenThumb offer its franchisees?

The company is looking for professionals with business acumen, previous experience of managing a team, and preferably with sales and marketing ability. You will need to employ staff to carry out the lawn work, to handle customer enquiries and to generate sales leads.

GreenThumb created its franchise model in 1997 and it is a system with a highly successful track record – one that the financial institutions also hold in high regard.

All GreenThumb franchisees benefit from support and mentoring from dedicated head office staff. Other franchisees are also a great source of support and inspiration.

As the network matures and franchisees look to sell their businesses, the return on investment that a GreenThumb franchise delivers is becoming ever more apparent. It is this fact that is attracting shrewd investors to purchase an existing franchise, safe in the knowledge that the business model is proven to generate significant returns.

Resales are available at various prices and locations around the UK. In addition to comprehensive franchisee training at head office, you will also usually receive help from the vendor during a handover period so as to gain first-hand experience of your already-established business.

Even with resales, there is real potential for growth. As an example, one franchise recently became the first in the national network of 200 franchises to reach 10,000 customers, and remains one of the fastest growing.

This franchisee calculates that, even with 10,000 customers, he has only achieved 5% penetration in his area – which means 95% of the homes in the area still do not use GreenThumb.

Nationally, GreenThumb expects to reach 500,000 customers within the next year, but it is estimated that 16 million homes in Britain have a lawn.

Remember, GreenThumb is not looking for franchisees who want to treat lawns – many of its franchisees never have. GreenThumb wants business people with proven management and sales ability.

How to become a GreenThumb franchisee

Interviews for prospective franchisees are held at GreenThumb's state-of-the-art headquarters in St Asaph, Denbighshire, north Wales. There you will meet the franchise team, who will answer any questions you may have and assess your suitability.

Before reaching this stage you need to ask yourself questions like: 'Do I have the support of my family? Do I have the right skills to grow and run my own business? Am I experienced enough to tackle the challenges ahead? Do I have the drive? Can I manage a team? Am I prepared to run my business using systems put in place by the franchisor?'

If GreenThumb's team of experts believe you have what it takes to become part of the franchise network, you will be allocated a territory and the team will work with you to create a business plan.

GreenThumb will encourage you to carry out your own due diligence to find out more about being a franchisee, including, most importantly, talking to existing franchisees.

Once legal documents, including the franchise agreement, have been finalised, you will undertake two weeks of training at head office, learning about lawn care and how to develop and operate a GreenThumb franchise, before commencing the business you have purchased in your territory.

If you think you have what it takes to become part of one of the UK's most prominent franchising success stories, please contact GreenThumb to find out more.

For more information contact:
Mark Hallam, Franchise Manager
Tel: 01745 586041
Email: franchise@greenthumb.co.uk

CASE STUDY

GreenThumb

GreenThumb is Britain's original, biggest and most profitable lawn care franchise. It pioneered lawn care in the UK and has been much imitated as a result.

With more than 200 franchises nationwide, the 25-year-old company provides around 2 million lawn treatments every year to keep lawns all over the UK looking lush and green.

Due to the economies of scale its size allows, GreenThumb's lawn treatments actually cost less than a customer would pay to buy the materials at a DIY store and do the job themselves. Treatments start from just £15 and customers can pay monthly through an affordable and convenient direct debit facility.

Despite the economic downturn, the company has grown every single year to a current annual turnover in excess of £60million.

As the network matures and investors are looking for a business that will generate a significant return, even in difficult economic times purchasing an existing GreenThumb franchise is becoming ever more appealing as their impressive track record shows.

Resales are available at various investment levels and in varying locations across the UK. Virgin territories are also available at £31,700+VAT.

Statistics show how GreenThumb franchises consistently show better growth than rival franchisors in the sector.

The company's continuing success has brought huge benefits for franchisees who chose GreenThumb over its competitors in the lawn care sector.

Franchisees: Ian and Jacqui Balmforth
Location: Shropshire

When Ian Balmforth and his wife Jacqui bought the GreenThumb Shropshire territory in a resale, the business had just 500 customers and a turnover of just £61,000 a year.

Today, nine years later, they have around 6,650 customers, an annual turnover in the region of £800,000 and a staff of 16.

Ian, a former consultant with BT, says: 'GreenThumb has secured the growth. Over the years we have done everything GreenThumb suggested with their marketing mix and, as a result, the business has grown.

'It really did do what it said on the tin. We concentrate on customer service and expansion through marketing and recommendation. We have no doubt that this is a business that will continue to grow.'

Franchisees: Gary and Karen Cothliff
Location: Kendal and South Lakes

Gary and Karen Cothliff are now in their second year as GreenThumb franchisees in the virgin territory of Kendal and the South Lakes. They started with no customers, and by February, the end of their second year, they expect to have more than 1,000.

While many potential franchisees check out other franchisors in the sector to make comparisons, Gary and Karen decided GreenThumb was the one for them.

Karen says: 'We were GreenThumb customers ourselves and knew they were a good company with a fantastic product. We went to a seminar for potential franchisees at GreenThumb's headquarters and knew we were making the right decision. We have no regrets.'

Franchisees: David and Graham Sanders
Location: Kent/south London

Brothers David and Graham Sanders bought their virgin territory on the Kent/south London borders in February 2009.

At the end of two outstanding years they had 1,600 customers, and since then their customer base has increased to over 2,000.

Graham says: 'By our anniversary next February, we expect to have increased our customer base by more than 600 in our third year.

'GreenThumb has a system that works, but I think it also helps to have been in business before. We were not interested in running a "man and a van" operation. We want to grow this business as quickly as possible but at the same time make sure our customers are satisfied with the service.'

David and Graham are so happy with their GreenThumb franchise that they have already added a couple of neighbouring postcodes to expand the territory.

These franchisees are well on the way to generating significant wealth from this highly investable franchise proposition, just as many in the GreenThumb network have already.

COMPANY PROFILE

Greensleeves

Greensleeves, the lawn treatment experts, provides lawn treatment services to homes across the country. It offers a variety of services, from a seasonal treatment programme through to specialist applications such as scarification and re-seeding. Greensleeves uses the best quality products with 'no scorch' technology, along with controlled-release granules that provide a steady supply of nitrogen to the lawn. This allows for a long-lasting greening of the lawn and is perfectly safe to children, pets and plants. The company has been treating lawns for 12 years and has gone from strength to strength, with locations rapidly appearing across the United Kingdom.

Healthy growth at Greensleeves

In financial year 2011, Greensleeves saw its turnover increase by £800,000 to £3.4 million. In addition, Greensleeves' customer base soared, as it had in recent months, rising from 30,000. The company now has over 40,000 retail customers and 61 franchisees, a number that is growing with of new recruits coming on board all the time.

Looking at the past year, Greensleeves' Managing Director David Truby is justifiably proud of all that the franchise has achieved. He explains how the business really took off last year. 'Our profile was raised a lot more last year,' he says. 'We had a very productive spring with lots of work for both new and existing franchisees. This carried on as the year went on, and by the summer, we found that that we were very resilient against the effects of the recession, with constant requests for lawn treatments.'

A quality service

Because of the repeat demand, Greensleeves was easily able to meet its targets. When asked about the secrets of Greensleeves' success, David raises two important contributing factors.

One is the quality of customer service. 'The quality of people we recruit is very high. They must be professionally minded and ambitious, with a real drive to grow their own business.'

No horticultural background or expertise is required to start a Greensleeves franchise, although some management experience is an advantage. 'With our customer service, we look at this as our point of difference from our competitors,' explains David. 'We guide our customers through every step of the lawn-treatment process from the beginning to the end. That way, our customers are totally comfortable with us, and with the work that we do for them.

'This has led to many referrals through word of mouth, which, in turn, has led to lots more business.'

The other factor is that this is an excellent value-for-money business that can be used by anyone. 'It's not a service for the wealthy, but for everyone,' says David. 'The products we use allow for excellent results on lawns. But the price is surprisingly inexpensive: on average we charge £125 per year per customer, which normally accounts for four or five visits. Our service is affordable and very good value, and that's another reason why it has been so well received by the public.'

Opportunities for new franchisees

With over 60 franchisees established in the UK, Greensleeves is still seeking new recruits to join this fast-growing, dynamic business. There are nearly 100 territories available throughout the country, as the potential for work is as high as ever. Each new franchisee is allocated a geographical area that holds a potential client base of at least 80,000 customers.

The cost of a Greensleeves franchise is £24,950, which includes the provision of a full equipment package comprising machinery, stock, IT software and signage. In addition, franchisees are supported by an individually tailored marketing launch worth £7,000 that can include leaflet distribution, adverts and a website, among other initiatives.

Training and ongoing support

It is not necessary to have a background in the lawn care industry, as all franchisees are provided with full training. The initial training takes place over a period of 14 days and deals with all aspects of the franchise, putting new franchisees on the path to becoming lawn experts.

In addition to tuition on lawn care treatments and procedures, franchisees will learn about marketing, management skills, IT and business development. David Truby, managing director of Greensleeves, says: 'We understand that investing in a franchise and running your own business can be a bit daunting at first and that is why we are on hand at every stage of the process to ensure that our franchisees feel fully supported, trained and confident in running their businesses.'

Following the initial training period, franchisees will receive regular, hands-on support from the Greensleeves team. One of the Greensleeves managers will pay a visit to franchisees, on a quarterly basis, for meetings on progress and any assistance that is required. Greensleeves also has a very informative website and freephone number 0808 100 1413, which the public can use for information and to contact the company with any enquiries.

The benefits of being a Greensleeves franchisee

So what are the main benefits of becoming a Greensleeves franchisee?

'Apart from the generic advantages such as becoming your own boss and taking control of your working destiny, Greensleeves is a very secure business to be in,' says David.

'We have lots of long-term customers and also lots of new ones signing up all the time. This is because of our good value and high-quality service. Our franchise also appeals to family partnerships. We are a family-type business, as we have fathers and sons, sisters and brothers, and husbands and wives becoming franchisees. There is also the attraction of working outdoors. It's a very pleasant environment to be working in, because this is an outdoor-based business rather than an office-based one. In spring and summer, this is especially pleasant. It's also a very sociable business, because you are dealing with people all the time, speaking to them, and making sure that you provide the highest standards for their lawn care.'

David adds that there are a number of main unique selling points to Greensleeves.

'I feel that our technical programme and customer service are better than our competitors'. We have a strong, sound brand that we build from both service and quality. We are building the foundations for a business that is going to be even more successful in the future.'

After a fantastic 2011, this year looks set to be another good one for Greensleeves. 'Our main aim is to repeat last year in terms of performance and quality,' says David. 'We also hope to have more franchisees on board.' In addition to this, David adds that Greensleeves hopes to grow its customer numbers even further and to go beyond the growth turnover of £800,000. 'We want to consolidate and develop our brand, while raising our profile even further.'

Greensleeves, Unit 6, Technology Park, Station Road, Skelmanthorpe HD8 9GA
Tel: 0808 100 1413
Email: franchise@greensleeves-uk.com
Web: www.greensleeves-uk.com

CASE STUDY

Greensleeves

Franchisee: Steve Hook
Location: North Somerset

Franchisee in focus

In the first edition of this book we looked at how Steve Hook, at the time the newest member of the Greensleeves franchise, had achieved great success within just a few months of setting up his franchise. Now, one year on, we catch up with Steve to see how life has changed for him as an established Greensleeves franchisee.

Steve joined the Greensleeves franchise on 1 April 2010, but his track record shows him to be anything but an April fool – in a period of just over one year he has grown his franchise dramatically and now services a customer base of 500 clients.

Backtracking to 2010, Steve's induction into the lush green world of Greensleeves franchising came about after he decided that he needed a change of career. Steve's background stood him in good stead for the Greensleeves franchise. Steve has a degree in agriculture and had also been a sales consultant in the advertising world. This proved to be a useful combination for Steve as he looked for a franchise that could draw upon his experience and knowledge.

'I was becoming a bit tired of being in the advertising world for agriculture,' says Steve. 'I was looking for something new to do, and around that time I was starting to investigate franchising as a possibility.'

'Having browsed the web for possibilities in the lawn care and agricultural sectors, I came across a few that I was interested in. Given my background, I knew how to sell and market products and services – the issue was that although I had lots of ideas for starting a business of my own, I had less idea of how to get them off the ground. The good thing about a franchise is that all this is done for you.'

After much research, one of the franchisors that stood out was Greensleeves, and a meeting with managing director David Truby and his colleague Phil Paddock made Steve believe that this was a strong contender for his best option. Steve recalls: 'I spoke to several other lawn care franchises, but Greensleeves gave me by far the best impression. I went to see David and Phil for a two-hour meeting which turned in four hours plus. I knew within a few minutes that I could work with them. They were extremely professional, open and responsive.'

Steve adds that because the business model is in place, this takes the stress away of worrying whether your new business will work. 'Although in one sense you are thrown in at the deep end, Greensleeves will talk to you, prepare you and give you a list of potential clients when you begin – so there is no danger of worrying about what to do at the start.'

Steve also found that Greensleeves was very supportive during a slightly turbulent start to his franchise. 'During the period when I was signing up, unfortunately my father passed away – however, Greensleeves was very understanding about this, and I managed to begin trading with my franchise on 1 April 2010.'

Like other franchisees, Steve found that the franchise training course (which spans 10 days) proved to be both enlightening and useful. 'The course covers all the aspects that

you need to know before you can begin work. It is structured in a certain way so that you get dedicated periods of time on a particular aspect.' With that in mind, the training course devotes two days to the treatments needed, one day to marketing, another to technology and so forth. 'The training course is very good,' says Steve. 'You couldn't do without it.'

Steve is full of praise for the support that Greensleeves provides. 'The support is excellent,' he says. 'At the beginning, when you are feeling your way into the franchise, the support is dedicated to making you feel as comfortable as possible. For example, someone from the head office will come down once a week for the first month to see how you are getting on. And after that, they are always there when you want them. If you have a problem, they are always on the end of the phone.'

The marketing assistance is also very helpful, as Greensleeves promotes the franchise in a number of ways, such as on the web, and through leaflets and brochures. 'All the support is done in a way that all you need to concentrate on is to bring in as many customers as possible.'

Steve is emphatic about the high level of customer service that Greensleeves provides. 'My main task is to give people the beautiful lawns they are looking for, and in turn, this will help me gain as many customer numbers as possible,' he says. 'Even though I started only last year, I have managed to get 500 customers already. The Greensleeves offering is very simple. They believe in customer service and so provide excellent service at good prices. I am a strong believer in customer service – you cannot treat customers like cash machines, and because we deliver such a high standard, this is what brings in repeat business.'

Steve views his high levels of customer service and proactivity as the cornerstone of his successful growth. 'The main growth in year one came from canvassing – approximately 50% of my customers came this way. I made sure that all my friends knew what I was doing. I gave my customers good service, called in unplanned on problem lawns and made a fuss of them. I tried to maximise income by ensuring as many customers as possible booked a scarification and/or aeration treatment – 65% of my customers had at least one, and as a result lawns improved quickly.'

Steve's objective for the future is to grow the business further. 'My first target is to get to 750 customers, employing one full-time person as well as me. I am on track for this. I currently have a customer base of 480 and I employ a person three days a week. After I have achieved this goal I will review, but long term I aim to increase and employ more people. Joining a franchise was a big leap of faith, but looking back on it, it has worked out for me beautifully. I was bored in my last job. I am now much happier: I am selling a service people want and are very happy with in general.'

When asked what he liked most about owning a Greensleeves franchise, Steve is full of enthusiasm. 'I love that it's down to me – I decide what is going to happen and when, and I am able to take long-term decisions which steer the future of my business. I receive excellent support from HQ to bounce ideas off and I am very positive about the future. Setting up my Greensleeves franchise is the best thing I ever did; it really isn't bad when the last thing you have to do before you go to work is put on the factor 30 sun cream! Don't get me wrong: it is a challenge, but you get out of it what you put in and I am enjoying every minute.'

For further information about Greensleeves or becoming a Greensleeves franchisee please call 0808 100 1413 or visit www.greensleeves-uk.com.

HOME IMPROVEMENTS

Granite Transformations
EnviroVent

COMPANY PROFILE

Granite Transformations

The Granite Transformations franchise model has proved remarkably successful, since the concept first emerged back in 1996. Worldwide, there are now 200 franchised showrooms, fitting 7,500 installations every month and generating annual sales around £200 million. In this country, whilst the kitchen furniture market has suffered a downturn, sales across the Granite Transformations UK network have remained strong, with one-third of franchisees exceeding £1 million in annual revenue and overall net profit more than 50% up on 2008 figures.

This success has been built on the brand's distinctive 'top that fits on top', an affordable worktop replacement system that appeals strongly to homeowners looking for an instant kitchen makeover. Granite Transformations' worktop material has a distinctive slimline profile that allows it to be bonded directly over existing kitchen worktops. Despite its light weight and slim dimensions, the material is tougher than natural stone and is available in a choice of granite, quartz and recycled glass compositions, each blended with high tech polymer for exceptional performance and durability.

The UK franchisor, Rocksolid Granit Europe (RSG) subsequently expanded its franchise package by adding a profitable new revenue stream, through the introduction of replacement kitchen doors to the product mix. This logical extension to its retail offering has enabled Granite Transformations franchisees to offer customers both worktop and cabinet re-facing in a one-stop solution, with doors likely to contribute as much as 50% of franchise revenue.

'The affinity between worktop and cabinet re-facing is perfect and it enables our franchisees to provide a total kitchen makeover with just one sales call, usually carrying out the installation in one or two days,' says RSG's Chief Operating Officer, Danny Hanlon.

Latterly, in conjunction with parent company Trend, RSG has also introduced 'mosaics on a mattress' to the retail offering, whereby Granite Transformations franchisees can now install Italian glass mosaic tiles over existing splashbacks. The industry-first installation system dramatically cuts tile laying time and enables a perfect finish every time, adding another 'instant makeover' element to the brand proposition.

Yet, while kitchen makeovers are the mainstream business for most franchise owners, Granite Transformations' agglomerate material is equally at home in the bathroom, shower or wet room, and many adventurous homeowners are exploring its versatile décor possibilities. Indeed, TV property expert Sarah Beeny has used Granite Transformations material on a number of exciting bathroom makeovers, which are being showcased in her Rise Hall restoration show.

To support its franchise owners, RSG offers an award-winning marketing programme, which includes national TV and press advertising, an active brand PR campaign, tailored local publicity and website domains, extensive point-of-sale material and sales presenters for home visits. Added to which are computerised benchmarking and lead tracking systems and a product that franchisees will tell you 'virtually sells itself'.

What's more, that franchise package has become more affordable since RSG waived the need for new franchisees to rent, equip and staff a separate production workshop, in addition to a retail showroom. Apart from reducing set-up and running costs, this option appeals to those who are less comfortable with the technical side of worktop fabrication.

There is also the further cost-saving option of a concession-type showroom, rather than high street premises. Typically located within a garden centre or other high traffic area, a franchised concession site means there is no shop lease to sign and substantial savings to be made in such areas as business rates, service charges, legal fees and fitting out, substantially reducing the initial investment.

These lower-cost franchise packages and a recession-proof business model have all helped to recruit a steady stream of new franchise owners, currently running at a rate of one a month. With upwards of thirty franchised UK showrooms already and each exclusive sales territory covering at least 100,000 households, there are still gaps to fill in achieving total nationwide coverage, but new Granite Transformations franchise opportunities will eventually become thin on the ground. So, now might be a good time to join the 'makeover revolution' and get on board with a brand that's clearly going places.

"We're still looking for enterprising men, women and couples, who wish to run home improvement businesses themselves and who are not afraid of hard work," concludes Danny Hanlon. "We can offer flexible franchise packages, a continually evolving product offering and the reassurance of a successful global brand."

For further information and a full-colour franchise brochure, call 01892 509 680, email franchiseleads@granitetransformations.co.uk or visit www.gtfranchise.co.uk.

CASE STUDY

Granite Transformations

Franchisees: Whitwood Family
Locations: Norwich, St Ives

Whether or not industry surveys always reveal the fact, franchising appeals strongly to husband-and-wife partnerships and families. The traditional family business with its ' & Sons' suffix once formed the backbone of British retail and service industries, before 'plcs' came to dominate, and it still plays a key role in the franchise industry. Members of one family often play various roles in a franchise business, running the showroom, operating a workshop, keeping the books, making the sales calls. Typical perhaps is the Whitwood family from East Anglia, which together has built a thriving home improvement business in Norwich and now St Ives, Cambridgeshire.

The Whitwood family members, father Malcolm and brothers Oliver and Tom, are Granite Transformations franchise owners, amongst the early adopters in fact, and they fabricate, fit and market replacement kitchen worktops and doors. Advertised under the slogan 'the top that fits on top', Granite Transformations' hardwearing, diamond-polished work surfaces fit neatly and unobtrusively over existing worktops, creating virtually instant style makeovers, while replacement cabinet doors complete the makeover effect.

'When we first saw the Granite Transformations concept at a trade show, being from Norfolk we were quite sceptical. Does it really do what it says it does?' recalls Oliver Whitwood. 'We didn't take any leaflets and might have missed the opportunity, but later we saw it at another show and got hold of the franchise information. By 2004, we'd opened our first showroom in Norwich.'

Although all three Whitwood men are skilled joiners, they came to their franchise business from different directions. Dad, Malcolm, had his own woodworking firm, working with the lads' grandfather, where the boys often helped out on site. Oliver was destined for the forces, however, until a sporting injury dashed his hopes, later becoming a patisserie chef. Younger brother Tom previously worked with an outdoor pursuits company in Wales and France.

"Dad and I decided to invest in a Granite Transformations franchise, but we thought it would be great if we could all work together, so we enlisted Tom as Workshop Manager," says Oliver. "We attended the initial training programme and found the technical side quite straightforward, as you might expect, but we appreciated the franchisor's input on business operations and sales and marketing. We didn't have the finances to invest in a major local advertising campaign, so we built the business through leaflet drops, exhibiting at county shows and word of mouth recommendations, as well as attracting passing trade."

This approach has seen a steady increase in business year on year, with annual revenue close to £500,000 at the Norwich showroom. They average five worktop installations per week, with every other job additionally involving replacement kitchen doors; because the houses are generally bigger in Norfolk, the typical spend is somewhat greater than average. Despite the natural reticence of local people, it seems customers love the Granite Transformations product, especially as they like things to last, and they appreciate the polite, helpful and extremely proficient customer service provided by the Whitwoods, with feedback averaging eight out of 10 on the satisfaction scale.

Nor is this franchise family content with just residential installations. They were responsible for fulfilling one of Granite Transformations' largest commercial contracts, at the stylish OPEN Youth venue in Norwich, and are eyeing up sales opportunities presented by local factory conversions and a nearby pioneering eco-town.

They have now expanded from a smaller industrial unit in Norwich, to larger premises with double the showroom space and three times the workshop size, and last year opened new retail premises in the bustling market town of St Ives, near Cambridge. To finance this, they traded off some of their existing franchise territory around Peterborough, in order to achieve consolidated sales coverage across a more cohesive geographical area, with showrooms strategically located at the edges. The St Ives site has proved a wise investment, with installations in the southern part of their franchise territory already rivalling the Norwich operation and the main workshop economically serving both premises.

"We are not afraid to get our hands dirty and pitch in with the installations, but our growth target is to double turnover in the near future, by which time we shall be recruiting new staff," predicts Oliver. "Don't expect any fanfare and fireworks, we have always adopted a cautious attitude, building up our business gradually, and we shall be sticking to that formula."

COMPANY PROFILE

EnviroVent

Breathe life into your career with EnviroVent
Ideal for those with a passion for sales, EnviroVent is an award-winning home-improvement franchise that provides energy-saving ventilation solutions for homes and small offices. This is a unique opportunity to join an established manufacturer whose products not only eliminate the misery of condensation and mould but can also help to alleviate the symptoms of asthma and other respiratory problems.

Because Air Matters

Ventilation is a necessary part of modern life. As we construct or refurbish our homes in line with stringent building regulations to become more energy-efficient, the improvements made by adding cavity wall insulation, loft insulation and double glazing can actually work against us. By implementing these various improvements we have effectively 'sealed up' our homes, and by doing so create poor ventilation, which can lead to condensation and mould problems. As the average person spends up to 90% of their time indoors (of which up to 70% is spent inside their own home), good indoor air quality is vital to a healthy living environment.

Eco-friendly innovation
EnviroVent manufactures innovative and sustainable ventilation solutions that are designed to outlast a property, with minimal use of energy – all backed up by a five-year guarantee. What's more, each product in EnviroVent's sustainable Lifetime Range is manufactured in the UK, at the company's Harrogate factory.

" *We knew almost immediately that EnviroVent was the right franchise for us and the products fitted our own green ethics.* **"**

Helen Mould, EnviroVent North Wales and Wirral

EnviroVent is a home-based franchise opportunity that offers you:

- a market that is 80% untouched and free from franchised competition

- unrivalled and well-structured training with ongoing support

- unique, patented and environmentally friendly products

- over 20 years' experience in the industry

- marketing materials worth around £4,000.

For further information about EnviroVent's franchise opportunity please contact Phil Harrison, franchise business development manager, on 01423 810810, email PHarrison@envirovent.com or visit www.homeventilation.co.uk

THE QUEEN'S AWARDS
FOR ENTERPRISE:
INNOVATION
2009

Time for a fresh start?

Breathe some life into your career!

Are you interested in helping people to:

✓ **Improve their health?**
Help to alleviate the symptoms of asthma and allergies.

✓ **Improve their home?**
Banish condensation and black mould for good!

✓ **Cut their heating bills?**
Improve energy efficiency around the home.

EnviroVent are a company who design, manufacture and install award winning sustainable ventilation solutions here in the UK. We have built up a successful business supplying to the social housing sector but there are over 21 million private households who still need ventilation. We re offering you the opportunity to be part of an award winning company, the chance to run your own territory and buy into a growing market.

Interested? Contact us now.

0845 27 27 807

or visit www.homeventilation.co.uk
and go to our Franchise Opportunity Section ◄

The Package

Potential Earnings

Year 1	▶	£20,000 +
Year 2	▶	£60,000 +
Year 3	▶	£80,000 +

✓ Home based franchise

✓ Exclusive territory - 1 million population

✓ 20 days support and training in the first year, then 4 days support per year thereafter

✓ Bespoke web based software package including training

✓ Central marketing call handling

✓ Deposit on a sign written van up to £660

✓ ...and much more!

The Costs

Franchise Fee
£18,950 + VAT

Management Services Fee
8%

Marketing Levy
2%

CASE STUDY

EnviroVent

Franchisees: Peter and Helen Mould
Location: North Wales and Wirral

The franchise owners for EnviroVent north Wales
and Wirral, Peter and Helen Mould, have seen their
lives transformed since buying their franchise last
year. They decided to look for a suitable business
franchise, one that they could manage together,
following Helen's redundancy from the civil service.
Both have strong principles when it comes to
environmental issues and are keen advocates
of 'green products', especially within the home.

Peter had previously worked as a domestic energy assessor and was on the look-out for an
opportunity to make a bigger impact.

Peter said: 'We think it's a good "couples" franchise, but you have to enjoy spending a lot
of time together and be clear about responsibilities. Having two of us to bounce ideas off
each other and to see things from a different perspective or to cover different tasks has been
useful. Having an interest in this area, particularly the "green" aspect, has been helpful to us
as it means we can really sell the benefits
of the products.'

'And with a surname like Mould,' adds
Helen, 'we knew that this had to be the
right business for us!'

Franchisee: Iain Mantrippe
Location: north west London

Iain Mantrippe bought the EnviroVent
franchise for north west London as a
result of being a very satisfied customer.
He contacted EnviroVent when a flat that
he owns and rents out had problems with condensation and mould.

Iain explains: 'I was sceptical; I didn't think that EnviroVent's Positive Input Ventilation Unit (PIV) would be sufficient to solve the problem, even with the 100% satisfaction guarantee.'

EnviroVent's PIV unit successfully did the job, eliminating the problem of condensation and mould.

'I was so impressed,' says Iain, 'not only by the product but also by the service, that I started to look into the franchise opportunity. I also discovered that in 2009 the company had won the Queen's Award for Innovation and that the philosophy and ambition of EnviroVent matched my own. In order to learn more, I booked myself on to an EnviroVent franchise discovery day. Eight weeks later I began my training, started to take appointments and surveyed my first property!'

Franchisee: Stuart Wright

Stuart says: 'After seeing the company at a discovery day, I knew straight away that an EnviroVent franchise was for me. It already had a successful business solving condensation and mould problems within the social housing sector, and in 2009 it established a franchise operation targeting private rentals and the home owner market. I could see a huge opportunity here selling EnviroVent's innovative and sustainable ventilation solutions, which  already had a proven track record within the social housing sector, to private landlords and home owners.'

In order to capitalise on the opportunity to maximise revenues, Stuart embarked on a strategic plan so as to respond quickly, efficiently and effectively to a deluge of free survey requests from people whose properties were suffering from condensation and mould.

Innovative thinking
Stuart concludes: 'As EnviroVent continues to develop new and exciting ways to promote the business, I think we are a perfect match in ambition. A prime example of this is that I recently noticed that the local landlord fairs had dried up due to government funding cuts. I decided to team up with a local events company to run them privately, along with the assistance of local authorities who promote the events to all of the private landlords in their respective regions.'

Achieving much of his success by making it a policy to educate as many people as possible about the effect that poor indoor air quality can have on their health, Stuart has built up a very impressive franchise with a turnover in 2010 in excess of £300,000. He is on target to beat this figure for 2011, as well as increasing his profit margins and average order values.

The most successful garment alteration franchise in the UK and Ireland

Who?

- Are you ambitious to run your own business?
- Customer driven and well organised?
- Can you follow a proven business system?

How?

All Zip Yard franchises are finished to a distinctive specification and you are presented with a fully operational and fully supported business with trained staff and comprehensive brand marketing from day one.

Support Includes:

- Marketing and promotion tools
- Group purchasing power
- Internet and web support
- Ongoing training programmes
- Continued concept and product development
- Day to day troubleshooting

Total Cost:
Approx. £33,000 + VAT plus shop fit*

- **One-off licence fee**
- **Franchise package:**
  - **Corporate branding**
  - **Production equipment**
  - **Comprehensive marketing launch programme**
  - **Opening stock**
  - **Bespoke electronic point of sale package and software**
  - **Computer**
- **Training and project management**
- **Ongoing business support**

"After meeting the franchisor, Nigel Toplis, we were very impressed by the professionalism of the franchise. Since opening the reaction from customers has been amazing and business is going so well that we are looking to open a second Centre, and possibly a third after that."
Richard McConnell, The ZipYard Altrincham

For further information call
Janet Matthews on 01530 513307

e: jmatthews@thezipyard.co.uk   w: www.thezipyard.co.uk

*The exact shop fit cost will be determined by the size and standard of the premises

Your Local Specialist

Ableworld Franchise Opportunity

Ableworld, one of the UK's leading mobility retailers, is looking to recruit a limited number of franchisees to join their franchise network in the growing mobility sector

According to government statistics, in 10 years time over 25% of people will be over 65 and the figures for those over 80 and 90 are even more striking. *Ableworld's* products and services are designed to capitalize on this growing market and you can capitalize too, as an *Ableworld* Franchisee.

FRANCHISEES WILL GET

- Two integrated businesses for one price
- The opportunity of earning up to £95,000p.a. by Year 3
- Use of the *Ableworld* ™ brand in an exclusive territory
- A first class training and support programme
- And much more…

FRANCHISEES WILL NEED:

- Drive, energy and enthusiasm
- Customer service mentality
- A passion for helping people
- The desire to want to run their own business in a growing market

Your Local Specialist

For more information call **01270 627 185** or visit **www.ableworldfranchise.co.uk**

THE Christmas Decorators

Unique franchise investment opportunity
There is no other franchise like this in the UK.

Low cost investment
Franchise set up costs £14,999 + VAT.

Start your business working from home
No need for premises or expensive overheads.

Earn 12 months of income in just 3 months
Pay yourself the same in three months what other franchises of similar investment would pay in 12 months

Fun and exciting
Earn a living from making properties look amazing for Christmas.

No hard selling
The market place is massive and this is a highly welcomed service. It's also contagious – once one property has it, everyone around also wants it.

Almost 100 per cent customer retention
Christmas comes every year and so does the re-installation for existing customers as well as your new ones.

First-class training and support
We can teach anyone how to do it, as long as they have a keen eye for what looks good.

Ongoing training and support
Lots of training throughout the year, as well as on demand support, ensures your success.

Be in business as a Christmas decorator, in your area, for as little as £14,999 + VAT

RETAIL

The Christmas Decorators
Ableworld (UK) Ltd
FFS Brands Ltd
The ZipYard

COMPANY PROFILE

The Christmas Decorators

Welcome to a genuinely unique franchise investment opportunity

Professional Christmas decorating is a growing market sector and a unique opportunity that provides a very lucrative income by capitalising on the indulgence of the wealthy private sector and the 'must-have' requirements of the commercial and public sector.

Running an independently owned franchise business with The Christmas Decorators provides endless opportunities and is much more than a proven business model. It can be a way of life and the chance to be part of something that is not only very special but also, despite all the hard work, great fun.

Being your own boss

If the freedom to run your own business, be your own boss and enjoy the resulting financial rewards and lifestyle is appealing to you, then The Christmas Decorators franchise could be the ideal solution for you.

The Christmas Decorators has a wealth of business knowledge gained through practical, hands-on experience, and since 2008 has worked extremely hard to build a network of successful franchisees by working alongside them with a superb, structured support package to ensure their success and develop the brand for everyone's benefit.

The Christmas Decorators and you: a commitment

The Christmas Decorators have extensive knowledge of franchising our business and have thousands of satisfied, returning customers year on year. We know the Christmas industry and we will pass on to you our knowledge and expertise on how to build a successful business.

We are the recognised market leaders in this sector and our position and reputation has been earned by our in-depth knowledge of the industry and the market-place, by consistently exceeding our clients' expectations and by our commitment to building the brand by being the very best.

This makes The Christmas Decorators the ideal partner for anyone considering investing in a franchise, particularly if you have a creative side, a passion for Christmas and would enjoy making money by delivering an amazing and unforgettable experience to your clients.

Rewards

The rewards for hard-working, dedicated and enterprising franchisees can be significant, but the choice is yours as to how successful you want to be. The Christmas Decorators can be built around your existing lifestyle or your personal aspirations and can be operated as a purely seasonal business, but the more effort you put in out of season with the commercial sector, the more successful you will be and the greater the rewards will be.

The market place: sources of income

The list of potential clients and opportunities is endless and the following are a selection of where some of our clients come from:

- hotels

- restaurants

- golf clubs

- health spas

- wine bars

- shopping arcades

- shopping centres

- town councils

- designer outlet villages

- airports

- convention centres

- office blocks

- offices

- beauty salons

- theatres

- private residences.

The list of clients includes many of the UK's most prestigious brand names and A-list celebrities and sports stars.

The franchise package
The £14,999 cost of the franchise package includes:

- franchise license

- initial and ongoing training

- operations manual

- initial launch

- launch support

- ongoing support

- search-engine optimised website

- stationery

- residential brochures

- commercial brochures

- image portfolios

- branded uniforms

- access to unique and bespoke branded products at imported prices

- two conferences per year

- laptop and software.

Company background
Founded in 1999 in Aspen, Colorado by husband and wife team Nick and Sarah Bolton, the business flourished before being introduced into the UK in 2005. The service was readily accepted by many wealthy clients in the UK.

It is fair to say that the way the business has developed and expanded is very different from the original concept and that it has undergone substantial growth and development in the UK and expanded rapidly into the commercial sector. The Christmas Decorators had been heavily featured in many of the leading lifestyle magazines and tabloid newspapers, and has been featured in several documentaries on both local and national TV channels.

For more information, or to download the prospectus, contact:
Maurice Kelleher
Tel: 0151 734 4300
Mobile: 07711 843129
Email: maurice@thechristmasdecorators.com
Or visit our website at www.thechristmasdecorators.com and follow the links.

CASE STUDY

The Christmas Decorators

Franchisee: Trevor Grinsted

For most of his working life Trevor has held retail management jobs at various levels. Although enjoying the challenge of fast-paced retail, achieving budgets and showing progress, he always felt that if he put just as much effort into a business he owned he would earn substantially more money.

After almost three years as a store manager Trevor reviewed his options and decided a franchise was the way to go. It provided an opportunity to own a business that would produce an income based on the effort put into it, but with the guidance of a franchisor who offers support and a proven business model.

A profitable choice

When asked why he chose a franchise with The Christmas Decorators, Trevor replies: 'Because I am highly ambitious, saw the potential in the industry and above all love Christmas. I am not afraid of hard work and it was made clear that I wasn't entering a get-rich-quick scheme. However, I compared what I was earning in retail in 12 months with what I could earn inside three months and there was no comparison. Couple that with what I can do with the other nine months, and it was very attractive.'

Trevor continues: 'The team at head office, along with the existing franchisees, had a passion for Christmas that became infectious, and now I am in the position that I am reciprocating this for the new franchisees this year. You only have to ask, and help is at hand.

'Christmas has always been a big deal in the USA,' says Trevor, 'and it is slowly getting the same way in the UK. I took the point of view that if I was to get into the industry now it will only grow in the coming years. As I say, I'm highly ambitious!'

How did you raise the finance?

'From my own funds. I had savings accumulated over the years in retail and decided to spend some of it on an opportunity.'

Early days

Trevor financed his business from his own savings. 'From a financial point of view I was lucky to be in a position that I didn't have a bank loan to pay each month,' he says, 'but having never been in business for myself before, there was a level of anxiety. Am I spending too much for this? Is there enough profit in that deal? I beat the turnover target I set myself and managed to make a good profit in year one, having learned a lot from the experience.'

'I was suddenly thrust into a new world,' he continues. 'How many lights do I need to light a 40-foot oak tree? How many baubles go on a 7.5-foot internal Christmas tree? How do I use access equipment safely and effectively without spending over the odds? It was a lot to take in. However, I am glad I joined in May, which gave me time to learn.

'Physically I couldn't have survived without a good team, which is where my managerial experience came to the fore. One of my team is so enamoured with the company he has recently secured a franchise of his own.'

A great sense of achievement

Trevor is very motivated by his business and feels a great sense of achievement. 'Everything I do is my decision; I believe it's the right thing to do and I have the flexibility to suit myself. Since everyone in The Christmas Decorators is also their own boss and we have compatible goals, the franchise team works in a synergistic and supportive way which is really refreshing and different from other experiences I have had in the past.'

Trevor advises anyone thinking of buying their first franchise to do their research and ensure that franchising is the right solution for them. 'Check it fits your skill set and is the kind of role you would enjoy. Also, ensure you have sufficient funds in reserve to see you through those initial times – things might take longer than your plan indicates. Be realistic but not pessimistic. The more effort you put in, the better the results.'

One business, many plans

'Last Christmas was amazing. We helped 20 clients and exceeded the turnover target. We also logged over 100 enquiries that we couldn't help. I was determined to service a certain number of clients well, rather than a lot of clients averagely,' Trevor explains.

'For the coming Christmas we will be better prepared with a larger, fully trained team to help between 40 and 50 clients. The last year has been analysed, a steep learning curve has been traversed and changes have been made so that the coming Christmas runs much more smoothly, with a higher profit margin.'

Trevor's business won't be going slow during the other nine months of the year. 'We are looking for opportunities to help pubs with roof lighting and weddings and we also feel that there is an opportunity around the Olympics this summer.'

'Years three, four and five have been planned financially,' continues Trevor, 'but I'm sure this will change several times before they arrive.'

Would Trevor do it again? 'Without a doubt. I relish being my own boss and this is the opportunity I was looking for. I have recommended The Christmas Decorators to management in the retail companies I used to work for and there is a lot of interest. We really are a company to watch!'

COMPANY PROFILE

Ableworld (UK) Ltd

Company background
Ableworld is one of the leading mobility and homecare retailers in the UK, providing quality products and services to the ever-growing elderly and disabled market. The trusted Ableworld brand was created over a decade ago in the north west of England, and since 2008 has been offered as a franchise opportunity.

The market for Ableworld's products and services
The market for mobility equipment such as scooters, wheelchairs and stairlifts is estimated to be worth at least £1.5 billion in the UK and is growing year on year. The population of the UK is set to rise to by over four million in the next 10 years, and by nearly 10 million in the next 20 years.

People are living longer and there is a demographic bulge (the so-called 'baby boomers') reaching an age where mobility and homecare products are frequently needed.

In addition to these powerful demographic factors the government's stated aim is to help older people to live independent lives in their own homes. All of these factors mean that more and more people will need products and services such as:

- rise-and-recline chairs

- mobility scooters

- walking aids

- bathing aids

- stairlifts.

All of these products are provided by Ableworld and its network of franchisees.

Ableworld's unique offering
Ableworld is unique among mobility retailers in being the only bfa-registered franchise in its field.

The Ableworld franchise proposition is unique in the retail mobility sector in that it offers not one but two income streams in one package. A full Ableworld franchise gives potential franchise partners two viable, complementary businesses. First, there is the retail outlet – a mobility superstore that sells everything to help the elderly and disabled. Second, there is the stairlift business, which, using only high-quality branded equipment, provides home owners with a variety of stairlift options.

What will the franchisee's job entail?

For the retail side of the business, you can think of the job as being similar to a specialist retail manager. Building trusted relationships and giving high levels of customer service before, during and after the sale are paramount.

On the stairlift side of the business, franchisees will need to be able to quote, install and repair the equipment. A background in light engineering is an advantage, although full training will be given. Another option includes hiring an engineer if the franchise partner prefers to concentrate their efforts on the sales and management side.

As several of Ableworld's franchise partners have proved, a partnership of two people pooling their skills and experience works very well.

The franchise package

Some potential franchisees can be put off investing in retail franchises because of the high levels of minimum investment required.

In contrast, a full Ableworld franchise is only £29,950 and the business can be started with as little at £70,000 for a medium-sized retail outlet and stairlift franchise.

The following are highlights of the full franchise package:

- exclusive use of the Ableworld™ brand within a generous protected area

- a comprehensive operations manual

- full training on Ableworld products, systems and business

- advice on site selection

- help in negotiating the best property deal

- Ableworld LinePlans© to organise your store

- marketing launch pack

- comprehensive stationery pack

- help in arranging finance

- training on accounting and setting up your business

- assistance in setting up your VAT and your first VAT return

- introduction to and acceptance by key industry accreditation bodies

- setting up of accounts with suppliers

- intensive support during your first week

- 12-week diary of steps to take when you first open

- highly experienced industry mentors to guide you

- the back-up of a professional head office.

CASE STUDIES

Ableworld's first franchise partners

Franchisees: Andy Rees and Barry O'Donnell
Location: Birkenhead

In 2008 Andy Rees (pictured), who had been in the Royal Navy and had run a furniture business, saw the enormous potential that exists in the mobility and home care sector. Together with a trusted ex-service partner, Barry O'Donnell, he diligently researched the market and eventually decided that he wanted to team up with Ableworld.

Ableworld had grown steadily since its foundation over 10 years earlier, but did not have a franchise operation at the time. However, both parties could see the benefits of a franchise arrangement and one was agreed. Andy and Barry duly opened their store in Birkenhead in 2008. Three years later, they are running 30% above budget and have just renewed and extended their franchise.

Andy says, 'Franchising is a great way to start in business because you get the expertise and backing from people who have "been there, done that". They have systems and processes which have worked in the past and which we have proved can work in the future. Of course it's hard work, but then so is working for someone else – the difference is that you get to create wealth for yourself and your family rather than someone else.'

Ableworld decided, on the back of its success with Andy and Barry, to go into franchising in a more formal way. The company successfully applied for membership of the bfa in 2010 and started its nationwide search for other franchise partners to join it in this growing sector.

Ableworld's latest franchise partners
Franchisees: Mark Hennis and Naomi Moore
Location: Newark-on-Trent

Mark Hennis and Naomi Moore of Newark-on-Trent are the latest additions to the franchise network of specialist mobility retailers Ableworld.

Mark and Naomi previously ran a successful country pub on the outskirts of Newark and decided that for their next venture they wanted to go into a business that has a social as well as a commercial focus. Mark told us, 'We wanted to run a business that is ethical and fulfils a need in the community in which we live. We have seen plenty of poor service in the retail sector and we hope to bring our experience in the hospitality trade into a new sector.'

Naomi, who previously worked for the NHS, added: 'We want to build links, and more importantly trust, within our local community in our business. We will be providing a one-stop shop for our customers where you can purchase something as small as a pill box or as large as a stair lift and everything in between.'

They have also been very creative in getting their store noticed by the local community including having a 'Santa' travelling up and down on a stair lift outside the store over Christmas! Apart from their inventive marketing strategies, Mark and Naomi have also shown the enthusiastic and tenacious approach needed when starting a new business.

COMPANY PROFILE

FFS Brands Ltd

Southern fried success

Southern Fried Chicken continues to expand its network of stores, both internationally and in the UK.

In the early 1970s, British entrepreneur Arthur Withers spotted a gap in the burgeoning takeaway fast-food market and decided to bring 'fried chicken' from the US to Britain. Arthur trademarked the name Southern Fried Chicken (SFC), developed his own recipe and began travelling the country selling vending licences to existing food outlets so that they could then sell his chicken. Over the next 30 years Arthur expanded his business until nearly 200 add-on licensees and fully branded stores were selling SFC products across the UK.

Southern Fried Chicken provides fresh foods, hearty portions, good service, fair prices and a multi-choice menu, which combines the most successful quick-service restaurant products. All these add up to good value for money for customers, and generate increased brand loyalty.

Succulent pieces of fresh chicken are marinated to give flavour right through to the bone. They are coated in breading made from the finest ingredients mixed with a unique blend of herbs, spices, and SFC's exclusive Lemon Pepper. They are then pressure fried to perfection. Pressure frying ensures that as little oil as possible is absorbed into the product, giving a delicious grease-free product. But SFC hasn't just stopped there; it is constantly trying to improve its products to make them the best it can.

The Southern Fried Chicken store is also characterised by quality. SFC's scheme designs have been applied to create clean, spacious and comfortable restaurants, and are suited to all types of premises and existing architecture. SFC's theme designs provide that touch of originality that draws customers to return time and time again.

In 1996, Arthur's son Andrew persuaded his father to allow him to open franchises overseas – something Arthur had always been set against. It was this move that led to SFC's continued success, and in 2005 Andrew finally bought out his father and assumed the role of managing director.

Now Andrew wants to regain control of the UK market. Following his international success, he believes that SFC is perfectly positioned to meet its British competition head on, a process he started by appearing on the popular Channel 4 television show *Undercover Boss*. Andrew got to hear what SFC franchise owners really thought about how the company is run, but was also able to see for himself what could be done to improve things.

'*Undercover Boss* was a unique opportunity that allows you to see the day-to-day running of the stores without interference. To go in as myself would mean booking an appointment, whereby the franchisees would make a special effort to clean and tidy up, have the best staff in on that day to do everything by the book, and so on. Going undercover gives an accurate portrayal of the running of the stores as they actually operate, which is invaluable for the head office,' said Andrew.

After a challenging and enlightening few days Andrew decided it was time to reveal his true identity to some of the unsuspecting people he met. In an emotional and empowering climax he revealed what he had learned from the experience, the changes he decided to make and how he wanted to show appreciation to some of the great people behind the brand. Andrew had this to say:

'My experience on *Undercover Boss* is difficult to sum up in just a few words. I would, however, say it was definitely an experience. It was fantastic to get the opportunity to see our brand in its true form, both the good sides and the bad, and has left me motivated and inspired. Obviously, the whole experience was very draining, physically with the late nights and the early starts, and emotionally in meeting the people who rely on our franchise to succeed in order to support their families.

'The whole adventure gave me a tremendous boost in making improvements across the board in order to get the franchise chain back on track and where it should be, and to make things better for those who have invested in my brand for their livelihood. As a business owner, to do the show was one of the best decisions I ever made, and I think all bosses, given the opportunity, should jump at the chance.'

CASE STUDY

FFS Brands Ltd

Young siblings expand growing franchise portfolio
Franchisees: Romina, Lorenzo and Luca La Bella
Location: Norwich

Norwich-based sister and brothers Romina, Lorenzo and Luca La Bella have expanded their growing franchise portfolio in the region with the inclusion of up-and-coming British quick-service restaurant Southern Fried Chicken (SFC).

The siblings, all in their 20s, have invested in excess of £200,000 in SFC, which recently underwent a major brand revamp following its managing director's appearance on Channel 4's *Undercover Boss*.

The La Bella family, who already own six businesses in Norwich, including Papa Johns and Subway, will be the first to bring the revamped SFC brand to the region, and simultaneously be supporting local chicken farmers by using chicken from a co-operative of farms in the area.

The new franchise, which officially opened in the Mall Kitchen Food Court in March 2012, is the first of its kind in Norwich and comes under the siblings' umbrella company, LRL Legacy Ltd.

The La Bella family chose to invest in SFC after identifying a gap in the market for a quick-service restaurant that offers locally reared and sourced poultry. The business also differs from its competitors in that it prepares all its food freshly on the premises and does not use reconstituted chicken meat in any of its products.

Commenting on the expanding portfolio of businesses, Romina La Bella, 29, said: 'We are delighted to be taking on SFC as part of our expanding business portfolio. Our experience in the quick-service industry will complement this new venture as we look to turn the business into a success.

'In today's economic climate, quick-service restaurants are a booming industry. Our family has already tapped into some leading franchises, such as Subway and Papa Johns, and we are confident that SFC will follow in the same footsteps as these established and successful brands.'

Andrew Withers, managing director of SFC, commented: 'We are delighted that the La Bella family has chosen to invest in SFC. The La Bellas are among the first few to tap into the new SFC brand and recognise its potential. We have great plans to grow the business and aim to become one of the leading quick-service restaurant brands in the UK over the next five years.'

Withers added: 'It's also very special for my family to have an SFC presence in Norwich, as Norfolk is where the business dream began. Moving from wartime London, Dad enjoyed years of a much quieter life on a farm caring for and raising chickens before moving to the US and coming up with the SFC idea.'

COMPANY PROFILE

The ZipYard

The ZipYard is the most successful and fastest growing garment alteration franchise in the UK and Ireland where growth has been built on the back of quality, speed, convenience and value – together with a network of hard-working franchise owners.

The market potential is huge and all centres are expected to be profitable in the first year. Interestingly the clothing alteration business is not economy driven! When times are good more and more people buy new clothes that need altering to size. When times are not so good people get clothes altered or repaired to last a little longer.

People no longer have the time or the skills to tackle even the simplest of hems, let alone risk damaging a favourite or expensive garment, and at the ZipYard we have taken a different approach to the garments alteration business.

Highly visible, strong, bold branding separates the ZipYard from competitors and helps to dominate in the high street. All centres are finished to the highest standards and include state of the art machinery, computer systems and, in most cases, seamstresses work in full view of the public so customers can see for themselves the high standards of workmanship.

The ZipYard business model has been created, tested and developed to ensure franchise owners have the very best opportunity to be successful in the shortest period of time. Your investment delivers a fully operational and fully supported business, with trained staff and comprehensive marketing from day one – plus all ZipYard Centres are finished to a distinctive specification – customer-friendly, highly branded and very visible.

A word from franchisees
Franchisee: Garry Millington
Marine engineer and ex-navy serviceman Garry Millington gave up a life on the ocean waves to settle down in Llandudno and set up his ZipYard Centre on 31 May 2011.

Garry has set up and sold other successful businesses during his career, but decided the time had come to put down roots, settle down and make the most of the excellent customer service skills he has developed along the way.

What made you chose the ZipYard?
'There comes a time when you have to take stock of your life and think about the future, and for me the opportunity to buy the ZipYard franchise for the Llandudno area came just at the right time. I like the concept and can see how in today's modern times people either don't have the time or the knowledge to do their own alterations.

'I've enjoyed going all over the world to famous marinas and being part of the whole yachting scene working for people who demand the very best in life. They expect nothing but the highest quality of service and I bring this level of service to my customers.'

Experience suggests that a unit of 650 to 850 square foot is the ideal size for a centre and we look to locate each centre in an area that gives high visibility and is within easy reach of car parking.

The ZipYard is a 'turnkey' franchise and the package supplied includes industrial sewing machines, a blind hemmer, over locker, buttonholer, ironing station, electronic point of sale system, bespoke till and software package, accessories, consumables and computer.

We pride ourselves on the look and feel of our centres and to this end we provide a professional shop fit consisting of external and internal signage/fitting room/counters/flooring/fixtures and fittings, opening starting stock and corporate branding. Plus there is a comprehensive marketing programme to launch the centre with 50,000 leaflets, giveaways, official opening package, etc.

Franchisee: Richard McConnell
Richard McConnell, 32, owner of the ZipYard in Altrincham, used to be a driving instructor before following his wife Marie's hunch to buy a ZipYard franchise.

Richard is originally from Northern Ireland and opened his ZipYard franchise on 12 September 2011.

'I gave my future a lot of thought. We felt the time was right to seize the moment and invest in a reliable business with potential for growth.'

Why the ZipYard?
'Marie spotted the potential for the ZipYard as a result of her own personal experience. Her wedding dress needed alterations, and although the work was done well, the seamstress' working environment didn't inspire much confidence.

'The lady was working from home, and when Marie handed over her wedding dress it was plonked on the kitchen table – where upon the family cat jumped straight onto it.

'If you've spent a lot of money on an item of clothing you want to know that it is being repaired in a clean, professional environment by someone who knows what they are doing.'

And the future?
'It's exciting for us to be opening a ZipYard Centre and our plan is to open branches in prime retail locations throughout south Manchester.'

What is the total cost?
There is a one-off licence fee of £15,000 plus a fee for training and project management of £5,000.

The internal fit out and merchandising costs approximately £13,000.

So total costs are £33,000 plus the shop fit (plus VAT of course) – which will vary depending on size, structure and condition of the unit.

Who are we looking for?
We are looking for prospective franchise owners who will be dedicated, passionate, focused and hard working as we are.

You do not need to be familiar with repairs or alterations and we're not looking for tailors.

Successful franchise owners will be ambitious to run their own business, customer driven, well organised and keen to follow a proven business system.

Our business ethos is based on the principles of excellent and responsive customer service, speedy turn around, quality materials and staff loyalty augmented by efficient and proven business systems, marketing and promotional collateral and on-going in-centre support from the whole ZipYard team.

Contact: Janet Matthews
             t: 01530 513307
             e: info@thezipyard.co.uk
Total Cost: Approx. £33,000 + VAT plus shop fit
Type: Retail

CASE STUDY

The ZipYard

Franchisee: Richard McConnell
Location: Altrincham

ZipYard Altrincham: England's first clothing alterations franchise
Richard McConnell, 32, opened his clothing alterations, repairs and tailoring franchise, The ZipYard, in Altrincham in September 2011. Although well established in Ireland, Richard's business was the first ZipYard Centre in England, bringing on-site repairs

and alterations to the high street in purpose-designed premises with fully trained staff.

Originally from Derry in Northern Ireland, Richard moved to the UK in 1997 to study for a Management and Accountancy degree at the University of Huddersfield.

Richard is married to Marie and their first child, Darcey, was born in October 2011.

Education and early career
After university, Richard travelled and worked across Australia, Asia and Europe, often taking up jobs involving either door to door or telephone sales. 'It takes real inner strength to do those kind of jobs, because you are constantly being turned down. You have to put up with a lot of rejection and negativity but it does build character!'

In 2003, Richard moved back to Huddersfield to work in recruitment for four years until deciding to branch out and become a driving instructor.

'I was 24 years old and I wasn't enjoying the groundhog-day feeling of working in an office. I craved a new environment and wanted to get out and meet people. I was looking for work when an advert for becoming a driving instructor in the local newspaper grabbed my attention.

'I liked the flexibility that the job offered along with working my own hours and being my own boss.'

Richard joined a franchise operation for three years before setting up his own independent driving instruction business for five years.

What led you to switch from being a driving instructor to running a ZipYard centre?
'My wife and I wanted to start a family, but my hours as a driving instructor were really unsociable, mainly during evenings and weekends. We didn't think this would fit in well with

family life so I started looking around at different opportunities. We had saved up a bit of money and thought that investing in a franchise was a less risky option.

'We did lots of research in the franchise press and online, and looked into a wide variety of franchises.'

Why did you choose ZipYard?

'My wife noticed the ZipYard advert and she thought it was a fantastic idea. We did some research and quickly realised that there was no real competition in our area. Most of the time clothing repairs are done as a bolt-on service at dry cleaners. The turn-around time isn't very good and they don't offer a very wide range of services.

'We went to meet Nigel Toplis, the franchisor, and we visited a centre in Wales. We were impressed by the professionalism of the franchise. The brand is very strong and the shop fit is amazing, from the fitting rooms to the equipment and layout. They really know what they are doing and can cater for every kind of alteration and repair on site.'

What kind of support have you had setting up your franchise?

'Both myself and my wife, Marie, have received comprehensive training, at the ZipYard training centre in Belfast and more 'hands-on' experience in a working centre. The training covered everything from administration and office processes to employment contracts, employment law, pricing, tills, equipment maintenance and the general day-to-day running of the centre.

'Nigel and his team helped us to source the right premises and even helped us to negotiate the lease. There are so many areas that I knew nothing about, such as break clauses and other contractual technicalities where Nigel's team have been invaluable. I'm so glad we weren't on our own.'

How is it going?

'It's going brilliantly and we are getting busier every week.

'The reaction from customers is amazing. They seem genuinely ecstatic that we are here and their faces light up when they come in to the centre. They are delighted that we can breathe new life into clothes that they can't wear or that are damaged in some way.'

What are your future plans for the business?

'Once we've got one centre up and running to full capacity we would love to open up a second one. Marie would also like to get more involved with the business once Darcey has grown up a bit.'

Would you recommend a ZipYard franchise to potential franchise owners?

'Absolutely, no doubt about it. It is one of the most unique franchises available, with a professionalism and quality that just shines through.'

TRAVEL

GoCruise

COMPANY PROFILE

GoCruise

Why start up your own GoCruise franchise?

The cruise business is booming! It is fast becoming the most lucrative sector in the travel industry, and you can become part of it as a GoCruise franchisee. Since the earliest days of sailing there has been something special about travelling by sea. It's about fresh air, breathtaking views, new cultures and wonderful discoveries.

The cruise industry has continued to grow, despite recent economic challenges, and is one of the only sectors of travel to see such growth. More and more customers are choosing to cruise (either as a repeat of the holiday they know and love, or as a first-time experience), based on the value for money that this type of holiday represents.

GoCruise, which is part of Fred. Olsen Travel Ltd, is one of the UK's largest specialist cruise agencies. It has seen significant business growth, giving it a great base from which to include even more value for its franchisees.

The franchise package

GoCruise will set you up with your own territory containing at least a quarter of a million households and show you how to run your business from the comfort of your own home or premises.

Whether full-time or part-time, no previous experience is necessary, as we can teach you every aspect of this exciting business. You will be shown how to establish your market, get the phones ringing and book your customers' cruises. We will also supply you with consumer leads.

GoCruise ensures that you have at your disposal literally hundreds of amazing cruise offers from all the major cruise lines, and continuous support in order for you to make the most of them. For a modest outlay, your GoCruise franchise is an exciting and fun-filled business opportunity, with a potentially high financial return, complete with an invaluable mentoring system – giving you peace of mind.

GoCruise's induction training includes elements of online booking systems and product training to encourage faster intake of the knowledge that you will use as a specialist in your business.

GoCruise franchisees

Naturally, we want to make sure that this is the right opportunity for you, and also that you are the perfect candidate to join the GoCruise team. The following are just some of the qualities you will need to run a successful GoCruise franchise:

- drive and determination – you get out what you put in

- commitment and enthusiasm for hard work

- a professional approach

- excellent management skills

- enjoyment of networking and getting yourself out and about in your local community

- passionate about selling

- commercial awareness and business acumen.

How much can you earn?

As with any business, the more motivated you are in the marketing and management of your business, the greater the return. The cruise lines pay remuneration by way of a commission on each sale.

If you have a general business understanding, you are keen to learn, are enthusiastic and hard-working, then there is no limit to the amount of money you can earn from a GoCruise franchise.

High commissions

As part of the Fred. Olsen Travel Group we at GoCruise benefit from the group's bulk-buying power and we receive some of the highest commissions in the industry – on average between 10% and 15%. You will receive continuous updated offers and the latest marketing material direct from the cruise lines.

You make money, we make money

GoCruise makes money only when you do. It is in the franchisor's interest to support and assist you as much as possible in a mutual goal of selling cruises. It's a win-win partnership when you become part of the GoCruise team.

Sell with confidence

GoCruise is a fully bonded member of ABTA (Association of British Travel Agents), ATOL (Air Travel Organisers Licence), ACE (Association of Cruise Experts), LCA (Leading Cruise Agents) and a full member of the bfa, which means you can relax in the knowledge that all your clients are protected. This means you can sell with confidence.

Where do I go from here?

If you feel that you have got what it takes to be a successful independent GoCruise specialist, then call us now in confidence to arrange a meeting. The number of franchises available is limited to ensure exclusivity, so don't delay.

Tel: 0800 954 0067
Email: sales@gocruise.co.uk
Web: www.cruisefranchise.co.uk

CASE STUDY

GoCruise

Franchisee: Jane Chadwick

A GoCruise journey

Jane Chadwick joined GoCruise as a franchisee in April 2006 and has never looked back. She had been made redundant some 18 months earlier and was looking for something that was right for her.

'I had always wanted my own cruise business, but obtaining things such as an ABTA licence was far too daunting a prospect,' says Jane. 'I looked at many "home working" opportunities but none was right for me. None provided me the flexibility to run my business the way I wanted, to be able to work the hours I wanted to work, and to be able to be totally independent and not tied to promoting any given operator over another.'

GoCruise offered all of these factors and more. Jane says, 'I am happy knowing that my business is safe with the backing and support of Fred. Olsen Travel, with ABTA and ATOL protection, and likewise my clients feel at ease knowing that backing is in place.'

Training and support

Jane says that the training and support are 'second to none' and are adapted to the individual needs of each franchisee. 'Ship visits are always in good supply, allowing us to experience at first hand and provide a better insight into what makes one ship different from another.'

'I'm very fortunate to have worked in the cruise industry previously and I appreciate the fact that I am left to run my business very much the way I want to,' says Jane, 'but I know if ever I need help or support with any aspect of running my franchise, the franchise manager and head office team are there to assist.'

Award-winning business

'Motivation to work from home has never been an issue as I'm passionate about what I sell,' says Jane, who has earned awards for her outstanding business.

'Opportunities are there if you want to grab them with both hands. Who would have thought, when I started my own franchise, that I would have picked up the award and title of Cruise Sales Person of the Year at the UK Cruise Awards 2008 for P&O, Princess, Cunard and Ocean Village holidays, and been nominated as Agent of the Year finalist at the TTG Travel Awards in 2010? Hard work it might have been, but it wouldn't have been possible without the help and support of Fred. Olsen Travel and GoCruise.'

Franchisee: Martin Spence
Location: Farnborough, Hants

Martin Spence loves travelling, so six years ago, after 20 years as an engineer with British Airways, he bought a GoCruise franchise. 'I have never looked back,' says Martin.

'Having travelled all over the world I have now experienced many different cruises over the years. On my latest adventure I joined a working postal cruise in Norway where the ship delivered the post to local towns. The GoCruise franchise means I can combine my enthusiasm for travel with my own business, working from home in Farnborough.'

Martin loves the variety in his job, and as he serves his clients, he travels the world in the comfort of his home. 'Being part of the GoCruise franchise I have the opportunity to sell all types of cruising to all types of people to a whole host of destinations worldwide. From tall ships to river cruising, from family cruises to luxury cruises, from singles to groups, I have the facility to book most of the world's cruise lines from the comfort of my home.'

'I am a cruise expert,' says Martin, 'and offer a very personal service to my customers, who come back to me time and time again because of my service, my advice, my recommendations and my in-depth knowledge of the cruise industry. I will match customers to cruises and will very often offer bespoke packages to ensure the customer gets exactly what they want from their holiday.'

Training is half the fun

'Working in a fun industry, I have been lucky to have been on familiarisation trips two or three times a year, as the cruise lines are firm believers that it's easier to sell a product you have sampled first hand yourself. With the GoCruise software I can run my business from anywhere using my laptop, always marketing my business in my local territory and networking at every opportunity.'

However, adds Martin, 'I will be the first to tell you the first year is a challenge building up your customer database, but with determination, commitment and enthusiasm for hard work. I would also tell you that that first year is definitely worth the rewards later on.'

Where do I go from here?

If you feel you have got what it takes to be a successful independent GoCruise specialist then call us now in confidence to arrange a meeting. Unfortunately the number of franchises available is limited to ensure exclusivity, so don't delay.

Tel: 0800 954 0067
Email: sales@gocruise.co.uk
Web: www.cruisefranchise.co.uk

FRANCHISING OPPORTUNITIES